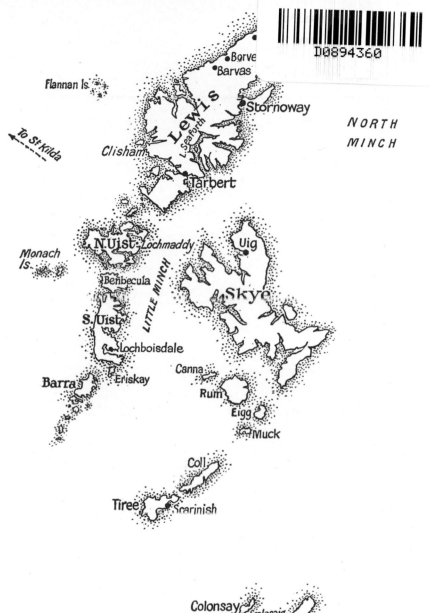

•Borve
•Barvas

Flannan Is.

NORTH
MINCH

L E W I S
•Stornoway

L. Seaforth

To St Kilda

Clisham

Tarbert

N. Uist. Lochmaddy
•Uig

Monach
Is.

Benbecula

Skye

LITTLE MINCH

S. Uist

•Lochboisdale

Canna

Barra
•Eriskay

Rum

Eigg

Muck

Coll

Tiree
Scarinish

Colonsay
•Scalasaig

Oronsay
Jura

Feolin

Port Askaig•

Portnahaven•

Islay
Gigha

Port Ellen

The Sunset Coasts

Sunset over Kirkwall Harbour, Orkney

The Sunset Coasts: Bird's Eye View

Vivian Bird

Kineton: The Roundwood Press

1970

Vivian Bird has also written:

BIRD'S EYE VIEW: THE MIDLANDS (1969)

PORTRAIT OF BIRMINGHAM (ROBERT HALE LTD)

First Published 1970 *by The Roundwood Press* (*Publishers*)
Limited, Kineton, Warwick.
Copyright © Vivian Bird, 1970

SBN 900093 14 5

Set in 10 on 12 point 'Monotype' Times New Roman, series 327
and printed by Gordon Norwood at The Roundwood Press, Kineton, in the
County of Warwick. Plates made by The Process Engraving Company,
Coventry.

Made and Printed in England

To
Edith and Jennifer
who came some of the way with me,
and to
Molly
who didn't.

Contents

Illustrations

Acknowledgments

I wish to thank the Northern Ireland Tourist Board and the Irish Tourist Board (Bord Failte Eireann) for the assistance always readily forthcoming when I visit their territories, and with the latter to mention particularly Liam Earley, their Birmingham manager, who is more than an Irishman, he's a Corkonian.

To British European Airways and 'Tommy' Staddon, their Midlands sales manager my thanks are also due, and to David MacBrayne Ltd., particularly to their George Ward; to the Orkney Islands Steamship Company, and to Loganair.

My friend Norman Williams not only shared my walking in the Southern Hebrides; he again read the book in typescript and made corrections and suggestions.

For permission to quote from my own articles I am indebted to the editor of the 'Sunday Mercury' and the editor of 'The Climber'.

Permission to include extracts from 'Dauber' has been granted by the Society of Authors as the literary representatives of the Estate of John Masefield.

Introduction

THE YOUNG SHIRT-SLEEVED PRIEST dropped his end of the folded table he was helping carry, threw back his head, and laughed immoderately.

'You're just walking across the island in five hours, and you're writing a book about Barra,' he said. 'Oh no!'

'I didn't say I'm writing a book about Barra,' I told him. 'I'm writing a book about a journey, and Barra happens to be on my route.'

Let me anticipate similar criticism that I have treated a favourite place, a beloved island, in cursory fashion; that I have hastened through Harris, scampered through Shetland. Twenty-seven islands in four months is no way to explore the soul of any one of them, but my knowledge of many of them is based on more than this one journey — and in any case this is the story of a journey.

All my life I have found a natural affinity with the western and northern fringes of the British Isles. From the lovely countryside of West Cork to the austere moors of Unst the imminence of the Atlantic Ocean gives an integrity to Ireland, the Hebrides, Orkney, and Shetland. My love for the pellucid blue of northern skies, and the almost endless daylight of the northern summer, has sent me even farther afield — to Iceland, Spitzbergen, the Scandinavian countries, and four times to Finland, a country which would have occupied more of my time had it been easier of access.

The journey on which this book is based took me, in the spring and summer of 1969, from the westernmost village in the British Isles, Dunquin on the Dingle peninsula of County Kerry, to the northernmost headland of our islands, Hermaness on Unst in Shetland. My route lay along the western verge of Ireland, through the Hebrides, the Orkney Islands and the Shetland Islands, along what I soon came to regard as the Sunset Coasts.

Extremities have always fascinated me — North Cape, Norway, where I have been; Cape Horn, where I have not. To me the outermost headland is the same as the summit to the mountaineer, to be attained 'because it is there.' In 1968 I reviewed John Hillaby's book *Journey Through Britain* (Constable, 35s.) — splendid walking, excellent journalism. All it lacked was a basic idea. Land's End to John o' Groats lacks originality. A groove is worn between these two extremities from over use.

So I cast about for extremities of my own.

From Slea Head, near Dunquin, I saw the beam from Terracht in the Blasket Islands, the westernmost lighthouse in the British Isles; from Hermaness I heard the doleful wailing of Britain's northernmost lighthouse on the rock of Muckle Flugga, lost below me in the mist.

In between those two points this book will take you with me to the northernmost cape in Ireland, Malin Head; to the southernmost tip of the Hebrides, the Mull of Oa in Islay, and the northernmost, the Butt of Lewis. It will take you to that ultimate extremity of our islands, St. Kilda; and you will gaze down with me on Fair Isle from the aircraft flying me to Shetland.

My journey north by west was not leisurely, but it did what I intended it should. It has given me a thread on which to hang much that I already knew, an excuse for writing of experiences and impressions collected over thirty years and more. Ireland I know intimately from 62 visits during which I have slept in all thirty-two counties. Orkney I know so well that, while I would hesitate to write a book on its fertile and soft-contoured islands, I want to contribute something more permanent than occasional newspaper articles about a sea-girt world that has given me much happiness.

So the account of my 1969 journey will often hark back to earlier years, and some sections will be entire interludes from the past.

Travel and topographical books so often fall between two stools. They do too much — the writer lives his whole life in the Hebrides, or elsewhere; or he spends more time and money on his journeys than a reader can ever hope to do. Or they do too little — they are pure guide books without any atmosphere of travel at all; their terrain exists in a vacuum without the wind, the rain, and the cloud that beset the traveller or the sunshine that warms him.

I hope my readers can travel vicariously with me. If they wish to do more I suggest that my dash up the Sunset Coasts of the British Isles might well break up into the holidays of five years from the five sections of my book.

Since I wrote the pages on Ireland there have been tragic happenings in that country which call for comment from an English writer who has declared himself, as I have, so sympathetic to the Republic, and to a lesser degree, to republicanism.

The happenings of August 1969 have left me much less sympathetic. Civil Rights and Bernadette Devlin ran true to the despicable form I suggest in my text. What did shock me were the irresponsible utterances of the Prime Minister of the Republic, and the impudence of the Irish community in Birmingham, where I live, in staging a strike in favour of the enemies of the United Kingdom.

The British Press and television struck me as pro-Catholic throughout, if only in stressing Protestant intransigence in the face of certain peace-making efforts. Protestant belligerency in Northern Ireland should be appraised in the context of a situation where Catholic proliferation constitutes a cold but insidious war where they have no need for guns. I can offer only one hopeful suggestion to curb future trouble in Northern Ireland, and incidentally, throughout the United Kingdom — a tax on babies.

Which reminds me that one review of my book *Bird's Eye View: The Midlands* deplored the fact that my prejudices emerge occasionally. I should be ashamed, in 75,000 words or so, if they did not. They will be apparent from place to place in this book.

I   *Ireland*

Curraghs in Kerry

ALL DAY, AS I DROVE half way across Ireland, the sun had streamed down from a cloudless April sky. It even followed me to my evening meal in the Little Chef restaurant at Cashel of Kings in County Tipperary. Then suddenly the radiance was gone. I looked up to see why, and realised that as I tucked into my egg and rashers the shadow of the cross had fallen across my table.

Immediately beyond the back windows of the restaurant loomed Ireland's Acropolis, the Rock of Cashel. In bands of cream limestone and terraces of green grass it rose to the most breathtaking building skyline I know. The serrated jackdaw-haunted outline of Cormac's roofless chapel is flanked by a round tower with its conical cap — surely the world's loveliest architectural form. To the right of them, overtopping the surrounding wall, the slender shaft of a recent Celtic cross stood tall against the pale blue evening sky. The sun, moving westwards and filling the remainder of the restaurant with its radiance and warmth was, for the moment, casting the shadow of that cross on me.

In the Malvern Hills of Worcestershire in my native English Midlands we have the legend of the Ragged Stone. Long ago a monk, condemned for some misdeed to crawl on his knees up Ragged Stone Hill, leapt to his feet and cursed the hill and everyone on whom its shadow might fall. Among those unlucky enough to incur the Curse of the Ragged Stone was Cardinal Wolsey who, in his young manhood, was a tutor at Birtsmorton Court, east of Ragged Stone Hill. There, one summer afternoon, he fell asleep on the lawn to awake shivering in the shadow of the Ragged Stone. Though this

I

did not prevent his rise to eminence, his eventual downfall was certainly unhappy enough.

Surely, however, this shadow of the Cashel cross, falling gently across me as I ate, could be only a benediction. No harm could come from so exquisitely lovely a place as St. Patrick's Rock, where the saint had likened the three segments of the shamrock leaf to the Trinity. Not that the Rock of Cashel had always known peace since the day, so they say, when the Devil dropped it there, having bitten it from a mountain to northward, still known as the Devil's Bit. More sinister flames than those of a refulgent sunset had twice licked its walls since Conall Corc set up a fortress there in the 4th Century and the Kings of Cashel became kings of the entire province of Munster. In 1495 the Earl of Kildare burned out the cathedral on the Rock, excusing himself to Henry VII by telling him he thought the Archbishop was inside.

'All Ireland cannot rule this man,' expostulated the Archbishop.

'Then he shall rule all Ireland,' replied the King, though it was his son, Henry VIII who was the first English monarch to call himself King of Ireland.

The flames of war blackened the stones of Cashel in 1647 when Burner O Brien, the renegade Earl of Inchiquin, with a Parliamentary force, burned and sacked the Rock, putting the garrison and the townspeople to the sword.

I asked my waitress if working in close proximity to so famous and sacred a place meant anything to her. Maybe I was being patronising and expected 'No' for an answer, but I should have known better in Ireland.

'Sure,' she said, 'it's a wonderful spot. Me grandfather and me grandmother, me uncles and me aunts is buried up there and, please God, one day I'll sleep there with them.'

The gates into the enclosure were locked when we walked up the Rock after our meal, so we had to content ourselves with strolling over the hummocky grass beneath the western perimeter of the wall. The Rock of Cashel is one of the places on which I would stake my love for Ireland. My wife and I had seen it several times before, but it was my daughter Jennifer's first visit, and Ireland did not fail me.

The regal Rock rose there from the plain of Tipperary, lit by the westering sun beneath a tranquil sky clear but for the silver vapour-trails of aircraft following the sun across the Atlantic. In a field below were the jagged Cistercian ruins of Hore Abbey. To the left of the sunset the Galtee Mountains took on the purple of evening, a thin mist rose from the pastures and smoke stood up straight from the chimneys of the town as we turned back to the home of Paddy and Mary Duane where we were staying in the main street. Its frontage was orthodox enough, but after driving my car carefully through a narrow opening I parked it in Paddy's garden enclosed by the massive walls of a one time Dominican friary. From the bathroom window as I went to bed was a vision of fairy beauty, the Rock of Cashel, floodlit by the grace of the licensed trade in the town and of the House of Guinness.

The benediction of Cashel cross was still upon me twenty-four hours later and 120 miles farther west. I had wanted a spectacular sunset from Slea Head, the real starting-point of my journey North by West, and I was getting one. A great advantage in a holiday on the west coast of Ireland, especially early in the year, is the later hour of sunset. The one I was watching on April 4 was at 8.25 p.m. when in Birmingham it was timed for 7.30 p.m.

Slowly the sun sank behind Great Blasket Island, transmuted in its last lingering half hour from gold to fiery red. Farther in the Atlantic to the left of Great Blasket the prickly island of Inishnabro and gentler Inishvickilaune were already taking on the steely hue of nightfall, merging with a steel-grey ocean. Inishtooksert and the skerries of Blasket Sound lay dark on the opaline sunset sea. From where the foot of Slea Head plunged into the Atlantic the soft thresh of waves stroked the quiet air. The shrill cry of an unseen seabird broke in on the whimpering of a tiny dusk wind in the crannies of the cliff around me, and my meths stove spluttered merrily as I brewed some coffee.

By the time it was ready for drinking darkness had well nigh fallen and the white marble figures of the Calvary with whom I shared the headland looked ghostly across the road. Ours was but a tenuous ledge between the immovable bulk of the cliff and the immensity of movement below and beyond, its presence betrayed by luminous coils of foam. As I peered into this dark expanse of ocean a faint beam of light pierced the gathering mists — the ray from Terracht, outermost of the island group, nine miles off Slea Head, but hidden by the bulk of Croaghmore, Great Blasket's mountain.

The lighthouse on Terracht is the westernmost in the British Isles.

3

Slea Head, with Dunmore Head and Clogher Head, all on the Dingle peninsula of County Kerry, are the westernmost promontories of the Irish mainland, and we had come to them on this Good Friday of 1969 by way of another, more famous extremity, The South Pole — an inn at Anascaul, 20 miles eastward. On January 4, 1912, three well-muffled figures raised three cheers in the Antarctic wastes as they watched five others become smaller until they were swallowed up in the white desert — Captain Robert Falcon Scott and his four companions who were to reach the South Pole fourteen days later on January 18, 1912. The three who had waved them goodbye and now turned northward for a grim trek to base at Hut Point were the last men to see Scott alive —Lieutenant Edward Evans, Petty Officer W. Lashly, and Able Seaman Tom Crean. Their homeward journey developed into a fight for Evans' life, Lashly and Crean performing valorously in hauling him on their sledge.

On November 12, 1912, Tom Crean was one of the search party to find the bodies of Scott, Bowers, and Wilson near One Ton Camp. When his exploring days were over Crean became landlord of a pub at Anascaul in his native Dingle peninsula, where he was born at Gortacrone in 1877. Naturally he called his pub The South Pole, and the frontage still bears his name, while his photograph as a petty officer is in the bar.

'He died in 1938,' the present proprietress, Mrs Patricia Lenihan, told me. 'They do say he could have been saved. His appendix burst while they were taking him from one hospital to another. His widow lived to be 80, and two of his daughters married brothers named O'Brien from Tralee, and still live there.'

So, having established ourselves in comfort at Aisling Guest House in the township of Dingle, we had come to this western extremity of the British Isles and the beginning of my journey.

Next morning we drove again round Slea Head, past a close-knit hamlet where the miniature round haycocks were barely distinguishable last night from the thatched stone cottages, and so to Dunquin, the westernmost inhabited place in our islands since the last islanders were moved from the Blaskets in 1957. Another halcyon day was sailing in from the broad Atlantic, the morning melodious with lark-song and tremulous with the call of curlews. Down zigzag steps we reached the slipway where the famous curraghs lie upside down on frames beneath a beetling cliff alive with fulmars. Great was our luck

4

to see a curragh launched, with three taciturn ex-Blasket islanders at the double sweeps. Three students were embarking, one with a crossbow slung across his back.

'Are you after shark?' I asked with some memory of the shark hunters of Achill Island.

'No, rabbits,' said the young man disarmingly.

Ask a silly question, I thought. But the student was amplifying his answer. 'We're going out to the Great Blasket for three days bird watching. There was no myxomatosis there so the island swarms with rabbits, and the crossbow doesn't scare the birds like a gun.'

I was astonished, as the oarsmen bent to their task, at the speed with which their flimsy black shell leapt forward between the rocks, for the oars have no blades. During the next 45 minutes we watched the curragh's progress in the lee of the headland far to the left of the island, then, where it lost the mainland's shelter, taking a rare old dusting for a while on this calm morning before moving across the tide race in the sound towards the landing beach faintly visible below the scattered houses of the old settlement, with a criss-cross of stone walls marking the fields.

We were joined as we watched by two girls, students of Irish at local homes for Dunquin is a 'Gaeltacht' or Irish-speaking area. One of them, Margaret O'Connor, had braved the buffeting to Great Blasket just a year earlier.

'Holy Week it was,' she told me, 'and Holy Mother, me not able to swim at all. The men were taking sheep to the island for the grazing, and me just standing by when they asked if I'd like to go with them. Sixteen sheep there were, lying on their backs with their legs tied, though they began to wriggle when we were standing on end. We stayed still for a rest or for the tide out there before crossing the sound, and I thought we were all going to drown, but we got to the island in an hour. It was, mercy on us, quicker coming back without the sheep.'

Margaret told me that the local name for the curragh is 'naomhog' pronounced 'naovog' with the second 'o' long, and that the dark curly-haired man who had seen the curragh off that morning was the Tomos Keanen whose name was writ large in paint on the slipway wall. He had told me that he himself was not a Blasket man, but Margaret said of him 'He can make a curragh do anything.'

Several books have ensured the Blasket Islands their place in

5

history and literature — 'Twenty Years A-Growing' by Maurice O'Sullivan, 'The Western Island' by Robin Flower, 'An Old Woman's Reflections' by Peig Sayers, and 'The Islandman' by Tomas O'Crohan. Jennifer, who had been reading Peig Sayers' description of the curraghs, stooped beneath several and drew our attention to the Holy Water bowls fixed in the bows, though precious little must remain in them on passage to the Blaskets. As we ascended to the cliff top we left behind a peacock butterfly flexing its wings on one of a pile of oars. Spring had really come in from an azure Atlantic with its white lace fretwork of breakers bursting on the skerries, and the horizon hidden in a fine-weather haze.

Settled fine weather is a mixed blessing in Ireland as we saw when we drove round to Smerwick Harbour. From the Fort del Oro, a grassy almost circular cliff promontory accessible by a one man's path, where over 600 Spaniards, Italians, and Irish were massacred in November 1583 by English forces, we could see the Three Sisters well enough, sharp pinnacles rising over 450 feet above the cliffs. Across the bay breakers spouted white on Ballydavid Head, but beyond them nothing. The haze was denying us that magnificent prospect of Brandon, the mountain that rises 3,100 feet direct from the sea — a superlative view which I have seen in clearer conditions. It takes showery weather with alternate sunshine and shadow from high-piled argosies of cloud to distil Ireland's loveliest colours.

From Smerwick we drove to one of Ireland's famous national monuments, the Gallerus Oratory, very well signposted as are so many of the antiquities, and the Dingle peninsula is abounding in ogham stones, beehive huts, churches, wells, and crosses. The last lap to Gallerus necessitated our climbing a stone wall and crossing a small field pied with daisies. The oratory, built of drystone masonry in the 7th Century, is shaped like an upturned boat, and I would have confidence in its protective powers against a hurricane, though its plain floor space is only 22 by 18½ feet. From its lower exterior walls pennywort grows in profusion.

We sat in the enclosure bright with celandine and enjoyed the infinite peace of a perfect afternoon, disturbed, if that be the word, only by the distant bark of a dog, the shout of a man calling his cows, the lilt of many larks, and the constant fret of the sea in Smerwick Harbour, where the eastern shore is flat, and its stark individual houses with the absence of trees reminded me vividly of the clean

6

bland landscape of Orkney. Meanwhile Jennifer was being reminded of Easter two years earlier when we were in Cyprus by finding a lizard basking in the sun on a wall. We had spent Easter Sunday, 1967, driving from Famagusta to Larnaca where, beside the salt lake, and later on a beach where Jennifer was watching lizards, we were shrivelled with cold, so different from this summer-like Easter Saturday in Ireland which was to close with our third successive glorious sunset as, from Ventry Strand, we watched the sun roll down the unbroken slope of Mount Eagle.

Sunshine Across the Shannon

AS IRELAND BECOMES BETTER KNOWN there is growing controversy concerning the charms of the neighbouring peninsulas, the Ring of Kerry and the Dingle. With Killorglin, where they crown a lusty billy-goat King of the Puck Fair and hoist him high in a cage to preside over the festivities in the second week of August; with Coomakista Pass and its wide seascape including the Skellig Rocks; with sub-tropical Parknasilla, and the magnificent mountain prospect at Moll's Gap, the Ring gives 100 miles of fantastic beauty. Nor have I any snob objection to Killarney. True, the town is commercialised, but the lakes are bluer, the mountains a deeper purple, and the grass greener than in the English Lakes, the Scottish lochs, and the Welsh hills. Because these other countries of Britain have small lakes beneath towering mountains Killarney is not unique. This is left to the vast loughs in open country, Lough Ree on the Shannon, the Galway Corrib, Lough Neagh and Lower Lough Erne in the North, the fishing loughs of Westmeath, and Mayo's loughs, Mask and Conn. All these reflect the afterglow long past sunset, extensive mirrors on the fair face of Ireland.

But for all the charms of the Ring of Kerry I give the palm at two points to the Dingle, in Slea Head's rugged view of the Blaskets and the heart-throbbing wonder of Brandon rising from the sea.

With two such rivals as the Ring and Dingle among the five southwest peninsulas West Cork tends to be neglected. Yet stand as I have done among the butterwort and sundew on Mount Gabriel behind Schull, with Carbery's Hundred Isles to southward, and the Slieve Miskish and Caha Mountains looming across Dunmanus and Bantry

8

bays, and you will proclaim the scene unsurpassed anywhere. Courtmacsherry, Glandore, and Rosscarbery, where shoals of grey mullet and bass defy the fishermen to do his worst, these are entrancing spots, but Baltimore, the ultimate little town of its own promontory, is as charming as any in Ireland. It has that exciting distinction of being the portal to an offshore island for, from Baltimore the open boat, 'Naom Ciaran' (Saint Ciaran) leaves for Cape Clear Island where An Oige, the Irish Youth Hostels Association, has a hostel. Ireland's land's end is Mizen Head in West Cork, though the Irish equivalent of Land's End to John o' Groats is 'Mary's House to Donaghadee,' the SW-NE axis of Ireland, the former in West Cork, the latter in County Down.

They are even greater talkers in Cork than elsewhere in Ireland and will tell of characters like the highwayman O'Donovan who coined the phrase 'beyond the Leap, beyond the Law' — the Leap being a stream in a village of that name, westward of which was such tortuous woodland that O'Donovan was safe from pursuit there. Or you will have Cliona's Rock pointed out, off Castlefreke.

'She was a mermaid, a kind of siren,' Thaddeus O'Keefe told me at the Carbery Arms in Rosscarbery, 'and it was Cliona who eventually had Captain Sweeney. He used to ply his sailing boat from Rosscarbery to Cork with cargoes of potatoes, and he'd bring you a piano back if you wanted one. But his own instrument was the melodeon, and he'd sit playing it at the tiller. One day, off Castlefreke, he foundered, and Cliona got him.'

West Cork saw more of the 'Troubles' between 1916 and 1923 than most parts of Ireland, and though they are too sensitive to harass the English visitor, the Cork people will take great pleasure when an Englishman sings to them, in their own local anthem, 'The boys who licked the Black and Tans were the boys of County Cork.' In eastern counties of Ireland a roadside memorial stone or cross invariably marks the spot where someone died in a car crash; in Cork it commemorates death in war, like the stone south of the Pass of Keimaneigh inscribed 'Lieutenant Dennis Kelly, I.R.A., killed in action April 17, 1923'. West Cork is Tom Barry's country, of his book 'Guerilla Days in Ireland'; but above all else it is Michael Collins' country, where he was born at Clonakilty in 1890, and met his death in action at Bealnablath — the Pass of the Flowers — on August 22, 1922.

9

Collins was the greatest of all Irishmen, a born fighter, but with the quality of knowing when he was beaten, and not prepared to sacrifice an entire nation to his own vain hope. It was an easy matter for an ageing Churchill to offer up the blood of countless Englishmen in the last ditch after Dunkirk — a sacrifice averted only by the unforseen German attack on Russia. It was a more cruel decision taken by Michael Collins, aged only 31, in December 1921, when he signed the Treaty with Lloyd George's government, and thus saved Ireland a full-scale war. 'I am signing my death warrant,' he told Lord Birkenhead, and in eight months he died at the hands of his own countrymen, lying in the road returning the Irregulars' fire after his convoy had been ambushed. Ireland owes Michael Collins a more worthy memorial than the blue-grey Calvary at Bealnablath on top of what seems like the brick roof of a public urinal.

The spot was beautiful as I last saw it on a summer's day in 1965, lush with yellow irises, late primroses, lady-smock, bugle, and golden furze, with the sound of a stream burbling through marestails and rushes, probably the last sound Michael Collins heard before he died in the Pass of the Flowers.

But back to County Kerry and Dingle as we left it on Easter Sunday morning in 1969 along a road where churchgoers were streaming in to service on foot, on bicycles, by donkey cart, and even one group on a tractor, the men in sober black, the girls in their Easter bonnets. Across the peninsula we drove by the westward shoulders of the Slieve Mish Mountains, still blessed by our Cashel benediction of sunshine, to a memorable view, near Camp, of Tralee Bay. Tralee itself did not detain us longer than to set down a pair of Canadian girls, teaching at Alloa in Scotland, but now under the spell of Ireland which they proclaimed, rightly, lovelier by far than Scotland. We did pause awhile, however, at Ardfert, where thirstiness is next to godliness. They were just turning out of church, the women to go home, the men to queue, like a hundred black beetles, outside O'Flaherty's Bar, presumably awaiting O'Flaherty's own return from church. Matching their black habiliments, a congregation of jackdaws pursued loud and earnest debate on one of the greens, where farm implements lay idle.

A feature of the Irish countryside is the graveyards clustered around the roofless ruins of churches. At Ardfert they have a derelict cathedral as the focal point, built where St. Brendan the Navigator founded a monastery in the 6th Century. The cathedral was 13th Century, and I was spellbound by a doorway in the north wall, a kind of Romanesque-Hibernian ogee shape. I busied myself pretending to photograph the imposing gateway of Ardfert Abbey, home of the Talbot Crosbies, but surreptitiously fiddling with my camera I got a picture of the thirsty legion outside O'Flaherty's.

Six miles from Ardfert we brewed up for lunch at Ballyheigue, the northern extremity of Banna Strand, which would be a major tourist attraction on any Mediterranean coast, but which, in Ireland, is best known for a stirring event which happened at Easter 53 years before my visit. In the dark hours of Good Friday morning, 1916, a rubber dinghy bringing three men ashore from the German submarine U.19, capsized in the Atlantic surf breaking on Banna Strand. Like three drowned rats they struggled ashore, concealed their Mauser pistols, and sought a place where they could hide. This they found in McKenna's Fort, a circular earthern ring probably Danish in origin, and there, after drying out a little, two of the castaways left their companion, ill after 12 days and nights of sleepless sea-sickness on a cramped and rough submarine journey from Heligoland. He was Sir Roger Casement who had been, unsuccessfully, trying to recruit Irish soldiers, prisoners of the Germans, to fight in an army for the liberation of Ireland. His bedraggled comrades, en route for Tralee to seek assistance, were Robert Monteith, an I.R.A. agent, and Daniel Bailey, one of Casement's few recruits. In addition to exercising his blandishments on Irish prisoners of war, Casement had been negotiating for arms for the Easter Rising in Ireland, due three days after their landing, on Easter Monday. Here again he was unsuccessful, obtaining only 20,000 obsolete rifles instead of the 200,000 he wanted — though the number was immaterial, as British naval units captured the 'Aud' in which they were being consigned to Tralee Bay, and its German crew scuttled their ship in Queenstown Harbour on Easter Saturday.

Local people were astir early around Banna Strand on that fatal Good Friday. Farmer John McCarthy, rising at 2 a.m. to walk to a holy well to pray, saw the empty dinghy in the surf and found the Mausers. He despatched a neighbour to fetch police from Ardfert Barracks. At 4.30 a.m. another early riser, a farm girl, saw the trio, and it was this which led one Police Constable Riley to McKenna's Fort where he captured Casement who claimed to be an English author, Richard Morton. A code paper, a rail ticket from Berlin to Wilhelmshaven, and a diary helped establish the inefficient Casement's identity and treasonable purpose, and he was eventually tried and hanged on August 3.

Banna Strand was shining in the sunlight and the Atlantic waves lapping lazily as we ate our lunch. Groups of oyster-catchers, like little men in frock coats, were probing the wet sand with their orange bills, and a local resident told me that a monument had been erected to Casement at McKenna's Fort in 1968.

In between Casement's landing at Banna and his execution another drama of the sea was enacted off Marwick Head, Orkney, when, on June 6, 1916, H.M.S. 'Hampshire' was lost while carrying the British Secretary of State for War, Earl Kitchener of Khartoum, to Russia. His memorial on Marwick Head I have often seen, and would see again before my present journey was over. Now, in County Kerry, I ran to earth Kitchener's birthplace, four miles south of Ballylongford on the Listowel road. Up a drive I walked across a rushy field to a white house beside a red Dutch barn in an odorous farmyard.

'Yes,' said Thomas Dowd, shovelling manure, 'this is Kitchener's birthplace. In his day it was known as Gunsborough Lodge, now it's Coolbeha House. We still get about a dozen people enquire each year, though we've no mementoes of Kitchener. Yes, I was born here myself.'

The year 1916 would not let me alone on that bright afternoon. I had previously known of Casement and Banna Strand and of Kitchener's birthplace, but sheer good luck drew my eyes at a crossroads in Ballylongford, to a white marble tablet on a three-storey house. It read 'Erected to the memory of The O'Rahilly, born here 1875, killed in action in Dublin Easter Rising, 1916. Erected by the North Kerry Republican Soldiers Memorial Committee, 1966.' The O'Rahilly has always seemed to me one of the most attractive of the Easter Week fighters — the prefix 'The' denotes him the senior living member in direct descent from the clan chieftain. A member of the Irish Republican Brotherhood, he was prominent in 1913 in the formation of the Irish Volunteers, the body which ultimately rose on Easter Monday, 1916. With the failure of the 'Aud' gun-running, and the discovery of the Volunteers' intentions, The O'Rahilly was opposed to the Rising, and did a quick tour of the west trying to call it off, but when it took place he was in the General Post Office, Dublin, ready to fight. On the Friday of Easter Week, when the Volunteer garrison evacuated the blazing Post Office, The O'Rahilly took particular care of the 13 prisoners, and having safely disposed of them so that they afterwards paid tribute to his concern, he volunteered to try and penetrate Parnell Street to report on conditions there. No report ever came. The O'Rahilly was shot dead in Moore Street.

Estuaries always hold a fascination for me, the lordly Shannon more so than most. So extensive is it that people without a good bump of direction are never sure if they are looking upstream or downstream. It imposes a considerable barrier between Kerry and Clare, but this is being overcome by a 14-minute car ferry from Tarbert to Killimer, the cost being 15 shillings per car with passengers free, or 2s. 6d. per foot passenger. The saving distance is nearly 75 miles from shore to shore via Limerick and Clarecastle Bridge on the River Fergus. I hoped to use the ferry but it was not sailing, so we decided on a night in Limerick city.

The county of Limerick has, perhaps, the most gleaming white cottages in Ireland, and in Adare, to which signposts pointed on my right, it has the accepted prettiest village in Ireland. Another signpost — to Newcastle West — brought me a laugh with the memory in that town of the 'Dog Fair.' While Britain was engaged in a frontier war in India the town crier of Newcastle West proclaimed a 'Horse Fair' at which Her Majesty's Government would buy any horses brought in by the local populace for shipment to India as transport in the mountains. For some reason there was scant response to the appeal, but those who did appear with horses sold them and were paid generously on the spot by Government agents. Some months later another proclamation was made in Newcastle West. Her Majesty, Queen Victoria, being concerned that her subjects in West Africa were plagued with rats, was buying dogs for shipment to the affected colonies. A 'Dog Fair' would be held in the town and good prices paid for the animals. This time no one intended being left out, and on the appointed day all roads leading to Newcastle West were teeming with men and dogs. The town became a yapping bedlam. Time wore on but no agents arrived. Some of the dog 'owners', suspecting a hoax, asked others to hold their dogs for a while and decamped quietly. Morning became afternoon, afternoon evening, and the whole operation turned out a gigantic leg-pull. Newcastle West was left with a thousand or so stray dogs about its streets.

Limerick is a gracious Georgian city and seaport, the City of the Broken Treaty, and of the Flight of the Wild Geese, the city which has bestowed its name on a five-line verse, and given the world an expression for honest down-payment — 'on the nail.' The Nail, now in Limerick Museum in Pery Square, was a circular plate of copper, three feet in diameter, on top of a pillar at Limerick Exchange, on which bargains were struck. Bristol and Liverpool had similar 'nails,' but the expression was current before stock exchanges came into being.

Various accounts are given of the origin of the limerick — that one of the first concerned 'a young lady of Limerick,' or that a chorus 'Will you come up to Limerick?' was sung after extempore five-line verses from everyone in the company.

At the west end of Thomond Bridge, Limerick, is the Treaty Stone where Patrick Sarsfield signed the articles of capitulation after the siege of 1690-1, getting honourable terms from the Williamite General Ginkel, terms which were subsequently dishonoured, causing 11,000 Irish soldiers to join the French army, an emigration which became known as the Flight of the Wild Geese. Sarsfield is remembered in the name of Sarsfield Bridge across the Shannon, and on it the 1916-22 fight for Irish independence is commemorated in the statue of a Volunteer in the act of discharging his pistol — into the 'Gents' below.

We watched our fourth flaming sunset down Shannon from the Limerick quays, the orange, white, and green flying from all the flagstaffs on the eve of the 53rd anniversary of the Easter Rising, and bells were ringing with the deep resonance that bells have in Roman Catholic countries.

I have no sympathy with the Irish religion, but at heart, English romantic that I am, I am a Republican, and it was a thrill again to be in the country on Easter Monday, and to remember the men who, against all the odds, struck successfully for nationhood in 1916. The comparative handful of fighters at the General Post Office, and in several other strongpoints throughout Dublin, were regarded with scorn and annoyance by the majority of their fellow-countrymen and women, who saw in the Rising an embarrassment to themselves and

14

to their menfolk fighting in the Irish regiments of the British Army on many fronts against the Germans. Capitulation after six days was what the Irishman in the street expected, and there was little sympathy as Padraic Pearse, President of the Provisional Government and Commandant-in-Chief of the Republican Forces, handed over his sword in Parnell Street, and was marched with his men into captivity. Then came the trials and the executions of 15 Irish leaders, and at once, in the immortal words of Yeats,

'All is changed, changed utterly:
A terrible beauty is born.'

What the eloquence and the persuasion of the insurgent leaders failed to do with their countrymen the English did with their executions. 'One more martyr for old Ireland' is no empty heart cry. As Pearse, Thomas Clarke, Sean McDermott, and the others stood before the firing squads; as Count Joseph Plunkett, one of the signatories of the Declaration of the Republic, was shot on the morning after his marriage, as the wounded James Connolly was wheeled in his invalid chair to his death, public opinion changed in a twinkling, and after five more years fighting came the establishment of the Irish Free State.

One funny story remains from the Easter Rising. Plunkett's personal force of 56 men marched into Dublin from his farm at Kimmage. At Harold's Cross they commandeered a tram, and while one of their number thrust a shotgun into the driver's ribs and told him to drive to O'Connell Bridge without stopping, George Plunkett tendered fares to the conductor for 56 twopennies.

Ireland is free of the old English thraldom, but I sometimes fear she might put on another, far worse. The Shannon Electricity Scheme, at Ardnacrusha, near Limerick, was constructed by German engineers, and since then the Germans have insinuated themselves more and more into Ireland, in factories, guest houses and hotels, and particularly with the Volkswagen car, made in a factory near Dublin. Almost every other car on the Irish roads is a Volkswagen, and, to my horror, I found myself driving a German car on this journey. I had told Bord Failte I would prefer an '1100' such as I drive at home. I have strong views against the promiscuous driving of strange cars in traffic. 'But,' said Ryan's charming girl at Dublin Airport, 'We're out of 1100s. We've got a Cadet for you. Have you ever driven a Cadet?'

'I've never even heard of a Cadet,' I said truthfully.

'You'll manage,' she said with a melting smile, leading me to an enormous estate car tightly packed in a car park. 'Reverse is as far right as possible, and up.'

The gear slipped in like silk and I backed out impeccably. She was obviously impressed, and I didn't propose making a fool of myself before such a charmer. Quickly I loaded my wife, Jennifer, and our bags, and without asking any questions which would reveal my abysmal ignorance of matters mechanical I drove away. Believing in keeping going once under way I did not stop until I was well into County Kildare, beyond Naas.

'Look how they've spelt Kadett, Dad,' said Jennifer. 'It looks German.' And, by Heaven, it was. The car was an Opel.

I could not see at a glance how to get at the spare wheel or any tools provided, nor, though without trying very hard, could I raise the bonnet. In fact I had left it four days before I felt I should see what was under that lid, so, buying petrol at a garage in Tarbert on the way to Limerick, I had asked them to check my oil and water. They waited for me to raise the bonnet. When I admitted I could not they had a go at everything that pushed and pressed — unavailingly. A bystander or so tried his hand. Somehow it came out that I was a journalist, so the local reporter was sent for — and came. It then emerged that I came from Birmingham. Emissaries were despatched to local families with connections in Birmingham, and round they gathered. We had one of those delightful Irish hours of scintillating conversation — but I drove on without anyone having managed to raise the bonnet. Nor could two subsequent garages, and it remained a closed book until I returned the car to Ryan's.

Eight miles north-west of Limerick stands one of Ireland's most expensive tourist spots — Bunratty Castle — now only a massive keep where, since the Anglo-Norman invasion of Ireland, there has been a succession of castles fought over and in, captured, destroyed, and rebuilt. In 1646 the Papal Nuncio said of the Bunratty Castle of the day 'In Italy there is nothing like the palace and gardens of the Lord Thomond, nothing like its ponds and park with its 3,000 head of deer.' Today it is just a keep with an Irish folk village constructed alongside, the keep having been bought in 1954 by Viscount Gort, and restored by him and Bord Failte Eireann, the Irish Tourist Board — literally the Board of Welcome to Ireland. Mediaeval banquets are now held in the keep by candlelight with girl harpists and plenty of mead to drink, the cost about 50 shillings, or, if part of a one-day tour from Shannon Airport, including a night in a first-class hotel, between £9 and £10, entertainment definitely geared to American purses, as is most top-class Irish tourism. We were doing nicely on guest houses of impeccable standard and Bord Failte recommendation at 17s. 6d. to £1 bed and breakfast.

Not far beyond Bunratty on our journey through Clare, the 'Banner' county, we were passing another of Ireland's major dollar earners, the Dromoland Castle Hotel, which adds a golf course to its plush amenities and once staged an episode of 'The Saint' television series.

On through Ennis and Ennistymon we drove past the spot where, four years ago, we gave a lift to an old countrywoman, and, as ample reward, heard a corncrake rasping as we set her down. April may be a bit early for the corncrake, but the pied wagtails are a constant source of alarm, and pleasure, dicing with death on the Irish roads. They were still in evidence as we climbed up into the O'Brien country — Cornelius O'Brien M.P., who compelled his tenants to pay for a monument to him two miles or so from Liscannor, and is further commemorated in O'Brien's Tower, familiar to all visitors to the Cliffs of Moher. As the road rises inland of the cliffs the scenery becomes flat brown moorland, its only features an occasional wind-contorted thorn tree, and stone walls, some of them large slabs sunk upright in the ground, others the more orthodox dry walls of small stones.

Sea coasts are not particularly typical of their countries. Though the Cliffs of Moher are tremendous and awe-inspiring seen from the platform at the end of the road or from the crisp turf rising on either hand, I never feel involved in them as I do, for instance, in the great cliffs of St. John's Head, Hoy, in Orkney, beneath which I have several times felt reduced to lilliputian dimensions when sailing the Pentland Firth to and from Stromness. There are five miles of the Cliffs of Moher, fronting the Atlantic in a sheer wall rising to 700 feet, five separate headlands as you look south from the viewpoint, ledge upon ledge multitudinous with seabirds, and, in the inlet north of O'Brien's Tower, the famous kittiwake colony.

Interest quickens on the road from the cliffs towards Lisdoonvarna although it leads to one of the unfashionable areas of Ireland, the

17

Burren of north Clare, of which one of Cromwell's generals reputedly said 'There is not a tree to hang a man, neither water to drown him, nor soil to bury him.' It is typical thinking for a henchman of that ill-favoured death-dealing warthog, but who wants to think of death in a landscape filled with wonder, the like of which can be seen nowhere else in the British Isles? A desert of pale grey limestone karst, seeming always to have a dusting of frost on its weirdly-terraced hills, the Burren under the right conditions is the most beautiful part of our islands. My first visit to the Burren, in June 1965, gave me — walker that I am — a bias in its favour. I had stopped my car in Lisdoonvarna, the pleasant little spa which is the capital of the region, and walked up the main street prospecting for accommodation. As I regained the car, a native, standing idly by, said, 'Now, sorr, that's a foine grand military walk you have.' Now, on my journey 'North by West' I walked for an hour, letting Jennifer drive on towards Lisdoonvarna. Every thatched white cabin sent out the fragrance of its peat fire, the peat itself being neatly stacked usually on the other side of the road. A feature of these gleaming single-storey homes is the stone on top of each white gatepost, stones picked off the land and painted a bright colour. I had walked this road before, buffeted then, as now, by brisk ocean breezes, but having then good views of the Aran Islands on my left, with Inisheer, smallest of the three, a bare eight miles away. Today the anticyclonic haze was still veiling the distant view.

So the sunset we watched that night over Galway Bay was serene but unspectacular, unlike one, four years earlier, memorable in a lifetime of hill walking, which my wife and I saw from Slieve Elva, at 1,134 feet the Burren's highest hill. A huge motionless purple cloud covered the entire expanse of Galway Bay, but from behind it, like a stage backcloth, a flood of golden light fell on the Maamturk Mountains and the Joyce's Country, the Twelve Bens of Connemara, and the isolated hill of Urrisbeg out towards Clifden. Seaward of all this grandeur several ill-defined islands almost brought me to a belief in Hy Brasil or Tir-nan-Og, the legendary lands of eternal youth off the west coast of Ireland. Ultimately the sun dropped from behind its curtain, slashing a blood-red trail across the sea to the Aran Islands. On the coast road far below were tiny doll-like houses; up on Slieve Elva brooding space and loneliness, until three jolly boys cantered along a track on donkeys. My wife declares that the

18

young men of Clare are the best looking she has ever seen — and they keep up a strange tradition from the mists of antiquity. At every wedding in the Burren they arrive as the 'straw-men,' young unmarried men wearing tall conical straw hats, with straw tied round their bodies and legs. Unbidden they come, neither speaking nor accepting hospitality. Solemnly they dance with every guest and then depart without a word, their visit having, it is believed, ensured the fertility of the marriage.

Feeling the urge to walk again after a night in Lisdoonvarna I set out after an early breakfast on 12 miles across the hills, arranging to meet the car at Cregg beside Galway Bay. For 1½ miles I followed the Ballyvaughan road to a rough track on the left beyond a quarry. For miles that track runs between its stone walls with bogland and peat cuttings on either hand. As Slieve Elva rises to its summit on the right it sheds the coarse reedy vegetation — cut for thatching in the autumn — and the bare limestone begins to outcrop in layers and terraces.

From Balliny Farm the Burren lies ahead in all its cream-coloured charm, with Gleninagh stepping down in the typical terraces to the sea at misnamed Black Head. These hills are astonishingly barren — superficially. In fact, they constitute 50 square miles of natural rock garden, their crevices filled with white Scots rose, mountain avens, saxifrages, orchises, and the deep blue of the gentian verna — a botanist's paradise in late May and June. Here, too, can be found that special boon, a second spring. In early June, a month after they are gone in England, violet, and cowslip bloom in profusion in the Burren. Now, in April, only a dwarf blackthorn was in bud in the crevices. I was admiring his goslings when the farmer at Balliny told me that the hill foxes take toll of his poultry. 'And down the track towards Fanore,' he added, 'you'll meet badgers in twos and threes at dusk.' But I left the Fanore track on my left, and took instead the green road which runs across a northern extension of Slieve Elva, 2½ miles between stone walls, and magnificent top-of-the-world walking. Tumbling down to the rough road at Formoyle it crosses one of the few streams of this arid area, the Caher River, in a more fertile tract with a few trees and cottages.

The track soon leaves this oasis by an iron gate to climb and cross a shallow saddle of Gleninagh Mountain, and to come down, in another mile and a half, to the neat farmhouse of Feenagh, where

19

Galway sheep and shorthorn cattle find grazing. The farmer here surprised me by talking of 'winterage' on the hilltops. In the Burren, unlike everywhere else, they send the cattle to the tops in winter rather than bring them down. This is because the upland limestone holds more water in winter than in summer, and winters are fairly mild in Clare.

From Feenagh a hill road drops gradually to the right, but I turned left past one last cottage where the road became merely a field track rising to a pass between Cappanawalla (1,024 ft.) on the right, and Gleninagh (1,045 ft.). At the stony height of the gap a wide prospect of Galway Bay opened below, with a ruined keep near the seashore as a marker for the spot where my steep zigzagging descent through the limestone brought me to the coast road near a cottage at the place name 'Cregg' on the half-inch Irish Ordnance Survey map, and there the car was waiting to continue our journey to Galway.

The speleologist, seeking fresh underworlds to conquer, will find Slieve Elva riddled with caves — a Polldubh linear series; Fauna-rooska, 300 feet deep; and, on the southern slopes, the Coolagh River Cave, Polldonaugh, a complex system of which only two miles has been explored. Pollagullam on the eastern slopes, is accessible by rope ladder down a 100-foot tree-grown shaft in a hillside where, in June, a riot of purple and white orchises is a rebuke to the troglodytes who prefer to spend their days underground when there is so much beauty on the surface. The Burren is not climbers' country. There is some minor scrambling on the terraces, but the flat limestone is very easy, pavement-like walking, the deep crannies being only inches wide and filled with maidenhair fern and ivy, while every square foot of grass is bright with flowers that will keep your mileage down as you study or merely enjoy them.

Kinvarra, as you turn round the head of Galway Bay, has another Bunratty, and for my money the massive keep of Dunguaire Castle, standing between the road and the sea, has the greater authenticity. The menu at the Kinvarra banquet consists of Spanish wine, Galway Bay prawns, Inis Eoin lobster cream, hero's morsel, Kinvarra green salad, Tarragona candied cream, Dunguaire Castle pastries,and coffee with double cream. After the repast the young waiters and waitresses become Thespians, and put on something cultural from Ireland's 20th Century theatre.

Colour in Connemara

I SHALL NEVER forget my first visit to Galway, in July 1937. It coincided with Galway Races, and in late afternoon Eyre Square was pandemonium as the crowds dispersed. You didn't so much seek your bus as find a squad of strong men all making for your destination and commandeer one. Somehow we managed to get to Recess in Connemara.

There are two statues in my life. One is the incomparable Havis Amanda beside South Harbour in Helsinki, warmer and more exciting than most flesh and blood women. The other is vastly different, though equally lifelike — the quaint figure of Padraic O'Connor, the poet, seated in a rock garden in Eyre Square, Galway, in the act of composition. A battered trilby perches well back on his massive brow, he wears a cravat and holds his lapel with the left hand while writing in a notebook on his knee. His boots are extraordinarily good, and a stone bird and rabbit rest beside him.

Since I last saw him in 1964 Padraic has fallen among bad company. Behind him in a newly-erected section of wall is a bronze head of 'College Boy' Kennedy, on the spot where that grossly over-rated President became a freeman of Galway in 1963. The Virgin Mary I can accept in Irish homes, but it sickens me to see her so often juxtaposed, since Kennedy was assassinated, with a large colour picture of those naive features. I am pleased not yet to have seen brother Robert completing the Trinity. And Eyre Square now gives house-room to the John F. Kennedy Gardens.

Padraic O'Connor's other new neighbour, out in the stream of traffic, is Liam Mellows, though there is no English on the plinth where he stands in uniform, but bareheaded, and his name is rendered in Irish, O Maoiliosa. I respect Mellows as a fighter for Irish independence, but cannot forgive him for being among the most virulent of Michael Collins' enemies after the Treaty. He was executed by a firing squad of Free State troops in Mountjoy Gaol, Dublin, on December 8, 1922, for his part in the Insurrection of June 1922, when he was one of the Irregular leaders in the Four Courts fighting in Dublin.

As I was studying the Mellows statue a motor-cyclist passed with a girl side-saddle on his pillion — dangerous but modest. Another risky road habit of the Irish is cycling with an umbrella up in the rain. How they manage to cross themselves as they pass a church I do not know.

Galway is a foreign-looking city, a grey city with decaying dock-side appurtenances, and the only ship on the dockside was the Naom Eanna (Saint Eanna), the Aran Islands steamer, successor to the famous Dun Aengus.

The classic Galway story is that of James Lynch Fitzstephen, elected Mayor in 1493, who gave us the verb 'to lynch' when he hanged his own son, Walter, though modern usage of the term is somewhat different. Walter had killed a young Spanish guest in their home who had looked too kindly on his lady friend. As chief magistrate, the father sentenced his son to death, and when no executioner could be found, he himself enacted the role of hangman. A wall in Market Street where the execution was carried out bears a commemorative inscription above a skull and cross bones.

Fitzstephen would doubtless have seen Christopher Columbus who, it is said, visited Galway and prayed at St. Nicholas Church before setting out for America. Columbus was luckier than I am. In several visits to Galway I have always found St. Nicholas padlocked so that I have been unable to enter even the churchyard, let alone the church.

Salthill, Galway's western continuation, is a pleasant seaside place where we got excellent and cheap accommodation with Mrs McGwyn behind the church.

The coast road westward from Galway, which we took next day, might well have inspired Eva Gore Booth's poem on 'the little roads of Cloonagh.' 'And there are people on them, and many a horse and cart' she wrote, and how true this is of that road along the north

22

shore of Galway Bay. I have travelled it several times, and nowhere in the British Isles have I seen its equal in human and topographical interest.

On Easter Wednesday morning the human cavalcade was as intriguing as ever. A man leading a black cow at leisurely pace westward was passed by a woman in a black shawl leading her black cow eastward. 'Fine day, thank God,' said he, and 'Fine day, thank God' said she. From his bright orange cart, the donkey tethered to a telegraph pole, a weather-beaten old man in blue dungarees was heaving manure over a stone wall. Another was busily forking seaweed into an identical donkey cart.

'Where are all the cyclists going to?' asked Jennifer.

'Where are they all coming from?' asked my wife, for the bicycle traffic was as heavy going east or west. One rangy man held his handlebars with one hand, while with the other he held the forelegs of a goat slung over his shoulder.

One of the problems in Connemara is the name that should be given to the great mountain mass of that delectable land — the Twelve Bens or the Twelve Pins. Somewhere, so long ago that I have forgotten where, I read so authoritatively that it convinced me, that one should always say 'Bens,' never 'Pins,' and this I have continued to do. Barna, the first township from Salthill along the coast road, thinks differently — it has a pub called the 'Twelve Pins.'

Single-storey cottages stud this busy seaside road, old Irish homes with golden thatch or the modern bungalows towards which the government gives generous grants. Many of the old houses are painted a blue wash in honour of the Virgin, but all, ancient and modern, are practically lost among the stones, boulders, and rock outcrops which litter the landscape. Dry stone walls abound, many unnecessary as walls, but the best way to dispose of the embarrassment of stones. Neat raised plots of soil, black from the seaweed content, get some shelter from the walls against the gales that storm in from the Atlantic. Mrs McGwyn, our Salthill landlady, told us of the local devastation when Hurricane Debbie strayed too far eastward on September 16, 1961.

'The day it was when we were saying Mass for the Irish United Nations contingent we thought was wiped out in the Congo, and me sitting here watching the bank manager's roof lifting up and down.' All electricity wires were down, and candles, said Mrs McGwyn, cost

23

2s. 6d. each — an echo of the Galway Guide Book reference to 'the Great Storm of 1839' when 'in Galway and Oughterard all was misery and woe, and the wages of slaters and masons rose to the unprecedented height of 7s. 6d. a day.'

Some 15 years ago the Irish government tried to introduce a tomato industry in Iarconnaught — West Connaught, as this district is called — and, despite the gales, vestiges remain in the form of large glasshouses with boiler houses and tall grey chimneys dwarfing many of the cottages. 'The experiment failed,' a man working in his garden told me. 'In season, when our tomatoes were 3s. 6d. or 4s. a lb. Spanish tomatoes were coming in at 1s. 6d.'

Now we had just a merry breeze with blue skies to light up the myriad little loughs like jewels, winking eyes of azure and turquoise among the sepia bog and grey rock. Three times in my life have I been conscious of 'air like wine.' Two of these were in Ireland — alighting from a bus on a golden evening at Recess, and in Achill Island on a blue morning after a night of rain. Now that intoxicating quality was there again. Some years ago, on a Coras Iompair Eireann coach tour, I heard an American woman express astonishment that anyone could live among this seemingly inhospitable waste of stones. The Irish courier exploded: 'Not live here; why, in this air they never die.' Having said which he stopped the coach at the new church at Tully, an airy spot where the coast road turns inland to Screeb.

'This is the newest church in Ireland,' he announced. 'We'll go in and see it.'

And there, inside, to confound him, was a coffin with a group of mourners.

The fine weather was still bedevilling us, so that the Aran Islands loomed only ghostly to seaward, while inland we were denied possibly the loveliest view of the Twelve Bens. The road was less populous, and more tortuous as it struck inland. A car in front of us stopped at a track north of Costelloe and disgorged a passenger, a close-cropped youngish man in heavy walking boots with a pack and a hand grip. I picked him up, and he introduced himself as Thomas Anthony Mullen of Middletown, County Armagh, though presently 'of no fixed abode.'

'I wander around Ireland,' he explained, 'making notes of all the monuments I can find.'

Obviously a man after my own heart, a collector of epitaphs, but

24

something of a mystery no less. He produced a notebook and read a long inscription copied from a statue, in Banbridge, County Down, to Captain Francis Crozier, who sailed as second-in-command with Sir John Franklin on the ill-fated voyage of 1848 in search of the North-West Passage. I had seen Crozier's statue not four months earlier on a journey in County Down. Mr Mullen spoke, too, of the Spring-Rice memorials at Foynes, County Limerick, and of Liam Mellows' memorial at Castletown, County Wexford. He had established himself with me, though I would like to have known how he supported himself.

As we talked I turned left at Screeb across eight miles of mountain road to the Zetland Arms in the little community of Cashel, beside Bertraghboy Bay. My wife and I had come to Cashel 32 years earlier, in 1937, on our last holiday before we were married four months later — a July holiday when fuchsias rioted in the hedgerows and sunsets blazed in splendour on the gatherings at the crossroads, to which men came afoot and on bicycles to talk quietly in the dusk.

Mr Mullen left us when I pulled up at the general stores with the neat bungalow beside it where we had stayed so long ago. From the bright sunshine outside I passed into the gloomy shop and was soon attended by Jack Bolger, a tall lean Irishman. I told him I had stayed there in 1937 with the Kellys.

'They're still living in Galway,' Mr Bolger said. 'I bought this place from them 18 years ago. I suppose the biggest change since you were here is the seaweed industry. There are three seaweed factories within 10 miles, and the one at Kilkerran employs 50 people. It's a great boon to the poor people. They get £2 a ton wet or £5 dry for the seaweed they collect. With hard work a man can earn £20 in two days.'

It was a nostalgic journey for Edith and me as we drove along on the road we walked so long ago to Toombeola Bridge, beneath Cashel Mountain which we used to climb. One of those days which last a lifetime was August Bank Holiday Monday, 1937, and now we lived it again, on the road to Roundstone, and beyond, to Dog's Bay. On that far-off morning we were driven out from Cashel by a young couple from Portumna, and the four of us shared that white beach at Dog's Bay all day without anyone else in sight. In the Mediterranean or the Caribbean it would be world-famous, an anchor shape of sand dunes with Dog's Bay on the open Atlantic, and Gorteen Strand

25

facing the inlet of Bertraghboy Bay, white sand unblemished by pebbles or seashells, turning the deep blue of the ocean into an emerald fringe. Edith and I walked back to Cashel that evening, 12 miles or so, with the breeze singing softly in the telegraph wire, a sound to me inseparable from the western coasts of our islands.

Urrisbeg, the rugged mountain above Roundstone, is a paradise for botanists: the habitat of Mediterranean plants found nowhere else in the British Isles. As the road skirts it, now more open to the Atlantic, the quality of the air gives it the name of the 'Brandy and Soda Road,' and for us it was at its most heady, with one superlative view, at Mannin Bay, which nearly had me and the car into the ditch with its sheer compelling beauty. Sand almost white, yellowing a little below high water mark, was kissed by wavelets of jade. In slightly deeper water, weed on the seabed brought a quick change to indigo, and beyond it the bay was striped alternately with purple and bottle green.

High between Mannin Bay and Clifden Bay a blue-grey replica of an aircraft's tail commemorates a feat which reached fulfilment in this tract of rock and bogland. An inscriptions reads: 'This memorial honours the achievement of John Alcock and Arthur Whitten-Brown, the first men to fly non-stop across the Atlantic Ocean. On the morning of the 15th day of June, 1919, they landed in their aircraft 500 yards beyond the cairn which can be seen 1½ miles south of this point, having left St. John, Newfoundland, 16 hours 27 minutes before. The aircraft was a Vickers Vimy biplane, powered by two Rolls-Royce Eagle VIII engines of 350 h.p. each, and the average speed during the flight was 115 m.p.h. Dedicated June 15, 1959.'

A quarter of a mile downhill a Celtic cross commemorates two other men: 'In memory of Patrick Morrison and Thomas James of Ballina, Co. Mayo, who were killed in action defending the Republic on this spot, October 28, 1922, R.I.P. Erected by Connemara I.R.A.' This 'Republic' was obviously the unofficial anti-Treaty republic.

Clifden has always seemed incongruous to me, a little town perched between the Atlantic and the grey Connemara rock, with the Twelve Bens as a backcloth to a rather theatrical scene. It is a veritable temple of the winds, and cloud flying in from the sea, with dust spirals buffeting the market booths, suggested that our Cashel benediction was running out. I prefer my rough weather in country places, being strangely disturbed by the conflict between wind and streets of houses.

There were magnificent vistas to our left as we took the Letterfrack road — seaward down Streamstown Bay towards Omey Island, and later, from the Cleggan turn, across four miles of moorland to a seascape blocked by Inishbofin Island, a grand venue for a holiday thoroughly off the beaten track.

There are two surpassing viewpoints for the Twelve Bens. One we had visited that morning, near Costelloe — it forms the glorious dust cover of the 'Shell Book of Ireland.' I had stopped there for a colour picture of the foreground, the Bens being completely lost in the sunshine haze. Now, with deteriorating weather but better visibility we came suddenly upon the other viewpoint at a bend in the road two miles west of Letterfrack. Barnaderg Bay supplied the water for my picture, still finding sufficient blue sky to reflect, though cloud was now thickening over the Bens to the right. Diamond Hill, nearest of the mountains, dominated the centre of the view, and to the left of the gap where the road ran down into Letterfrack, rose Doughruagh and Althagaighera, with the great bulk beyond them of Mweelrea on the Mayo shore of Killary Harbour.

Ballinakill had a nice line in modesty on a sign which read 'Possibly the most interesting craft shop in the West.' Kylemore Abbey, a mile or so on, is almost certainly the most photographed place in the West, though I prefer the more open stretch of Kylemore Lough eastward of the castellated building which was erected by a Lancashire industrialist and is now the home of an order of nuns.

The British Isles have several 'deserts' — Rannoch Moor, Dartmoor, and the Great Desert of Wales between Tregaron and Abergwesyn — and well qualified to represent Ireland among them is the immense bowl of brown moorland with the Twelve Bens to westward, the Maamturk Mountains to eastward, and the Mayo giant, Mweelrea to the north. And here, in this austere wilderness, with only one habitation in view in any direction, a church has recently been built. They call it Creeragh Church, but in what Creeragh consists it is hard to determine, though the church serves 40 families from combes along Glen Inagh and farms beside Lough Fee. It cost £12,000 to build this church, which is described in a Dublin newspaper article as 'a peak with four combes, the southern face a massive A frame of laminated wood, its feet toughly anchored to the rock.' The congregation sit with their backs to the end at which they entered. This is mainly of glass, so, from the altar the priest, facing his flock, has a splendid mountain view through the plain glass beneath a window showing the Virgin in a scarlet Connemara shawl. One of my minor hobbies is the study of comments in church visitors' books, and Creeragh promised something interesting.

'Thy will be done' — was this straightforward reverence, unconscious humour, or tongue in cheek? After all, Creeragh Church cannot be everyone's cup of tea. 'Nothing like it in Scotland' — does one read an unwritten 'Thank Goodness?' There are surely no two ways of reading 'Like a little Heaven,' or the Keats quotation 'A thing of beauty is a joy forever.' 'Fab, but wasted out here' a Dubliner had written, failing to appreciate that the situation makes the church, and that it would pass unnoticed in a city. 'It shelters the sheep from the wind' might well find the apologist replying 'I am the Good Shepherd.' The last entry was 'Queer,' and it got my sympathy. Somehow Creeragh Church failed with me — unlike a not dissimilar church of wood and glass which I visited in Finland in 1964, where the altar cross was not in the church, but in a natural grove of silver birch trees just outside the glass east end, and red squirrels were playing about the arms of the cross when I was there.

Leaving Creeragh Church on its tawny moorland, we soon had on our left hand the dark waters of Killary Harbour, a fjord running eight miles inland, and separating Galway from Mayo, which county we entered where the Erriff River tumbles down the Aasleagh Falls beneath the Devil's Mother Mountain at the head of the inlet, which was once a station of the British Atlantic Fleet. Killary Harbour is, indeed, the drowned lower valley of the Erriff, and we looped round on to the Mayo shore where, in three miles, the road strikes inland between the Mweelrea Mountains and the Sheefry Hills to Louisburgh. Approaching the southern end of Doo Lough we encountered the classical place name, Delphi, bestowed on a fishing lodge by an Earl of Sligo under the influence of the Grand Tour.

Our six days of fine weather were coming to an end with grey cloud legions sweeping in from the Atlantic, the rising wind dispelling the haze so that we had glimpses of Inishturk, Cahir, and Clare islands, the last of these across the mouth of Clew Bay rising to 1,540 feet, and still having a population of 500 who live by fishing, farming,

28

and burning kelp. Clare Island, accessible by boat from Roonah Quay, once had its own queen, Grace O'Malley, who, visiting Elizabeth I, insisted on being treated as of equal rank. Grace is one of the great characters of Irish history, and many are the stories still told about her. She kept her ships tied to a hawser which passed through a wall and was secured to her bed. She fought, pillaged, did a bit of piracy, took up the cudgels for and against the English and for and against her husbands, and there is confusion as to whether she is buried on her island, in Clare 'Abbey,' or on the mainland at Burrishoole 'Abbey.'

In either case Mayo has her bones, Mayo, the county that embodies the particular attractions of Ireland. Great lakes like Mask and Conn, mountains with space around them like Nephin, Nephin Beg, and Croagh Patrick, the Holy Reek, where St. Patrick expelled the snakes from Ireland, place of pilgrimage each last Saturday night in July, with, it is said, 365 islands strewn haphazardly on Clew Bay to reward tired eyes if Garland Sunday dawns clear. Mayo has the best-situated village in Ireland with the ugliest name, Pontoon, on an isthmus between Lough Conn and Lough Cullin; it has Ireland's loneliest road — seen now, alas, in the rain — 20 miles from Mulraney via Ballycroy to Bangor Erris; and Ireland's remotest region, the Mullet peninsula. At Crossmolina Kevin Brown has a bar, but he is more than a publican, he is the local undertaker. An Irish works policeman in my newspaper offices married Kevin Brown's daughter at Christmas, 1967 and spent his honeymoon at Crossmolina. 'Sure,' he told me when he came back to work, 'We had a marvellous time. I drove the hearse for 16 funerals.'

Fairest of them All?

IN HER BOOK, 'My Ireland,' Kate O'Brien, the novelist, accepts rather than asserts that the accolade for scenic beauty must go to County Kerry. She gives second place to Antrim. Perhaps I am unkind to find this surprising, for it was among the Glens of Antrim that my love for Ireland first came upon me in 1935, strengthened by several evenings of sheer delight as, with three others, I rowed Paddy Hannon's cumbersome boat across a corner of Lough Neagh from Six Mile Water, Antrim, into the splendours of sunset among the woodlands surrounding Shane's Castle. Paddy would stand striking matches to guide us back safely into Six Mile Water.

As coast roads go the famous Antrim coast road rates high, but rocky coasts are much the same the world over, and I find no particular Irish quality in the Antrim coast road, while I am sure that the road from Belfast to Larne is the least attractive in Ireland.

Having paid her tribute to Kerry and Antrim, Kate O'Brien then puts in a claim for Sligo. Here I go joyfully with her, adding the lovely little neighbouring County Leitrim to make the most perfect microcosm of Irish scenery. One summer's morning in 1956 I walked out of Sligo town on the race course road, and, where Lough Gill first came in sight, its wooded islands floating on a calm expanse of pearl and pale blue, I stood entranced. Something of my wonder must have shown on my face, for a workman, digging a hole in the road, said, with a suspicion of bitterness, 'Sure, but you can't live on scenery, sorr.' He was not strictly correct, as the Irish Tourist Board would soon point out to him.

Driving into County Sligo from Mayo in 1969, we turned right short of the town on the Dromahair road and made a circuit of Lough Gill, where, pulling in at a viewpoint to let the April loveliness of the scene lap around us, we met one other man, tall, handsome, well set up and smartly dressed, who was watching a pair of yellow wagtails. We passed the time of day, and I talked of my present holiday in Ireland without revealing my wider knowledge of his country. I was, I told him, calling in the Bord Failte office in Sligo to see Eamonn Hoy.

'I know him well,' said my new acquaintance. 'Tell him you've been chatting beside Lough Gill with a Sligo man named Pilkington - doesn't sound a very Irish name to you, does it?'

'On the contrary.' I said. 'I know all about the exploits, nearly 50 years ago, of one Liam Pilkington, Commandant of the Third Western Division of the Irish Army in this area, though he was with the Irregulars on the wrong side after the treaty.'

My companion nearly stepped back into Lough Gill. Seldom have I seen anyone so moved.

'You, an Englishman, in 1969, know of Liam,' he said. 'He's my brother.'

So I mentioned my great interest in modern Irish history, in the 'Troubles.'

'Liam's still alive?' I asked.

'And, please God, he is,' Mr. Pilkington told me. 'After going through all the blood and fire of the Troubles he left Ireland disillusioned with the Free State, and joined the Redemptorist Brothers. He's now a priest, Father Pilkington, at St. Joseph's, Hawkstone Hall, in Shropshire.'

Only a few months earlier I had been at Hawkstone writing about the Hill family whose home it had been, not knowing that among those black-robed brothers was one who could tell such stirring stories of the Irish Troubles.

After the encounter with Mr Pilkington we drove through Sligo to Strandhill, the little seaside resort dominated by Knocknarea, the hill where Queen Maeve is reputedly buried, but our eyes were constantly turned north to Sligo Bay, where Ben Bulben, surely Ireland's most remarkable mountain, was faithfully reflected in perfectly calm water.

Sligo is the metropolis of the Yeats country, a pleasant little port: Sean O'Faolin, in a hilarious passage in his 'Irish Journey' describes its architecture as 'nineteenth century macaroni'. Walking its quiet streets in the evening my wife suddenly stopped and pointed to a sign above a shop — 'V. Bird and Son, Undertaker. Select Shrouds Supplied.' For 58 years Vivian Bird had been unique. I like it that way. There seemed to be living accommodation above the shop, so I hurried up some stairs and pressed the bell of a flat.

'Are you Mr. V. Bird?' I asked the man who answered my ring.

'I am,' said he.

'What does the V stand for?' I demanded.

'Vincent,' he replied.

I walked out relieved — and still unique — into the Irish dusk, returning to the Cafe Cairo in Wine Street, an unfortunate Arab name for a pleasant lodging, where I fell asleep reflecting that only in Ireland could I possibly find myself driving a German car and staying in a place named after Nasser's capital.

At all the Yeats shrines around Sligo celebrated in his poems, verses have been placed for the public to read — 'The Lake Isle of Innisfree' beside Lough Gill, at Glencar Lough, and at Drumcliff Churchyard 'Under bare Ben Bulben's head' where Yeats's gravestone bears that irritating and incomprehensible epitaph written by himself:

> Cast a cold eye on life, on death;
> Horseman, pass by.

Loveliest of the Yeats' shrines, both to the eye and to the ear, is Lissadell House, liquid-noted Lissadell, the grey mansion in the woodlands between the brooding prow of Ben Bulben and the sands of Sligo Bay, shining, as we saw them in the afternoon sunlight of an April day.

> The light of evening, Lissadell,
> Great windows open to the south.

No wonder this delectable spot nurtured a poet, Eva Gore-Booth, whose 'Little Waves of Breffny' breathes an air of her Sligo homeland. Lissadell bred, too, a rebel — Eva's sister Constance, who, as Countess Markievicz, was the first woman elected to the House of Commons at Westminster, as Sinn Fein M.P. for a Dublin constituency in 1918, though she never took her seat. She fought in the Easter Rising as second-in-command of the detachment at St. Stephen's Green, Dublin, where Max Caulfield in 'The Easter Rebellion' describes her on that momentous occasion. 'A grande

The westernmost embarkation point in the British Isles is the slipway at Dunquin on the Dingle peninsula of Co. Kerry, with a curragh about to leave for the depopulated Blasket Islands.

Dingle, the westernmost township in the British Isles, gives its name to a peninsula of outstanding beauty in Co. Kerry.   *Bord Failte Eireann.*

dame, born in Carlton House Terrace, London, a girl who had once curtsied to Queen Victoria, she now marched into St. Stephen's Green at the head of her troops, dressed theatrically to adorn the occasion in a dark-green woollen blouse trimmed with brass buttons, dark-green tweed knee-breeches, black stockings, and puttees and round her waist a cartridge belt from which, on one side, dangled a small automatic pistol and, from the other, a convertible Mauser rifle-pistol; the whole topped by a black velour hat trimmed with a spray of cocque feathers. It mattered hardly that the troops she led in through the gate were merely Boy Scouts and women; she nevertheless marched them in with the imperious confidence of a woman whose ancestors had been conquerors.'

From Lissadell we turned back through Sligo, headed south, and spent the early evening around two lovely lakes, Lough Arrow and Lough Key, before booking in for the night right beside the river at Carrick-on-Shannon in County Leitrim. Next morning, after a detour to see the Arigna coalmines perched on the hillside west of Lough Allen, we drove through Drumshambo and crossed into Northern Ireland by way of the Eireann frontier post at Swanlinbar in County Cavan.

*   *   *   *

We sat on the topmost haycock in the hilly field, my wife and I. To westward stretched a scene of splendour memorable even in this golden sunset land. Argosies of radiant clouds paid homage to the sun as it sank towards the great cliff of Sheean which towered grape-purple above the wider reaches of Lower Lough Erne — for we were in County Fermanagh, Ulster's beautiful lakeland. The waters in the sun's path shone as burnished gold, save where they were fretted by tree-clad islands and promontories pitch black against the kaleido-scope of colour. Sober and slate-hued to the right of the sunset, the rounded heads of the hills of Tyrone tumbled along the horizon. Below our field a belt of trees ran almost to the water's edge in Trory Bay. Stony foreshore alternated with marshy turf where the slender whiteflowered Grass of Parnassus sprang in profusion among the sweet-smelling water mint. Down there, too, were stately wine-red spikes of purple loosestrife.

Our eyes turned inevitably to the rushes where our rowing boat was moored. That boat had borne us on our most joyous excursions. From it we had bathed and fished, trawled for pike, and invaded slumbering islets, scattering the cows in the shallows. One five-mile pull against wind and weather back from St. Angelo neither of us would forget. Now, as we gazed, a ponderous heron flapped into the trees to the nest we had recently found, and leaping fish splashed soundlessly.

So we sat, recalling what Ireland had meant to us on several visits — days of fresh air on Antrim uplands and on Lough Neagh's broad bosom, walks on rough roads and rougher mountains in far western Connemara, on the softer hills of Wicklow, and on the plain of Tipperary ablaze with golden furze. We thought, too, of our honeymoon, only the past year in Fermanagh, staying at this same little lakeside farm at Trory, near Enniskillen, to which, and to our friends, Lena and Carney Templeman, also newly married, we had returned again. But now our second Fermanagh holiday was ending.

A dusk wind had risen during our reverie. A curlew trilled his homing song. A marauding owl swooped into the trees. Edith slid from the haycock and we took a last look up the lough as we turned downhill to the cottage.

'Shall we ever see it again?' she asked softly and sadly. As well she might. For this was August, 1939. War was only days off. Survival was doubtful, let alone enjoyment in the loveliest land we knew.

Well, we did survive, and two of our three children had good Irish names, Michael and Molly Deirdre. I had served in Northern Ireland during the war, and had been back many times since, but never again to Fermanagh. In 1963 it was 25 years since our honeymoon visit, a propitious time to go back. My friends of the Northern Ireland Tourist Board knew of the anniversary, and one day in early April of that year I had a phone call from Belfast. Would I like to spend four days in Fermanagh staying at the Imperial Hotel, Enniskillen, with a dozen fishing journalists? So there I was again, in the town islanded by two arms of the River Erne, home of the famous Inniskilling Dragoons and the Inniskilling Fusiliers.

Enniskillen has a population of 5,000, yet the first three people I asked knew my old hosts at Trory, Lena and Carney, now left the farm and living in the town. Somehow the war had broken communications between us, but now came a quick and rapturous reunion. The faded photographs of our two holidays in 1938 and

34

1939 were produced by Lena and, also somewhat faded, hanging above her kitchen fireplace as it had hung above our bed at Trory 25 years ago, was a card entitled 'Home Blessings:'

The Crown of the Home is Godliness,
The Beauty of the Home is Order,
The Glory of the Home is Hospitality,
The Blessing of the Home is Contentment.

So far, so good. There was no doubt of the success in the personal side of this rather risky return to past happiness. But the next morning, as I walked the five miles to Trory, even the sunshine could not dispel my disappointment at the deadly motor road which the once-pleasant country road had become. Momentarily my spirits lifted at the glimpse of the round tower on Devenish Island rising, ageless and with all the faery magic of Ireland, across a blue strip of water, only to slump again at the sight of the old cottage. As well-preserved as ever, and ivy-clad, it stood with grey slates, stucco walls, brown door, and three windows facing the road, but bereft of its sheltering pines. Gone, too, were the hedges, ready for a road-widening which would take its two remaining trees and a slice from the front garden.

Beyond Trory Church the lakeside meadows towards St. Angelo were slashed with a wartime aircraft runway.

'All nationalities landed here,' Lena Templeman told me, 'so we opened a cafe for them. One day three top brass came in for ham and eggs, and only afterwards did an officer tell us we'd served Prince Bernhard of the Netherlands — in your old sitting room.'

Even this aura of royalty failed to compensate. No longer tree-embowered, the cottage was not its long-remembered self. No one was at home, so I walked up our steep field until, standing where that haycock previously stood, I felt my happiness flood back, for here was that peerless panorama unchanged, the vision of a quarter of a century become reality again, with Lough Erne sparkling in the jewelled brilliance of a sunlit morning, and the mountains of Leitrim, Donegal, and Tyrone making a distant half circle of magnificent background.

This view epitomises the true beauty of Ireland. That 'little bit of Heaven that fell from out the sky one day' is not an extravagant notion. Ireland's great glory is her waters — her huge lakes in open country. Where the English and Welsh lakes and the Scottish lochs

35

lose the sun behind their surrounding mountains early of a summer's evening, Ireland's loughs reflect every cloud, every hue and tint of the sky until midnight.

Down to the reedy shore of Trory Bay I hurried, over violets, primroses, lady-smock; crushing the fragrant water-mint as I went. Peeping from the broader lough across the opening of the bay was wooded Tresna Island, once the kingdom of one of Ulster's great eccentrics, 'Orange Peggy' Elliott, Queen of Tresna. Born on July 11 in time to be christened on the 'twelfth,' Orange Day, Northern Ireland's national day, she was 108 when she died — on July 10, 1891 — so that she was buried on the 'twelfth.' Lena Templeman is her great grand-daughter, and she told me: 'I don't think it's true, as the guide book says, that every stitch of clothing she wore in her life was orange, but she never visited Enniskillen without wearing two great crossed orange sashes. She caused such a commotion whenever she walked through the town that my mother, as a young woman, hated walking with her. The 'twelfth' once brought tragedy to Orange Peggy when she stood one Orange Day, on the shore of Tresna unable to help, and watched two of her sons drown as they rowed out in a violent storm to save two soldiers whose boat had overturned.'

Orange Peggy used to wave an orange flag at every boat that passed Tresna, and she lies buried at Maghera Cross.

I had been wakened in my Enniskillen hotel by the sonorous beat of swans' wings as they flew along the River Erne. Now, as I contemplated Tresna, there came another sound to thrill me even more — the rasp of the corncrake, scarcely ever heard in England nowadays, but often in the west of Ireland. Indeed, in 1951 I heard one on the perimeter of Belfast's old airport at Nutts Corner. No matter that this shy bird is seldom seen; that his call is unmelodious; he is a survival for which Heaven be praised. His croak sounded a benison on this chancy pilgrimage of mine back through 25 years to the happy days of young manhood.

One thing remained to be done — to tread again the holy turf of Devenish Island hidden around the headland. We loved this green uninhabited island with its round tower, its 6th Century ruins of St. Mary's Abbey and the House of St. Molaise, and we rowed there each day on those two holidays of long ago. No boat was available now, so I spent the remainder of the day in an epic 70-mile hitch-

36

hike, helped by Northern Ireland's ultra-courteous motorists, up the east of Lough Erne, walking across bridged Boa Island to Beleek and Garrison, both on the border, with glimpses of Lough Melvin and the two loughs MacNean.

Next day another such journey revealed to me the charm of Upper Lough Erne, another paradise for the boatmen and the fisherman, in a walk from Lisnaskea across several bridged islands to Derrylin, where I was given a cup of tea by the Royal Ulster Constabulary in this most shot-up of all Northern posts by the I.R.A.

Finally I hired an outboard to take me the three miles from Enniskillen to Devenish, and, as we cleaved the still waters I felt the solace which Ireland bestows on the wayfarer. We went ashore through budding hawthorn and grazing sheep, with a goat or two. Devenish once had a large population of hares, kept there to be netted for coursing.

'They're wiped out,' Carney had told me. 'When myxomatosis took the rabbits the foxes used to swim to Devenish and kill the hares. I've often seen them.'

Now I was back on the island with lake water lapping its shores. In Ireland they're great ones for wishing. The visitor wishes down wells, in caves, clasps arms round a Celtic cross at Glendalough, squeezes through a cleft rock in Mayo, and at Blarney hangs from the castle battlements. All that a wish might come true. On Devenish it is an old stone coffin, lidless, among the abbey ruins. You lie in it, wriggle round three times, and your wish is granted. I didn't avail myself of the opportunity. After all, I was back in Ireland, back in Fermanagh, back on Devenish. What more in the world was there to wish for?

* * * *

We actually entered Northern Ireland at the Customs Post of Mullen, half a mile or so along the road from Swanlinbar. A wave of our brown pass provided by the car hire firm saw us through without ceremony. So we came into Enniskillen across the west bridge, with the Water Gate to southward and Portora Royal School to northward where the river begins to broaden into Lower Lough Erne. Among its past scholars Portora numbers Oscar Wilde and the Rev. H. F. Lyte who wrote 'Abide with me,' conscious perhaps that Portora means the 'Port of Tears' because from old Portora Castle, now a ruin, the dead were embarked for burial on Devenish Island, though it is hard to imagine the smiling Erne as a River Styx.

Enniskillen is lacking the wide main street customary in Irish towns, but beyond the far eastern end is Fair Green, from which spectators once watched executions at the gaol. The opening in the wall which gave access to the scaffold is now filled with a sculpted panel depicting Labour. Dominating Enniskillen from Fort Hill is a column to Sir Lowry Cole, one of Wellington's commanders in the Peninsular War. The town has always had a Protestant tradition, and only the spectacular Siege of Londonderry in 1689 took away the limelight from Enniskillen's own sturdy fight against James II. My friends the Templemans are stout Protestants, and I remember from 30 years ago how Lena would change the words of 'The Boys of County Cork' from 'the boys who licked the Black and Tans' to 'the boys who ran from the Black and Tans were the boys of County Cork.'

After a night's reunion with Lena and Carney, my first for six years, Edith's first for 30 years, we drove out next morning up the Omagh road and, staying left at Trory junction, visited the old cottage once again. Then on up the lakeside to Ballycassidy and Saint Angelo, the seat of a Church of Ireland bishop whom I remember seeing gaitered and seated in sepulchral black in a wooden armchair out in one of his cornfields while the harvest was gathered in.

A well-known story to the older generation in England is that of the four Macdonald sisters who, from humble beginnings as the daughters of a Methodist minister on circuits in Yorkshire and Birmingham, made splendid marriages. Georgina married the painter who became Sir Edward Burne-Jones; Agnes married Sir Edward Poynter, President of the Royal Academy; Alice married John Kipling and they became the parents of Rudyard Kipling, the poet; while Louisa married a Worcestershire ironmaster, Alfred Baldwin, and their son became Prime Minister and the 1st Earl Baldwin of Bewdley. Their saga may be said to have begun at Ballinamallard, just east of Lower Lough Erne from Saint Angelo, in the person of their grandfather, James Macdonald, born there in June 1761 to a poverty-stricken couple who had come to the smiling banks of Erne from the gloomy isle of Skye. In 1784 James was invited by John Wesley to become a Methodist minister, in which calling he was followed by his youngest son, George Browne Macdonald, born in 1805, who became the father of the four Macdonald sisters.

Killadeas is one of the great viewpoints for Lower Lough Erne, which always reminds me, with its many densely-wooded islands, of any scene among the Finnish lakes. We continued round the north shore, taking the road over Boa Island, but returning to the 'mainland' to stop at the entrance to Castle Caldwell and see the Fiddle Stone, erected by Sir James Caldwell in 1770 to commemorate a drunken fiddler who fell from a houseboat and was drowned in Lower Lough Erne. Still are legible the two lines:
> On firm land only, exercise your skill,
> There you may play and safely drink your fill.

At Belleek, famous for its fishing and its pottery, we crossed back into the Republic, and as we approached Ballyshannon I was living very much in the past. One day on our 1938 holiday at Trory we had gone by bus to Bundoran, the Donegal seaside resort, travelling from Enniskillen along the road on the western shore of Lower Lough Erne, which the 1st Lord Rothermere, a much-travelled man, considered the loveliest scenic road he had ever known. As our bus breasted a hill in Ballyshannon we had our first view of the estuary of the Erne with the shimmering sea of Donegal Bay beyond it. That view has remained in my mind's eye ever since, firmly entrenched there through some quality of the sunlight, and now we came upon Ballyshannon on a cloudy early afternoon, so my memory of that little town still comes from 30 years ago.

On the bridge at Ballyshannon there is a memorial tablet to William Allingham, the poet, a native of the town, and who but an Irishman could have written 'The Fairies'
> Up the aery mountain,
> Down the rushy glen,
> We daren't go a-hunting
> For fear of little men;
> Wee folk, good folk,
> Trooping all together;
> Green jacket, red cap,
> And white owl's feather.

Now, with Allingham, it was with us 'Adieu to Belashanney and

39

the winding banks of Erne' as we turned north towards Donegal town on a road which is but a poor introduction to one of Ireland's most ravishing counties. 'Donegal the Magnificent' it is called in a small book by James A. Moore, a writer I was subsequently to meet in Londonderry,

The coast of Donegal is so rugged and indented that limitless time would be necessary to visit every famous beauty spot. Already we had missed Rossnowlagh, and now we turned north for Ardara, missing Killybegs, Slieve League, and Glencolumbkille, thought I had seen them all before. One name normally neglected in Donegal's pageant of beauty is Bruckless, a grey little township of neat charm with a round tower among the daffodils in the church-yard. Two miles on we turned smartly right and inland, and somewhere near the watershed we picked up a woman outside her cottage and took her the five downhill miles to Ardara. Learning that we came from Birmingham, inevitably she had a relative in the Midlands — a daughter at Walsall. I find it a mistake in Ireland to mention my home town as it invariably leads to my discussing Birmingham instead of Ireland. Ten days earlier, on our first day of this journey, we were looking for New Birmingham in County Tipperary, so it was not unnatural that I should tell a man of whom I asked directions that I came from old Birmingham. I got the directions, but only after a lengthy discussion on a less salubrious part of Birmingham where one of his daughters lives.

We dropped our passenger at Ardara, declining her invitation to go and see Donegal tweed being made. Ardara is the centre of the industry, the tweed often being woven by skilled outworkers in the whitewashed cottages where generations of the family have plied the looms. At Owenea Bridge I forsook the main road, adventuring instead across five miles of minor road via Tully More and Tully Beg — though they made no noticeable impact on the loneliness of an austere tract of rock, heather, and little lakes. I was almost tempted to stay at a pleasant hotel at Maas where we rejoined the main road, but ahead lay the Gweebarra estuary, famed for its beauty, and with an afternoon turning brilliantly sunny it was a glorious sight, while inland came the first glimpse of Donegal's big mountains, Slieve Snacht (2,240 feet) living up to its name with a cap of snow.

At Dungloe we entered The Rosses, as stony as Iarconnaught, but incredibly more populous, with houses popping up everywhere on the most barren land, even proliferating in a white rash on Aranmore Island offshore. Driving through The Rosses is a hair-raising experience, for seldom can you see 50 yards of road ahead, and that disappearing skyward with the certainty of some twist or turn when you top the rise. This fascinating district is Paddy the Cope's country, from its remarkable character, born Patrick Gallagher at Dungloe in 1871, but remembered in Welsh fashion from the co-operatives he set up, as Paddy the Cope. This boy who, on leaving school, walked to Strabane hiring fair 50 miles distant in County Tyrone, and was taken on by a Londonderry farmer, became wealthy and famous enough to publish his autobiography, 'My Story.' I have a treasured copy, given me by my good friend Joe Harkness, a devout Northern Ireland Protestant from Rasharkin, County Antrim, and inscribed by the author: 'My dear Joseph, I hope you will like "My Story," Paddy the Cope, 9 August, 1958.'

Paddy's book begins 'The Rosses is on the west coast of County Donegal, Ireland. There are 109 townlands in The Rosses. Cleendra is one of them. Cleendra lies on sloping ground facing the Atlantic. I often heard that Neil Og's home is the highest house in Ireland, and many a pleasant evening I spent there listening to Neil Og and his sister, Maire, telling stories. They are both dead long ago. Whenever I visit Cleendra and look up at the ruins of that grand old home I feel sad. Hardly a day passes that there are not some of the Cleendra people standing or kneeling on the brae, watching across the Atlantic, some of the older ones wondering why they cannot see their sons, daughters, brothers, or sisters in that land across the ocean, as there are no hills, mounds, forests, or bushes between Cleendra and America. Oh! if the naked eye could travel 3,000 miles, wouldn't it be a grand sight?'

There is the same simplicity, as of a child writing a composition; the same peasant lack of pretension, but a feeling for words, landscape, and weather that comes through the opening paragraph of that more famous book from farther south, from the Dingle where we had recently been — Maurice O'Sullivan's 'Twenty Years a-Growing.'

'There is no doubt but youth is a fine thing though my own is not yet over and wisdom comes with age. I am a boy who was born and bred in the Great Blasket, a small truly Gaelic island which lies north-west of the coast of Kerry, where the storms of the sky and the wild sea beat without ceasing from end to end of the year and from generation to generation against the wrinkled rocks which stand above the waves that wash in and out of the coves where the seals make their homes.'

Paddy the Cope's father was known as Paddy Bawn (fair-haired Paddy) and his maternal grandfather as Sean Og (young Sean). After his spell on the Londonderry farm Paddy went to Scotland as a miner and he bought a suit at Broxburn Co-op, an ordinary-enough purchase, but it was to alter his entire life. Returning to Donegal to live, he persuaded some of his smallholder friends to join him in buying artificial manure wholesale, but the merchant would sell only to an organisation. So Paddy founded a co-operative. It paid off — henceforth he was known as Paddy the Cope. By 1906 the Templecrone Co-operative Society Ltd. of Dungloe had six branches employing 44 men and boys, a bakery employing 13, a mill 2, while 150 girls worked in a hosiery factory, co-op gloves were sold throughout Ireland, and there was an electricity power plant, an iceplant, and a herring curing station. Paddy opened up Burtonport, south of Dungloe, and brought in such cargoes as manure from Holland and 1,000 tons of cement from Denmark. One of his great exploits, in November 1945, was to sail a 60 h.p. boat without charts or Customs clearance from Burtonport to Ayr with a cargo of herrings for the Scottish Co-operative Wholesale Society.

In 1945 the Cope's sales turnover was £154,440; its wages bill £10,985, and it paid out £3,755 in a dividend of 2s. in the £1 on purchases. Paddy had transformed life in west Donegal. His book, first published by Jonathan Cape in London, in 1938, sold out the first edition. A second edition was published in New York in 1942, and by 1958 it was in its seventh edition, having also been published in translation in Sweden. Then the Templecrone Co-op published an edition of 10,000 — and when Paddy sent Joe Harkness his copy there were only 28 left unsold. Enough, one would think, to have satisfied Paddy the Cope. But no. In a letter to Joe, typed on Templecrone Co-op notepaper on August 8, 1958, Paddy had this to say: 'I have very little education. I did not tell half the story. There is another story now in the hands of the American publishers. In my opinion the following chapters are much better than those of my first book. Chapter 1. I met my wife Sally at Johnnie Mulhern's wake. 2. James Dillon, T.D., attacked me in the Dail. 3. Smuggled whiskey

42

in the coffin instead of the dead man. 4. I refused to pay harbour dues on a cargo of artificial manures. 5. I shot a shark in Dungloe Bay. 6. The English gentry sack their king — I am sure the Queen and 90% of the English people will like it.'

Whether anything came of Paddy's second book I do not know. He died a few years ago in his nineties.

* * * *

One of my most moving Irish memories concerns Joe Harkness. On the last day of an Irish holiday in April 1968 my wife and I drove from Cookstown, Co. Tyrone, to call on Joe at his sister's home in Rasharkin before returning to Aldergrove Airport for an evening flight home. We found him — in his eighties — in bed with a cold, but we sat and talked to him for an hour. As we were about to leave, he got smartly out of bed, stood on the carpet in his blue and white striped pyjamas, removed his night cap, took Edith by one hand and me by the other, bowed his head, and said: 'Father, I thank you that two good friends have come so far to see an old man. May they be blessed for it, and may their journey home tonight be safe. Amen.'

I have no religion myself, but its sincere manifestations from those who have always touch me deeply.

* * * *

The evening shaping up for another spectacular sunset, I would have liked to see it around Bloody Foreland, Ireland's north-west headland, which gets its name from the blood-red glow it assumes at sunset. But we had already driven too far during the day, so we settled down for the night at Dungloe and continued northward in the morning to Bunbeg, and into another area still closely associated with the man who developed it before Paddy the Cope was operating in The Rosses.

This was Lord George Hill, who lived at Gweedore House between Bunbeg and the majestic cone of Errigal (2,466 feet), possibly Ireland's most striking mountain. Accompanying a Viceroy of Ireland on tour as one of his staff, Lord George was so moved by the famine, typhoid, consumption, and wretched housing in Donegal

43

that he devoted his fortune to improving conditions in the north-west of the county. In 1838 he bought 25,000 acres around Gweedore, and living at Gweedore House above the River Clady, he spent 40 years promoting schemes for the betterment of his people. He visited all his tenants regularly, speaking to them in Irish so that they said he could not possibly be an English lord. For years, and throughout the Great Famine, he moved about in perfect safety while other landlords were being harassed, and even murdered.

He put up a premium on production to encourage industry, and built a quay at Bunbeg, bringing in vessels of 200 tons from Liverpool. To me that quay and the channel of approach through sheer rock is one of the wonders of Ireland. He set up a store for corn to discourage its use in illicit distilling, and built a corn mill, a saw mill, and a flax mill. That store has been converted into a 60-roomed hotel within the last couple of years, but Lord George's inscription in Irish above the old harbourmaster's office still remains, translating as: 'A just weight is a pleasure to the Lord, but an unequal balance is an abomination in his sight.'

I was sorry not to be able to get into Bunbeg Church to see the memorial erected by his tenants to their benefactor, but an idea for an amusing short story struck me as I studied the notice board outside the church. I offer it, gratis, to any latter-day George Birmingham who may read this book. There are, it seems, regular services in an island church offshore, the boat leaving Bunbeg quay one hour before the time of the service. That boat must contain most of the local Church of Ireland population. Imagine it, one day, in trouble, and the Bunbeg lifeboat, manned entirely by Roman Catholics, called to its aid — surely the stuff of which George Birmingham wove his humorous stories of Irish life.

We drove on, through desolate moorland, to Bloody Foreland, and turning east had excellent views of Inishbofin and its two attendant islets, with Tory Island (pronounced Torry) beyond it, ten miles out to sea, still the home of 300 hardy characters who subsist largely from lobster fishing. They pay neither rent, rates, nor taxes. When H.M.S. 'Wasp' went to collect certain dues in 1884 it was wrecked with the loss of all but six of the crew. Tory was the home of the Formorians, a legendary race of giant pirates, whose leader was the One-Eyed Balor of the Mighty Blows. He met his end through the theft of a cow belonging to the mainland chieftain MacKineely.

Learning that MacKineely was plotting a revenge, Balor crossed from Tory and beheaded him on a huge stone, now known as Cloghaneely, with red veins said to be the blood of the dead chieftain. The stone can still be seen at Falcarragh. Nemesis awaited Balor, however, in the person of the blacksmith grandson of MacKineely, who thrust a red-hot iron bar into the giant's remaining eye.

From Falcarragh and Gortahawk we circled back inland towards Gweedore, but stopping short beneath the slopes of Errigal, we turned left to Dunlewy which has an astonishingly ugly church, badly coloured, and over ornate for anywhere, let alone this wilderness. This is perhaps Ireland's high spot of savage scenery. Beyond Lough Nacung on our right bare jagged slopes swept up eventually to Slieve Snacht, its snowy summit matching Errigal which rose immediately above our left hand with its own white cap of quartzite and snow, westernmost of a magnificent ridge of snow-capped mountains switchbacking over several white summits for eight miles to Muckish (2,197 feet). As Lough Nacung gave place to Lough Dunlewy the gap of the Poisoned Glen appeared on our right between Slieve Snacht and the Derryveagh Mountains, a wicked defile which gets its name from a spurge growing there. Our primitive road climbed steadily through the heather to nearly 1,000 feet, a place of austere grandeur where we were assaulted with hailstones from a sudden shower. We had the world to ourselves, not even a sheep grazed in this inhospitable spot. Crossing the watershed, we turned downhill towards Kilmacrenan and Letterkenny, passing on our right the track leading to Lough Veagh. James Moore of Londonderry knows Donegal intimately, and this is what he has written of this area: 'The motorist or cyclist can proceed on a fair surfaced road that becomes stonier and rougher at every mile, to Lough Veagh, the most spectacular lough in Donegal, and indeed for that matter, in all Ireland. The mountains rise in steep slopes from the water's edge to a height of 1,500 feet. There are no cottages or farms to soften the wildness, and the place is solitary beyond expression. The lough is about four miles in length and nowhere more than half a mile in breadth. One of the classic excursions in Ireland is to walk by the path to the south-western end of the lough and then climb up to the Glendowan road. A gap called Ballaghgeeha Gap leads to the savage Poisoned Glen. From here you can follow the Devlin River down to Dunlewy. It is a marvellous walk, but one that should only be undertaken in company and then only by persons of the strongest physique.'

We stayed that night at the Fern Hotel, Kilmacrennan, where we were made most comfortable, and from which we were able next day to explore the Roscuill peninsula, a place of superlative beauty jutting northward between Sheep Haven and the western entrance to Mulroy Bay. The short circular drive from Rosapenna should be walked — if you will pardon the Irishism. Driving is so tricky that it takes the full attention of driver and passengers from this Donegal in miniature, ten miles which embody all that is endearing in that captivating county. Rosapenna itself has an immaculate beach and extensive sand hills.

Something has to be missed out in Donegal, and it was the Fanad country between Mulroy Bay and Lough Swilly. From a night across the border, in trouble-torn Londonderry, where a skeleton on the civic arms recalls the starvation of the besieged populace in 1689, and an inscription on the city walls 'Cowards' Bastion' marks the place that was the safest during the siege, we set out on a day's exploration of the Inishowen peninsula on our way to the northernmost point of Ireland, Malin Head. We were anxious to see Clonmany, described by Moore as 'perhaps the most dramatic village in Ireland,' a description of which it fell far short. We did, instead, discover our own contender for the most attractive village in Ireland, Malin, where incredibly neat cottages border a central green, colour-washed in many hues, but all perfectly tasteful. Crossing a ten-arch bridge out of Malin we skirted Trawbeaga Bay among the highest sand dunes in the British Isles.

On Malin Head, which one associates at once, from the Meteorological Office area 'Malin', with rough weather, it was so calm that we brewed up with the meths stove in the open just as we had eleven days earlier on Slea Head. We had come from Ireland's westernmost headland to the northernmost, and found it a much less ferocious place, shelving more gently to the sea than the Kerry headland. Tory Island and Inishbofin, to westward, are well south of Malin Head, but one last rock lay six miles north-east, the exposed ultimate speck of Ireland, the 113 acres of Inishtrahull, occupied until 1930 by 50 islanders who surely lived nearer the weather than any other community in our islands. Now it lay serene and deserted on a blue sea, while our gaze, sweeping eastward of it, rested, 45 miles away, on the hills of the southern islands of the Hebrides, Islay and Jura — the next leg in my journey up the sunset coasts.

Reflections in the North

I SPENT THE NIGHT OF APRIL 7, 1968, at Cookstown, in Tyrone of the Bushes. Alan Cook well deserved to have the town named after him for laying out, in 1609, the High Street, one and a quarter miles long, dead straight, and impressive because of its width even in a land where country towns are noted for the width of their squares, diamonds, and main streets.

In this commodious thoroughfare, against the war memorial which is a copy of the Cenotaph in Whitehall, it pleased me to take a photograph of a van with the name of a prominent Northern Ireland laundry on it, Lilliput. Dean Swift, creator of Lilliput, was, of course, an Irishman, born in Dublin. I watched a funeral procession of cars, nearly as long as the High Street itself, following a hearse, and I walked out the two miles to Lissaw rectory, where a resident banshee wails on the impending death of one of the O Corras family. It was a calm, peaceful April evening, with local residents beginning work in their gardens.

I could not know what Cookstown was nursing in its pleasant bosom. Yet exactly one year later, a Cookstown girl of 21, a psychology student and a political agitator currently engaged in challenging law and order throughout six counties, was returned to Parliament at Westminster as Civil Rights M.P. for the Mid-Ulster constituency. It has taken Bernadette Devlin, an unfledged rabble-rouser, barely of age, to reconcile me to Ian Paisley. He is strangely uncharitable for a man of God, but take away that dog collar and you remove most of my objection to him. He becomes just another outspoken Northern Ireland Protestant — a belligerent breed, but they have a case.

48

Sybil Head, Co. Kerry, north of the village of Dunquin, where Ireland thrusts farthest into the Atlantic.

Bord Failte Eireann.

This lane, beneath Ben Bulben in Co. Sligo, might well have been in the mind of Eva Gore-Booth from nearby Lissadell when she wrote her poem on "the little roads of Cloonagh."

Bord Fáilte Éireann.

Ireland is so obviously a geographical entity that Partition seems stupid. Yet the border exists, dividing the Six Counties from the Twenty-Six, and better it should continue than strife be fomented and blood be spilt to remove it. My Republican sympathies are against the border, but my anti-Catholicism makes me sympathetic to northern Protestants in the religious and social sphere, if not in the political. A difficult impasse, but, unhappily resolved somewhat now that so many Northern Ireland republicans have embraced Civil Rights, march with long-haired liberals and workshy students, have forgotten the splendid Irish revolutionary songs, and sing instead that dreariest of all international dirges 'We shall overcome' the layabouts' lament. Their politics have become economic, not nationalistic; they are following the Connolly line, not the Pearse line; they are — how do they square it with their Catholicism? — Marxists, not Romantics, and where Ireland is concerned I am an unblushing Romantic. It is good for a man to have one realm into which he can escape from the pressures and problems of his everyday world. Ireland is my escape.

There exists a belief that politics and religion should never be discussed by the visitor to Ireland. I have no inhibitions on these subjects, short of good taste, and the only time I have ever had a rough handling — intellectually only — was in Birmingham during a period of Civil Rights rioting in the North. I was with five Irishmen at an Irish Club getting material to write about Birmingham's annual St. Patrick's Day parade. We had concluded our business, and they asked my view, as an outsider, on the trouble in Northern Ireland. I gave it to them, attacking Civil Rights, but, as a republican prepared to put up with their Catholicism.

Stonily they said, in effect, 'Thank you for nothing. It's no use your accepting our Catholicism if you oppose our economics. It isn't a religious war in Northern Ireland; it's economic.'

Twice in Ireland I have seen the readiness of Irishmen with a vested interest in the tourist trade not to give offence to the English. At Jury's Hotel, Dublin, they put on a fine Irish cabaret — the accent on the Irish, not the cabaret, or I could not have enjoyed it as I did one night in 1964. The show ended, all the artists reappeared on the stage, and everything seemed set for the National Anthem, 'A Soldier's Song.' But the song they sang, with the audience standing, was 'A Nation Once Again.'

49

Good, I thought, two patriotic songs for the price of one, and cleared my throat to join in 'A Soldier's Song.' It didn't come. 'Why not?' I protested to the manager. 'Some English guests might take offence,' he said. 'Well,' said I, 'here's one English guest who takes offence at its omission.'

I like Davis's great song as much as the National Anthem despite its having been desecrated by drunken-sounding recording groups, but there must have been some seismic disturbance around Glasnevin Cemetery as the old fighters of Easter Week turned in their graves at this slighting of 'A Soldier's Song.'

One rainy day, travelling on a C.I.E. coach tour between Killarney and Cork, we were singing merrily when Paddy, the courier, suggested that I might sing an Irish song. 'Certainly,' I said. 'We've just entered County Cork, so I'll sing "The Boys of County Cork".' Paddy came as near a frown as an Irishman can. 'We're just after coming up to the coffee stop,' he said. 'We'll have the song later.' Somehow, for the rest of that day, Paddy contrived to prevent my singing, though a coachload of Americans would surely not have been unduly disturbed at some scathing references to the Black and Tans. But this was tourism. Politics must not raise its ugly head.

Incidentally, my own favourite of all the rousing and lovely Irish songs is one that is both rousing and lovely, the lay of Bold Phelim Brady, 'The Bard of Armagh.'

It was Northern Ireland's major geographical feature which first attracted me to the province of Ulster as long ago as 1935 — that large blue hole in the north-east corner, Lough Neagh, out of which it seems all the stout and whiskey could run to waste. I have remained faithful to Lough Neagh ever since, never missing an opportunity to gaze across its sea-like expanse, always thrilled by its placid beauty, though I have seen it in storm as well. Bordered by five of the six Northern Ireland counties, Lough Neagh is 17 miles long by 11 miles broad, and covers an area of 153 square miles. Ten rivers flow into it. It is pre-glacial in origin, but Ulster folk have their own theory for its creation. Finn McCoul, their giant hero, is reported to have made Lough Neagh by scooping up a handful of Ulster to throw at a rival giant in Scotland. It fell short, forming the Isle of Man, and if proof is wanted, the Isle of Man covers roughly the same area as Lough Neagh. Another story tells of a flood which spread from a spring to drown entire communities, and the poet,

Tom Moore, recalls this legend in the lines:
> *On Lough Neagh's banks as the fisherman strays,*
> *In the clear cool eve's declining,*
> *He sees the round towers of other days*
> *In the wave beneath him shining.*

Antrim town, in the north-east corner of the lough, has Ulster's finest example of a round tower, 93 feet high, and at Ardboe on the Tyrone shore is one of Ireland's finest Celtic crosses, 18½ feet high, and embellished with 22 carved scriptural scenes.

Lough Neagh is a delusion. Beneath its huge placid mirror, which reflects the most wonderful sunsets as the west catches fire beyond the Sperrin Mountains of Tyrone, is a vast wriggling mass of eels, 153 succulent, squirming square miles of eels. The eel is a creature of habit, and no little stamina. In its third year, a four-inch sliver of silver, it journeys thousands of miles from its native Sargasso Sea with the Gulf Stream in search of fresh water in which to spend the next ten years maturing. Then it again feels the urge for salt water. This regular routine makes it an easy prey, where the Lower River Bann drains out of Lough Neagh, for the eel fishery at Toome. In the autumn of 1964 my visit to the eel fishery coincided with the run of the mature eels back towards the sea.

'They travel most on stormy autumn nights in the dark of the moon,' Mr Sam Ellis, the fishery manager, told me. 'Eel-fishing itself is seasonal. Most of our job lies in keeping alive the 600 tons of eels we catch in the season, so that supplies can be apportioned out regularly throughout the year, mainly to the London area where they are particularly partial to jellied eels.'

This, then, is the end of the Lough Neagh eels. Their beginning, as tiny elvers with an Atlantic swim behind them, is at Coleraine, near the mouth of the Bann, where, each spring, some 25 million elvers are caught in traps and transferred alive 31 miles upstream to Lough Neagh, where they live for ten years unless the licensed fishermen get them. These brown eels are caught in the lough by 180 or so boats licensed by the eel fishery, which holds the eel fishing rights. From little creeks, bays, and backs all round the lough, the Quinns, Hannons, Devlins, Doyles and MacCartneys come out to lay their eel lines, two miles long with hooked side lines every seven yards. They sell their catch to the fishery, lorries collecting the eels and delivering them in galvanised iron tanks.

The major part of the catch is of the mature silver eels as they leave Lough Neagh at Toome. There the fishery depot keeps a battery of long funnelled nets, 10 feet in diameter, at the mouth of the river facing the lough. By day they are raised. Fishing is permitted only between sunset and dawn, and there is a close season from January 11 to May 31.

Each night's catch is kept in large floating tanks from which the eels are removed in huge nets for transfer to a tanker taking them by road to the Larne-Preston ferry. Then they are taken across England to Maldon in Essex where an associated company keeps them in perforated barges in both fresh and salt water until they are disposed of to jelliers and retailers.

Lough Neagh, for all that it is the largest lake in the British Isles, has to be sought out. It is rarely part of a mainroad view, but it is seldom two miles from a main road. An eel fishery van drove me 80 miles round Lough Neagh. At creeks and harbours on the Derry and Tyrone shores — Ballyronan, Newport Trench, Ardboe, Kilycolpy — we left the expected world of the British Isles for something primitive, Biblical scenes of lines of drying nets, with fishermen tying hooks to their miles of eel lines, and always the coming and going of boats out of the limpid water where sky and lough were indistinguishable. Near Maghery we drove through miles of lonely peat bog. In County Armagh they were busy in orchards picking and crating apples.

It was a misty October morning next day, good for some illegal fishing, as Ernie Gibson took the patrol boat on to Lough Neagh from Six Mile Water, Antrim. His mates John Kennedy and Jim Crawford swept the horizon with their binoculars. There is quite a bit of needle in the encounters between the Protestant Unionist water bailiffs and the Catholic Nationalist fishermen of the Tyrone shore, even though they do sell to the eel fishery. I was soon to see it in action.

Wooded promontories had faded into the haze. Fitful sunrays scattered handfuls of silver on the water. With a completely encircling 'sea' horizon still our spray brought no salt to our lips — Lough Neagh is an ocean of fresh water.

John had his glasses on two boats. As we approached, one of them made off in a great hurry. Jim waved a red warning flag, Ernie switched on our two powerful outboard motors, and I turned a back

52

somersault. On regaining my feet I found we were grappling with the runaway boat which had in it two sullen fishermen and a sheepish priest. They were, it seemed, merely observing a test with a new type of trawl net by the other boat. Their flight had been a bit of mickey-taking, but I think they were impressed at the speed with which we overtook them.

The rest of our day was uneventful. Occasionally we drew alongside a fishing boat with one man at the oars and another pulling up the line, flipping the little perch back into the lough, and the eels into a bin in the boat. In addition to its eels and the coarse fish one would expect, Lough Neagh is the home of the pollan, a fresh-water herring, and the donaghan, a pink-fleshed trout.

During my van ride round the shores of the lough the driver told me that it was the ambition of Mr Robert Frizzell, general manager of the Northern Ireland Tourist Board, to see a scenic motor road right round Lough Neagh. 'If I meet Mr Frizzell I'll give him a piece of my mind,' I said. 'A motor road would ruin the lough.' This was on Thursday. On the Saturday morning I flew back to Birmingham. On the Monday I flew out to Helsinki for four days in Finland as a guest of British European Airways on their inaugural Trident flight from London. Friday and Saturday nights I spent in Stockholm on my way home, and on the Saturday I attended a cocktail party in the home of the B.E.A. Scandinavian manager. Among the guests were many delegates to the annual conference of the Skal Club — of travel agents etc. — being held in Stockholm.

I had pushed my way out of the warm room and was cooling off over a drink on a landing between some stairs when another chap joined me.

'It's hot in there,' he said.

'It jolly well is,' I replied.

'You're English, then,' he observed.

'Yes,' I said, 'from Birmingham.'

'I come from Belfast,' said he.

'I was there last Saturday,' I told him, 'writing a story about Lough Neagh'.

'Then you must be Vivian Bird,' he said. 'I'm Robert Frizzell, general manager of the Northern Ireland Tourist Board.'

'Then don't you get putting a bloody motor road round Lough Neagh,' I said.

2   *The Southern Hebrides*

Afoot and Afloat

AT 9.30 p.m. ON MAY 15, 1969, the sun set in splendour amid a Valkyrian ride of golden-edged clouds behind the Rhinns of Islay. Beinn Tart a Mhill, the biggest hill on that peninsula, put on a grey cloud cap, the lights of Port Charlotte flickered fitfully across Loch Indaal, and the lighthouse at Portnahaven flashed its steady beam through the dusk towards the western window of the sitting room in the gaunt three-storey farmhouse of Leorin, two miles north of Port Ellen, the tight little township at the south of Islay.

Through the south-facing window another lighthouse beam winked from Rathlin, the island off the Antrim coast of Northern Ireland where Robert the Bruce met his spider. Not an hour earlier the westering sun had picked out in shine and shadow every cliff and and every cove on the north coast of that island just over 20 miles away.

Leorin, with its 1,400 acres of hill land for its 800 ewes, and 400 acres of cultivable grassland to provide fodder for his 80 Welsh Black beef cattle, was the home of my old Birmingham school friend, 'Puss' Dawson — the 'Puss' being compound of 'Perce' from Percy, and a Cheshire-cat-like grin which disarmed many opposing scrum halfs in the 1930s before wing-forward 'Puss' flattened them.

'Puss' had come to Islay, the southermost island of the Hebrides in 1951 from a farm in north Wales. Leorin farmhouse dominates an empty landscape, its only rival the slim distillery chimney at Port Ellen, its nearest inhabited neighbour a mile distant, while a further mile northward in a converted school, where the playground walls and a shelter belt of trees surround an oasis of green lawns, colourful gardens, and a stable yard that might be in Warwickshire, lives Mr Spencer Wilks, president of the Rover Motor Company, and co-originator with his brother, Maurice, of the Land Rover, which was first tested on Islay's hills and beaches. 'Puss' Dawson's home stands back off the top road between Port Ellen and Bridgend, an island road, straight and undulating, with its typical row of telegraph poles carrying their eternally tuneful wires over the horizon. Grey and stark, with nine bedrooms, three dormers, and a porch entrance which turns its back on the west wind, it towers above the plough-man's cottage and the drystone walls of a track which continues to the corrugated barns and the slated byres. These drystone walls of Islay, the larger stones at the base shading off to regular tops of smaller stones, are impeccably constructed, and put to shame the more haphazard work of Cotswold and Derbyshire stonewallers.

Beyond the outbuildings the hill land rises east and north through rushes, heather, and bracken, past the sheep pens to Leorin lochs from which water is piped to the Port Ellen distillery. Pink-grey outcrops of dolomite over 1,000 feet high mark the extremity of the Leorin acres, a deer-haunted solitude. To westward, below the pasture around the house, peat bog stretches a mile and a half to the Big Strand on Laggan Bay where Atlantic rollers break with ceaseless roar on seven miles of perfect beach.

I had not seen 'Puss' since 1956, nor even met his wife, Jane. With me on this visit, my constant walking companion, was Norman Williams, also a Camp Hill Old Edwardian, so there was much to discuss late into the night over the sweet-smelling peat fire. 'Puss' told us of days when Leorin employed 60 women at the cheese making, and of an earlier tenant who had marshalled 24 pairs of horses ploughing simultaneously to impress his bride. He told us too, of his early struggles in Islay, and of the tragedy that befell when his brother, Eric, died suddenly aged 34 in August 1954, leaving a widow and a baby son at Leorin.

'On the night of Eric's funeral it began to blow and rain heavily,' said 'Puss.' 'By morning a 50-acre field of oats was in bad shape, and with the summer of 1954 continuing its evil career, by autumn the field was written off, a loss of £1,200. As though this were not enough, the cattle, previously sound, showed 18 reactors in their annual tuberculin test in October 1954. These had to be destroyed, and though I got adequate capital compensation, I lost the income from them.'

Under normal circumstances these calamities would have shaken even the tenacious 'Puss' severely, but following the more grievous loss of Eric they lost much of their sting.

Most of all on that night of reunion we talked of old schoolfellows.

We played again the immortal games,
And grappled with the fierce old friends,
And cheered the dead undying names,
And sang the song that never ends.

In his Hebridean temple of the winds 'Puss' must often have recalled two lines of our school song:

Here no classic grove secludes us,
Here abides no sheltered calm.

But it was a tranquil night for our reminiscences, and before going to bed in the small hours we took a short turn up the road. At a point where we outflanked Rydha Mor, the southern headland enclosing Laggan Bay, 'Puss' waved his hand westward into the darkness which still had a faint tinge of afterglow, and said: 'From here, in good visibility, you can see Inishtrahull off the Donegal coast.'

Next morning I walked back up that road, in good visibility, and there, 45 miles distant, was that utmost northern rock of Ireland which I had last seen from Malin Head 32 days earlier on April 14.

Islay is in the Scottish county of Argyll, but already, on the aircraft coming over, I had sensed its great affinity with Ireland. Leaving Birmingham at 7.25 a.m., and Glasgow at 9.35 a.m., we had touched down at Campbeltown in Kintyre en route for Islay. British European Airways took over the service from Scottish Airways, and my friend, Tommy Staddon, the cheery B.E.A. sales manager in Birmingham, had told me how, in those early days, the D.H.89 aircraft on the route were known as McGeackey's Clippers after the Campbeltown ironmonger who was agent for Scottish Airways.

Now the lordly Viscount flies this sky road to the southern isles, and we had been joined at Glasgow by Jack Ridgway, B.E.A. station superintendent at Glenegedale Airport, Islay. Discussing the fact that Ballycastle in Antrim is only 26 miles from Port Ellen I learned from Jack that the Islay Gaelic is more akin to Irish Gaelic than to that spoken in the Scottish Highlands, and that the prolific Islay hare resembles the Irish hare, browner and larger than its grey Scottish cousin. Islay is also in the Malin Meteorological Office area.

'There used to be considerable commerce between Port Ellen and Ballycastle, particularly at the Lammas Fair,' Jack told me. 'Irish skiffs were always in Port Ellen. There's just an occasional excursion nowadays.'

He went on to tell of his own trip to Ballycastle in the summer of 1968.

'We ran into fog beyond Rathlin,' he said. 'We weren't at all sure where we were, when, peering into a slight clearing in the mist, I saw, of all things, a Viking long ship with a bank of oars. It was only a momentary glimpse, but, thank goodness, another chap confirmed it. We had a second short peep at it, and then a third, a longer one, which revealing our Vikings as competitors in a fishing contest with their rods protruding from Ballycastle breakwater giving the illusion of oars.'

Irish help was sought by the Celts of Scotland in repelling the Roman invader, and one writer makes so bold as to suggest that Islay was the hinge on which Roman fortunes turned sour, bringing about their recession in turn from Scotland, England, and Northern Europe. While the Celts contained the Legions on the Mainland, Cairbrea Riada, an Irish prince, and later the famous Finn McCoul protected the exposed Celtic flank from attack by Norsemen. Finn McCoul led an expeditionary force to Islay, made it his base, and drove out the Vikings from the islands, leaving mainland Celts to deal with the Romans.

Glenegedale Airport seemed little changed since 1956 except that the toilets are now labelled 'Fir' and 'Mnathan'. Ireland, of course, marks them 'Fir 'and 'Mna' as visitors occasionally find to their embarrassment because 'Mna' suggests 'man' and it means 'Women'. The longer 'Mnathan' has the same meaning, but is used more commonly in Donegal than farther south in Ireland. The airport also has a plaque commemorating the 'pioneer work and devotion to duty' of Captain David Barclay, M.B.E., of the Air Ambulance Service from 1933 to his retirement in 1965, when he unveiled the plaque. I have flown on ordinary B.E.A. services with Captain Barclay — in the Barra Heron.

A new cargo has been consigned fairly recently through Glenegedale — the scallops collected by local boats and boats from Mull and the Isle of Man, cleaned and processed on Islay, and flown out three tons a week to be enjoyed in Paris on the day after they leave Islay.

58

My one previous visit to Islay, in 1956, had been so hurried that the only sightseeing was a drive to the Mull of Oa, southernmost headland of the Hebrides, the breeding place of the red-legged chough which I had seen there, but a forbidding place, rendered no less so by the memorial to two American troopships, the 'Tuscania' and the 'Otranto', sunk off Oa during World War One. The epitaph to those lost in these disasters reads:

> *On Fame's immortal camping ground*
> *Their silent tents are spread;*
> *While Glory keeps with solemn round*
> *The bivouac of the dead.*

Now, on the first afternoon of our visit, Puss drove us to one of Islay's beauty-spots, Claggain Bay, on the east coast. From Port Ellen we took the 'Whisky Road' past the distilleries of Laophraig (Islay Mist), Lagavulin (White Horse) and Ardbeg. Islay has nine distilleries, conspicious in Port Ellen in particular by the pagoda-like towers of malting floors. How many excisemen it takes to control them I don't know, but we did seem to meet a fair number in a short while.

Dunyvaig Castle, in ruins near Lagavulin, has seen sterner doings than the distilling of whisky, none more ghastly than the summary hanging from the mast of his own galley, during the Great Civil War, of Colla Ciotoch, commander of a Royalist garrison in the castle, who had come out under a flag of truce to parley with the Parliamentarians of General Leslie's force.

It was no afternoon for grim memories however. Blue sky was reflected in sapphire sea; the emerald of the grass was duplicated in the tender spring green of the woodlands fringing the road with chestnuts, beeches, planes, and sycamores. Primroses and daisies lay thick among gnarled dwarf willow, scrub oak and juniper, while bluebells were more advanced in the glades than at home in leafy Warwickshire. But everything palled beside the gorse, which led me into raptures, and Norman into quoting Goldsmith's "Deserted Village" — 'with blossom'd furze, unprofitably gay.'

Gaiety came before profit on this delightful afternoon when deer were lying down with the sheep in the pastures. Even Kildalton churchyard was gay with daffodils, lady smock, celandine, and primroses in and around the roofless church beneath the green shade of sycamores, while the ear was delighted by the sportive notes of the lapwing, the liquid burble of the curlew, and the call of many Wordsworthian cuckoos 'breaking the silence of the sea, among the farthest Hebrides.' Kildalton Cross is the great feature in the church-yard, nearly 1,100 years old, and said, with St. Martin's Cross in Iona, to be the finest Celtic cross in existence. I am not very interested in antiquity or craftsmanship for their own sakes unless there is a good story too. Consequently such treasures do not register strongly with me, but I have memories of two finer Irish crosses — at Clon-macnois, and the High Cross of Ardboe beside Lough Neagh. With respect to Kildaton Cross I was more interested in the gravestone in the church floor inscribed: 'This is the burying place of Duncan McEwan, Tenant of Upper Laorin.'

'They'd have carried him across the hill,' said 'Puss'; a rough journey of at least seven miles as the crow flies. 'Puss' went on to tell us that all the men within a wide radius still follow a funeral on Islay, and it often goes a long way round to the cemetery to give everyone a chance of a spell as bearer.

Also in the church floor at Kildalton, and in the graveyard, are flat memorial slabs with sculptored knights, some with a long sword carved in relief beside them, others with the sword on a separate stone. These are gravestones of the Islay Clan MacDonald, with the Great Sword of Somerled, the emblem of power on land, while the Great Seal of Islay is a boat with the heads of Somerled and his three sons, the symbol of power at sea. In 1156 Somerled, King of Argyll and the Isles, anticipated the tactics of the Elizabethan seamen against the Armada, by destroying a fleet of Norse longships in their own little vessels, able to manoeuvre close in to the more cumber-some enemy. It was Somerled's grandson, Donald I, who gave his name to the Clan Donald. His descendant, John the Good, succeeded in 1329 and died in 1380, during which time the Clan Donald Lordship of the Isles extended from the Butt of Lewis in the far north of the Hebrides to the Mull of Kintyre.

Kildalton churchyard is gloriously situated. From it we were getting our first view, northward, of the Paps of Jura which were to dominate our stay among the islands. To their left there was a distant entrancing glimpse of Mull up the narrow Sound of Islay, and, as we drove on to Claggain Bay, our own immediate left was overshadowed by Beinn Bheigeir, at 1,609 feet the highest hill in Islay, but having all the rugged quality of a mountain, and attaining its height in a bare two miles from the sea. Claggain Bay has a pebble beach with semi-precious stones for the patient and the knowledgable, but the more distant scene eastward occupied me, with the low green island of Gigha ten miles away, superimposed on the Kintyre peninsula, and the jagged peaks of Arran towering in turn beyond.

While we were at Claggain that fine old vessel, the 'King George V' cruised past into the Sound of Islay. Known to many thousands, the 'King George V' is MacBrayne's usual boat on the day excursion from Oban to Staffa and Iona, completing the circuit of Mull. Several times I have done that cruise, so calm that we have landed on Staffa and entered Fingal's Cave, so rough that we could not even land on Iona. Now the 'King George V' was bound for Oban to do the cruise during the week-end with a special excursion from the Midlands, which I should have been accompanying as a journalist had I been available.

Returning towards Port Ellen we parked again at Kildalton, but this time our objective was a cross on a hillside. To it we climbed, past the Lily Loch, a tiny bright blue eye in the bogland, and through the bursting foam of blackthorn bushes until we reached the Celtic cross of silver granite on a cairn of grey granite, with daffodils, primroses, and violets at its base. The cairn bore the inscription: 'Here lies my beloved John Talbot Clifton, Explorer, Lord of the Manor of Lytham, Laird of Kildalton, died 23 March, 1928. The life is changed, not destroyed. Love never faileth.'

Obviously I was in thrall to the mysticism of the isles. Forty-one years earlier I had cut from a Birmingham newspaper a piece about an Islay man who had died, and, I seemed to remember, had his ashes scattered on the island hills. I had not thought of the cutting for years, but on Islay it came back to me and I had mentioned it to 'Puss' near Kildalton.

'I don't know about that,' he said, 'but a chap's buried up there on the hill — you can see his cross now.'

So we had come to John Talbot Clifton's grave. I had forgotten the name, but some vague memory of Lytham convinced me he was the man of my cutting, as indeed he turned out to be. He actually died in Teneriffe after being taken ill on a journey in the French Soudan. Among his exploration was a year living with the Eskimoes while trying to learn something of the fate of Sir John Franklin's ill-starred expedition; he was the first Englishman to voyage up the River

Lena in Siberia, during which journey he discovered a new species of wild sheep, and he acted as a war correspondent in the Boer War and the Russo-Japanese War. His resting place commands wide horizons, from the Scottish mainland and Arran to the mainland of Ulster and Rathlin Island, seen across the treetops of Kildalton Castle grounds and the blue inlet of Loch Cnoc.

'Will you leave this pair of wellingtons on the milk stand for Mrs MacDermott?' asked the woman in Port Ellen next morning, handing a parcel to the MacBrayne's bus driver. Norman and I were the only passengers as we drove towards Bowmore along the bottom road with the peat cuttings of Machrie Moss on either hand, fuel for the distilleries. We were bound for remote Portnahaven, a journey that would keep us close to the shore of Loch Indaal, in whose calm waters the clouds were faithfully reflected. This shallow bay, eating into Islay from the south, leaves an isthmus barely two miles wide between it and Loch Gruinart, biting in from the north. On this isthmus, in the year of the Armada according to Bartholomew's half-inch map, the native MacDonalds defeated an invading force of MacLeans from Mull in Islay's major land battle.

Our dead straight road crossed Islay's two largest rivers, the Duich and the Laggan, before we entered Bowmore, the island's administrative capital with a population of 900 and a round church just 200 years old, built in this fashion, they say, so that it has no corners where the Devil can hide. In fact, Bowmore offers few hiding places — its Main Street is wide and there are no trees around the village. What a transformation, then, in the three miles to Bridgend, Islay's sylvan paradise, shaded by the woodlands round Islay House, where the little River Sorn trickles down to the sea. Four red mail vans were standing at Bridgend, and it certainly is the central point of the island.

The bus route continued, an open road round the head of Loch Indaal, where oyster-catchers were shrieking about the machair. Turning south into the Rhinns, we followed the shore to a short stop at Bruichladdich where a puffer lay at the distillery pier — the ideal craft for the shallow waters of Loch Indaal. The street names were in Gaelic and I called on the bus driver to interpret.

'Bruichladdich means the brae beside the shore,' he said. 'Sraid Na Sgoile is School Street, and Cnoc Iain Phail is Paul Jones Hillock.'

Paul Jones, thus commemorated, was the American pirate so

active in these waters around 1777 that forts were built for protection against him on the northern shore of Loch Indaal. The story has it that this 'Bloody Yankee' anchored off Bowmore, the loch being too shallow for him to sail nearer Islay House on which he had designs. So he rowed his cutters towards the head of the loch, but these went aground on the ebb. Two curious local men who rowed out to them were made prisoner and taken back to the pirate ship when the tide turned, to be cast off eventually in a coble which drifted ashore.

The Islay-West Tarbert packet boat was once attacked by Paul Jones, intent on robbing a Major Campbell who was bringing back to Islay not only his bride, but all his wealth and valuable antiques from a long sojourn abroad. The major was prepared to put up a fight, but was dissuaded by the captain of the packet so that Paul Jones got his booty without bloodshed, and Campbell reached Islay penniless, though from his lands on the island he was able to recoup his fortunes.

We left the bus at Portnahaven, its terminus on the extremity of the Rhinns, having first called at Port Wemyss. These twin villages of one-storeyed white cottages with their backs turned to the sea get some slight protection from two islands just offshore, MacKenzie's Isle, and Orsay where the lighthouse stands. From the shelter of these natural breakwaters the village boats once put out profitably to the cod-fishing, now no longer pursued.

Norman and I humped our packs on our backs and set out on the serious business of walking with a light breeze from the Atlantic, open on our left hand to the coast of Labrador, though warmed on this side by the Gulf Stream. We have walked together this past 20 odd years, before which we served in the same Royal Artillery regiment during the war, including a 14-month sojourn in Orkney. As boys we were at school together and later worked in Birmingham offices almost next door to each other. His idiotic pipe apart, Norman is a splendid companion, erudite, trusting to my map-reading and route-finding even through the darkest of nights, and ready to raise his voice in song come what may. I know plants by their English names; he by their Latin. I never carry a penknife, tools, or a key; Norman has pockets full of the lot. We are much of a size and our strides match admirably, though sartorially we are an incongruous couple. I am an unabashed scruff in my walking togs. Norman is a civil servant, always immaculate, and the only chap I know who seems to be wearing a bowler hat even when he isn't, both in town and country.

'Can two walk together except they be agreed,' he remarked as we left Portnahaven, adding that this was a quotation from Amos 3.3. Our long partnership suggests that perhaps they can.

Now we proposed nothing more than ten miles up the west coast and across the Rhinns to connect with a bus at Port Charlotte at 4 p.m. The narrow road was liberally provided, as next day we found, too, on Jura, with lay-bys for passing vehicles, each one marked with a black and white post visible across the bare landscape from the last. The roadside ditches were golden with kingcups, apart from which it was pleasant but uneventful walking until we came to the recovered grasslands round the rare farms. Then the day became noisy with the croaking of the elusive corncrake, ventriloquial and unmelodious but how reassuring! The corncrake has been practically driven out of England by mechanical farming, but on these western fringes he persists, along the sunset coasts he holds his own. Wheatears flirted their white rumps on rocks among the heather, and another indifferent songster clacked away busily from the fences — the stonechat. That aerial acrobat, the lapwing, had a lot to say whenever we strayed too near a nest, and from time to time the liquid dying fall of the curlew's call brought melody to the otherwise undistinguished birdsong.

We had time in Port Charlotte to look round the cheese factory.

'We take all the milk produced in Islay,' said James Kissock, the manager, 'two thousand gallons a day which gives us one ton of cheese. Today's milk is tomorrow's cheese, though it takes from five to eight weeks to mature. We have ten employees and hope to expand. All our production goes now to a Glasgow wholesaler and it's distributed by him. We make butter from the whey.'

Islay cheese is the traditional Scottish Dunlop; sweeter, smoother, and softer than Cheddar. Dunlop cheese was first made by Barbara Gilmour, a farmer's wife from Dunlop in Ayrshire who took refuge in Ireland from the fighting between the English redcoats and the Scottish Covenanters. It was on her return to Scotland in 1688 that she perfected her cheese — maybe another gift from Ireland. In 1880 an American cheesemaking expert, a Mr Harris of New York State, gave instruction to the Scottish cheesemakers, thus giving uniformity to Dunlop cheese.

A Connemara scene near Clifden of peat cuttings blowing with bog cotton beneath a wide Atlantic cloudscape. *Bord Fáilte Éireann.*

Lough Neagh, which washes the shores of five of Northern Ireland's six counties, is famed for its glorious sunsets over the distant mountains of Co. Tyrone.

Northern Ireland Tourist Board.

I made some reference in front of Mr Kissock to Coll Cheese, which, I had read, used always to grace the cheese board in the House of Commons dining room.

'I made cheese on Coll in 1948-49,' Mr Kissock told me. 'My wife is a MacLean of Coll. The population in 1949 was 197; now it's down to 155, and cheese is no longer made there commercially.'

Coll is one of the few Hebridean islands on which I have never set foot, though I once welcomed its rugged protection from a westerly gale when bound for Iona from Oban. The Gaelic is always spoken in the Rhinns between natives, as we discovered on the bus which took us from Port Charlotte to board MacBrayne's M.V. 'Lochiel' at Port Askaig at 5 p.m. Our driver of the morning had only one other passenger, an elderly contemporary with whom he chatted in Gaelic. 'We were at school together,' the driver told us, 'and Gaelic was our only language in those days.'

Norman and I intended sailing from Port Askaig to Scalasaig, 14 miles northward on Colonsay, to do an evening walk round the nine circular miles of road on that island. As we had risen early the previous day, and gone very late to bed, we wanted also to get as long a sleep as possible — problematic because we were sailing from Colonsay with the 'Lochiel' for Jura at 6.45 a.m. on the following morning, Saturday. To sleep ashore would mean a very early awaking, so we hoped to sleep aboard though the 'Lochiel' has no passenger sleeping accommodation. Nevertheless, we were prepared to doss anywhere.

Our fellow bus passenger mentioned that he, too, was boarding the 'Lochiel' at Port Askaig—as night watchman. A pensioner, he did this three nights a week, travelling by bus from the Rhinns, crossing to Colonsay, doing his stint of watching, and returning to Port Askaig by 7.45 next morning on the 'Lochiel's' passage to Jura. Perhaps he was a friend at court. But no, we must have a word in Port Askaig with MacBrayne's agent, Mr MacMillan. We did, in his cosy home beside the quay. He remained non-commital. Captain MacLeod was something of a disciplinarian, as well a ship's master should be. We must get his permission. Mr MacMillan would introduce us to the chief steward as intermediary.

Somehow we missed the chief steward during the 'Lochiel's' short stay at Port Askaig. So we sailed still nursing our problem, and went below for a meal. Half way through the meal and the passage,

Captain MacLeod came to his table, a veritable twin of Sir Winston Churchill in his familiar seagoing costume — and seemingly as tough a nut to crack. I hoped to catch his eye, but eventually had to make a direct approach without any encouragement. Could we sleep aboard?

'I think that might be arranged,' said Captain MacLeod, who went on affably to tell me that he is one of the MacLeods of Skye though Glasgow-born, and that it was 46 years to the day that he had first gone to sea, a deck boy for 30 shillings a month with the Canadian Pacific on the run from Glasgow to Montreal. I asked him about big seas.

'I suppose the biggest I've known were rounding Cape Horn,' he said, 'but it was always a true sea with us on the easterly run. The Pentland Firth's a wicked place; I did two years through it from Glasgow to the Baltic. On January 15 last year I lay in Port Ellen on the 'Lochnevis' during the great hurricane that did so much damage on the islands and in Glasgow, and I had to keep the starboard engine going astern all night to relieve the strain on the ropes. Port Ellen's a bad place in a nor-westerly gale, and Colonsay can be tricky in a strong westerly or south-easterly blow.'

Our worry on Colonsay was rain; only a gentle weeping of the clouds though, and as there was no need to take our packs ashore and get them wet it did not deter us. The road lay due ahead, inland from the pier, leaving an obelisk atop a hill on our left, and on our right a First World War memorial cross with 16 names, six of them McNeills — a high proportion of an island population now reduced to 150. Passing the hotel in an area well blessed with trees, we continued along a road we would have preferred to walk when the wild yellow irises were in flower, for their spear-like leaves filled the ditches and the road verges. Several cuckoos were calling. We even saw a pair alight in a tree with their peculiarly clumsy action, using their wings to steady themselves. Several snipe boomed around as we passed the road on our left leading in five miles to Colonsay's sister island, Oronsay. At low water, for about three hours each day, an extensive sand bar, the Strand, allows passage on foot, or preferably by pony and trap, between the two islands. Visible at low tide half way from Colonsay to Oronsay is the base of an ancient sanctuary cross, and fugitives having reached the Oronsay side of it could claim immunity from justice after a year and a day.

Saint Columba — as peripatetic as Queen Elizabeth I — is said to have landed in Oronsay on his flight from Ireland, but, finding that he could still see Irish hills, he put to sea again and reached Iona.

Not far beyond the Oronsay turn, around Machrins, we came in sight of the western ocean. Machrins has an 18-hole golf course; it also has the Lifting Stone, a boulder on which the young men of Colonsay used to test their strength, though so many did themselves injury that Lord Colonsay had the stone buried. It has since been disinterred. We swung on through the soft evening, down to the opaline sea at Port Mor, with a view of Iona 20 miles northward off the Ross of Mull. Through scattered Kilchattan we went, and so north of Loch Fadda, a narrow reed-fringed loch which almost cuts Colonsay in two. We passed the old corn mill and at Kiloran, which gives its name to a beautiful Atlantic beach and to Lord Colonsay's exotic gardens, we turned south again across the bridge over the loch. The road now began to rise and a rough track came in over the hills on our right at a bend, while the good tarmac road continued on what, on my map, appeared a lesser track towards the coast north of Scalasaig. There was no doubt of our position — a road running down round the eastern end of Loch Fadda to Colonsay House helped us check it. So this track, beside a lochan with many inviting fish rings, winding into the hills, must be what my map called the A870, and it should take us in less than two miles back to Scalasaig.

We took it, at times only a couple of wet cart ruts among rock outcrops, with the yellow-green rosettes of butterwort starring the rough going underfoot. Reaching the watershed we could see that indeed we should come out at Scalasaig, but it was Jura that caused us to stop in our tracks, spellbound at an awesome sight in the deathly-still dusk. An unseen sun was setting below pink and purple rain clouds hidden by the hills on our right, but the bulk of Jura loomed blood-red ten miles or so across a steel-grey sea.

Darkness had almost fallen as we passed the hotel, but finding a lamb in difficulties, without use of its back legs, we clambered up a bank to the nearest house to report it, and were cordially invited into the home of Miss Mary Clark and her brother Robert, from whom we learned that our rough hill road was the Bruich-a-Vannan, by which, in 1902, King Edward VII and Queen Alexandra had travelled to visit Colonsay House. A bumpy trip they must have had, no matter what their transport. We had noticed something man made on

Ben-na-Guderain, north of Scalasaig, and this, said Mr Clark, was a toposcope which gave the distance to Malin Head, Donegal, as 64 miles, and from which he had seen Ben Nevis.

The Clarks' brother, Donald, had been captain of the old 'Dunara Castle,' a name to bring a thrill to an island-lover, for this vessel had run regularly to remote St. Kilda before the evacuation, and Miss Clark had herself visited the island. After tea and cakes with our kind hosts we walked back to the pier and the 'Lochiel' to find two comfortable beds made up on settees in the saloon.

An inquisitive seal was bobbing around as we sailed from Colonsay at 6.45 a.m. on Saturday, with shower smudges on Jura and out to sea, but plenty of blue between the clouds. Going on deck I could identify most of the islands visible, and was particularly interested in the symmetrical bulk of Scarba, separated from the north of Jura by the Strait of Corrievreckan with its notorious whirlpool. One lower island to the left of Scarba in the Firth of Lorne beat me — I have since discovered it was one of the Garvellochs. I had seen the other man on the boat deck come aboard at Colonsay, so asked if he knew what the island was.

'Sorry,' he said, 'I'm not an islander. I come from the Midlands — Charles Orme from Uttoxeter in Staffordshire.'

I told him I came from Birmingham, and, making conversation, added that I refer to Uttoxeter whenever I address Women's Institutes and similar organisations on my macabre hobby of epitaph hunting.

'I mention Uttoxeter to place Rocester nearby when I quote an epitaph from Rocester churchyard.' I said.

A quizzical look had come into my companion's eyes.

'Are you a writer?' he wanted to know, 'and did you once mention that epitaph in a newspaper article?'

I agreed that I was, and that I did.

'Then just a moment,' he said, and went below — to reappear with a copy of George Eliot's novel 'Adam Bede,' from which he produced a neatly-folded page of the Sunday Mercury for September 11, 1966, featuring an article by me on the 'Adam Bede Country.'

'Uttoxeter is on the fringe of the Adam Bede country,' said Mr Orme. 'I've always felt I should read the book, and I kept your article in it. I thought I'd get my chance, and I've managed to read 'Adam Bede' this holiday.'

Not the least pleasing feature of this bit of recognition was that Norman had strolled up. On our walks in the Midlands I have often been identified by readers, but this occasion, Norman admitted, beat all the others.

Charles Orme was not the first man to produce a novel on board ship off Colonsay. In 'Mr Standfast,' John Buchan's famous hero, Richard Hannay, also produced two 'dingy red volumes' as he sailed from Colonsay after a frustrating day on the island. He was on the track of Gresson, a spy, who had taken a job as purser on board the 'Tobermory' doing her normal run round the Hebrides. Buchan has the ship heading north: 'Morning found us nosing between Jura and Islay, and about mid-day we touched at a little port where we unloaded some cargo and took on a couple of shepherds who were going to Colonsay . . . The big droving season was scarcely on yet, and the sheep for the Oban market would be lifted on the return journey . . . There was a kind of apple-green light over everything; the steep heather hills cut into the sky like purple amethysts, while beyond the straits the western ocean stretched its pale molten gold to the sunset.'

On the next day, Hannay, who wants to send a significant telegram to one Ochterlony at Kyle, cannot get into the telegraph office on Colonsay because it is in full view of Gresson on the 'Tobermory,' and Gresson is beginning to suspect Hannay. Not until nearly sailing time in the evening does Hannay find the local schoolmaster 'near the back end of the clachan,' and persuade him to send the telegram for him. Then, as a blind, he buys two sevenpenny novels from the schoolmaster and, returning on board the 'Tobermory,' produces them when Gresson demands angrily what he was doing holding up the boat, which then sails north.

'We left Colonsay about six in the evening with the sky behind us banking for a storm and the hills of Jura to starboard an angry purple. Colonsay was too low an island to be any kind of breakwater against a westerly gale.' So the 'Tobermory' moves out of our area.

Reference by Buchan to the sheep droving reminds me that 'Puss's' shepherd, Willie Campbell, told me that his grandfather, Angus Campbell, a cattle dealer, would regularly swim his cattle the three quarters of a mile from Port Askaig to Feolin on Jura, walk them across Jura, nine or ten miles, and then swim them again to the Kintyre mainland, roped and accompanied by a boat.

I had been doing some early morning thinking on our plans for the weekend. It had seemed, before we came north, that having landed from the MacBrayne boat at Craighouse, Jura, at 9.50 on Saturday morning we were stuck on that island until MacBrayne got us off on Monday afternoon. This would possibly have enabled us to travel the 20 miles of road up the east coast to Ardlussa, where I could add to my collection of photographs of centenarians' gravestones the daddy of them all — the stone to Mary MacCrain who died, aged 128, which adds the information that one of her ancestors, Gilour MacCrain 'spent 180 Christmases in his own house.'

With luck in weather, a lift, and accommodation, we might even have made the far north of Jura to the cottage at Barnhill where George Orwell wrote '1984' in such splendid isolation. But it was a chancy business with a Scottish Sabbath intervening. Islay was a fairer prospect for the week-end, so when I learned that Western Ferries crossed from Port Askaig to Feolin and back on Saturday afternoon I nipped ashore at Port Askaig to enquire their timing. This was 2.15 p.m., 4.30 p.m., and 6.30 p.m. from Feolin. So we decided to content ourselves, on Jura, with a 10-mile walk across the south of the island from Craighouse to Feolin, and thus get Sunday on Islay.

Our cruise round to Craighouse gave a preview of the road we should walk back, featureless miles of brown moorland above low cliffs sloping steadily up to the high mountain mass of the Paps of Jura. Islay puts on its sternest face from the eastward, with only the white walls of the lighthouse on MacArthur's Head to vary the dark rugged and uninhabited hillsides beneath Beinn Bheigeir and its neighbouring summits.

Going ashore at Craighouse we bought some rolls and called in the hotel to ask if they would fill our flasks, one with tea, one with coffee. The manager told me he was not elated at the increase in motor traffic in Jura, actual and expected, from Western Ferries services. 'They're just casual lunch calls,' he said, 'and in a place like this one can't cater for casuals.' I imagine he has a loyal clientele of fishermen, deer stalkers, and people who just like Jura, this spacious mountainous island with a population of only 250.

With a wave to the distillery workers Norman and I set out for Feolin, our road climbing steadily from an area of mature trees to one of sapling conifer plantations. For a mile or more we gained height, and I was content to conserve my breath and let Norman do the talking. It was magnificent walking weather, bright sun, drifting cloud, and a cold wind from the north which once brought a sharp shower with sleet among the rain. Once a car came from a farm and passed us bound for Craighouse. Away on the mountainside the gleaming pillar of a vertical waterfall was all that broke the sepia monotony of the heather, though the seaward view was splendid. Around Jura House at Ardfin we saw our second human in the green tunnel of trees that arch across the road with a stream dropping down a glen beneath them. From the trees on our left came the whine of an electric saw. As we moved on towards open country again we passed one last cottage with a well-tended garden where two children were playing — lonely children they must be in that little-populated island.

Beyond Ardfin a standing stone pointed a slim finger skyward, the Camus Stack, 12 feet high, evidence that Jura has been populated a long while, for the stack is said to pre-date the Pyramids of Egypt. Our route, previously south-west, now turned north-westerly up the west coast, with the Sound of Islay narrowing and becoming turbulent, a six knot tide race contending with a bounding head wind funnelling from the north. We had a session of singing the school songs of long ago, but I was anxious about that ferry, an anxiety which grew as our road descended to the shore. No cars had overtaken us making for Feolin, there was no habitation within five miles of the ferry house which I had seen from Port Askaig and which constituted all there was at Feolin, and Norman was sprouting a blister. When the ferry house turned out to be uninhabited and locked I looked longingly across the boisterous water at the lilliputian bustle of Port Askaig, enlivened occasionally by an explosion and a burst of smoke from the road works above the harbour. In the meantime we ate chunks of the Islay cheese given us at Port Charlotte, drank coffee, and settled down in the sunshine and the shelter of the ferry house to wait.

I was glad eventually to see the Land Rover. At least if the driver couldn't cross the ferry he could take us back towards Craighouse — for there was no road beyond Feolin. But the Land Rover ran off the end of the road and bumped away along the beach like a demented dodgem car, avoiding debris thrown up by the sea and down by the cliffs, obviously bound for the keeper's dwelling which we now noticed over a mile away. However, two more cars came along, and a third, and the ferry made it on time, though its course across the Sound was crabwise. It grounded on the shingle, opened its doors and the cars drove in, one with the hotel manager at the wheel, while another driver, a distillery worker from Craighouse, was taking his wife for her weekly shopping trip to Bowmore on Islay. He had a season ticket, £5 for three months — the cost of a casual single crossing for a car being £1 plus 2s. 6d. per passenger.

I need not have worried about the weather. Only one day in the three months service so far had the 'Sound of Islay' —as the ferry is called — failed to cross. Port Askaig is the most photogenic place I know — usually a colourful steamer or ferry boat alongside, white cottages, the Paps of Jura across the Sound, eight hours from Port Askaig by ferry to the 2,407-feet summit of Ben Chaolais and back for the average hill walker, and all the elevation a photographer wants from the wooded drive to Dunlossit House. The zigzag drop to the quay was undergoing widening to take the traffic from the larger ferry, the 'Sound of Gigha,' which loads on the mainland at Ceann-na-Craige in West Loch Tarbert, and brings lorries across so that the names of mainland transport companies have become familiar on Islay roads. Loads of malt or barley for the distilleries are the main inward cargo, with whisky the principle export.

We toiled up that devastated road amid dust, cranes, dumpers, tractors — even an explosion to shift more rock — and basked in the sun among some roadside rhododendrons. Ahead of us the Bowmore road climbed through the gleaming cottages of Kiells, a beguiling sight on that breezy afternoon. There ultimately we went, booked bed and breakfast with Jessie and Donny Carmichael, and were given a room with a magnificent view eastward, round the rump end of Jura whence we had come, to the distant isles of Gigha and Cara superimposed on the Kintyre peninsula.

"Islay is Heaven"

Blows the wind today, and the sun and the rain are flying,
  Blows the wind on the moors today and now?
Where about the graves of the martyrs the whaups are crying,
  My heart remembers how.

Grey recumbent tombs of the dead in desert places,
  Standing stones on the vacant wine-red moor;
Hills of sheep, and the howes of the silent vanished races,
  And winds austere and pure.

I KNEW from the moment we set out between that double row of white cottages at Kiells in the morning sunshine, with the west wind trilling a merry song in the roadside wires, that this would go down as one of our memorable days afoot. The croaking of the corncrake had wakened us, and a large brown hare was lolloping unafraid among the lush grass, silvered by the gusts that swept down the pasture beneath our window. Mrs Carmichael's breakfast stamped her as one who believes that an army marches on its stomach, and she had filled our flasks with coffee to go with the cheese and rolls left over from yesterday. We had intended walking beside Loch Finlaggan while on Islay, and this was our opportunity as it was not more than two miles distant by road.

One regret only went with me on that sublime morning. Robert Louis Stevenson had described it so felicitously in his poem 'Exiled' that I knew, when I came to write, I must rely largely on him, so there he is at the chapter heading.

We turned off the Bowmore road at a track marked 'Loch Finlaggan' where we could soon see Finlaggan Farm at the head of the loch. Turning left at some derelict lime kilns, we raced a shower to the shelter of some trees around the farm. On an island Sabbath I was loth to disturb the occupants, but I hoped someone with whom I could chat would emerge while we were cowering beside the wall, though blue sky was proliferating over the moorland hills to windward and the cloud evaporating on us was moving away eastward. As the squall passed across it the loch turned from blue to silver-grey, brushed with darker catspaws, and back again to blue. These waters in open country are quick to reflect the mood of the weather, and we were certainly lucky in the variety we were getting.

Meanwhile we had entertainment enough nearer to hand. A wildly-screeching hen came running from the farmyard with a lordly cockerel in fast pursuit. They disappeared round a building, for the cock to return in a few moments crowing loudly of his conquest, followed by a chastened hen ruffling her violated feathers. Up the track a male hare harried a female to and fro, finally chasing her into the tall pasture intent on the same fell errand as the cock. 'The ubiquitous male,' said Norman.

When the rain ceased and we made ready to move on someone did emerge from Finlaggan Farm — Donald Currie, the farmer. I asked him about the kilns we had passed.

'Aye,' he said, 'it must have been pretty industrious round here a century ago when there were lead mines above the eastern shore of the loch. They closed about eighty years back.'

He suggested we take the western shore by the old road to the deserted clachan of Seanghart, and we told him we should walk upwards of fifteen miles during the day.

'I'm away into the hills to look to my sheep,' he told us. 'I'll have walked ten miles before I come home' — a vastly different attitude towards walking from our Midland farmers.

Just below the farm, at the north end of Lough Finlaggan, is Castle Island, and, stepping carefully through the reeds, we reached it almost without wetting our boots. It is a place hallowed in the history of the western isles, for there the Lords of the Isles were proclaimed. Alasdair Alpin MacGregor, historian of the Hebrides, describes the ceremony, 'The proclamation rites at Finlaggan were conducted by a bishop and several attendant priests in the presence of the representatives of many West Highland and Island families then powerful and prominent. The bishop annointed the new Lord at a spot where lay a square stone bearing a deep imprint the size and shape of a man's foot. Robed in white the legal claimant stood with his right foot upon it. A white wand was placed in his right hand and in his left the claymore of the forebear whom he was now succeeding.'

The 'Lord of the Isles' in Scott's poem of that title, at the time of Bannockburn, is Ronald — 'the heir of mighty Somerled.'

> *Ronald, from many a hero sprung,*
> *The fair, the valiant, and the young,*
> *LORD OF THE ISLES, whose lofty name*
> *A thousand bards have given to fame,*
> *The mate of monarchs, and allied*
> *On equal terms with England's pride.*

When swords are drawn, in the true fashion of Scottish clan skullduggery, at the feast to celebrate Ronald's wedding with the Maid of Lorn, his vassals of the Isles prepare to support him:

> *Brave Torquil from Dunvegan high,*
> *Lord of the misty hills of Skye,*
> *MacNeil, wild Barra's ancient thane,*
> *Duart, of bold Clan Gillian's strain,*
> *Fergus, of Canna's castled bay,*
> *MacDuffie, Lord of Colonsay.*

On Castle Island in Loch Finlaggan the Lords of the Isles held their Council, summoning to it four thanes, four arnims or sub-thanes, four squires, and others. There was a judge of any disagreements on each island, and officials of the Lordship approximated to those of Saxon moots, still picturesque survivals in some English towns. MacFinnon, for instance, was Keeper of Weights and Measures, while MacDuffie of Colonsay was hereditary Clerk to the Council. There are exquisitely carved stones in the chapel ruins on the island, most of the memorials to wives and descendants of the Lords of the Isles, the Lords themselves being normally buried on Iona.

We pushed on to Seanghart through the heather and bogland with many a backward glance at those all-pervading Paps of Jura, monarchs of the entire scene, and seeming to belong to Islay as the narrow Sound was hidden. Cloud shadows sailed over the moorland, and whenever the pasture around Finlaggan Farm was lit by the sun we were entranced at its brilliant emerald green. There must, throughout the islands, be many melancholy remnants of human habitation like the roofless crofts of Seanghart, and they reminded me vividly of a similarly deserted clachan on the east side of Bressay in Shetland, facing the bird island of Noss. Beyond them we lay for a while, sheltered from the cold wind by an outcrop of rock, soaking up the sun, and indulging in erotic fantasies about the Paps — trying to build on to them the outline of a recumbent woman. Some lower hills were perfectly placed for her rib-cage, and the heights south of Glen Asdale made an admirable curve of thigh with the leg drawn up, but she remained uncomfortably rugged round the navel, and, unhappily, headless.

I was recalled from such thoughts by the cobalt blue of tiny plants of milkwort among the heather, which gave place to verdant pasture again, grazed by red cattle, as we passed beyond the tail of the mile-long loch, where a stream ran down through Glen Martin, its trees speckled white with the blossom of hawthorn, to become the River Sorn. Descending among plaintively-crying lambs and cuckoo-haunted trees to the tarmac road from Ballymartin Farm, we found a comfortable resting-place against a stone wall near the main road at Esknish. There we made further inroads into my Islay cheese and washed it down with Mrs Carmichael's coffee, at peace with the world, pleased just to watch the thrushes pecking among the daisies and lulled by larksong.

A mile of main road — as distinct from mainland road vile with traffic — brought us to Ballygrant, passing on our way two tractors Sabbath-breaking on a small steep field, with the biggest following of gulls I have ever seen, even at an island ploughing. Ballygrant has the Dunlossit Limestone Crushing Plant, the only quarries on Islay, which produce 12,000 tons of ground limestone annually for agricultural purposes in the south Hebrides in addition to supplying Islay's requirements in road stone, with crushed stone for building. We turned right behind the quarry, leaving our main road, and soon reached a left turn and a gate to a drive beneath tall trees where a congenial notice read: 'No Motors. Except on Business.'

So we entered the Dunlossit Estate, the property of Mr Helmut William Bruno Schroder, the merchant banker (who died shortly after this chapter was written) a wooded wonderland after our bare moors of the morning. But another transformation awaited us. In

76

barely a hundred yards the drive curved to the right, and facing us across a low stone wall, given that sharpness that always comes through a tunnel of trees, was a sapphire gem, Ballygrant Loch. We leaned on that wall in utter amazement, spellbound by the tree-fringed Shangri-La before us. If ever you go to Islay don't miss this view of Ballygrant Loch; but go, I implore you, when the sky above is blue.

Just up the drive to the left beyond the viewpoint, a picture of utter contentment in the dappled sunrays falling through the branches, sat a bare-kneed cyclist tending a billycan of water on a fire. In the rippling sunlight, with the love-in-the-mist haze of the wood smoke, he appeared at first an insubstantial figure, but as he brewed his tea and munched a concoction of banana and jam spread on a biscuit he materialised as a down-to-earth lover of happy living, an elderly sun-tanned cyclist from Glasgow way who holds Islay to be a heaven on earth.

'I keep this bicycle here on the island, and I get across whenever I can,' he told us. We chatted at some length about islands and island-going, and I can't remember how we came ultimately to be swapping stories that had nothing to do with our present sylvan environment, but I liked his one about the window cleaner.

'A beautiful young woman came into her flat one hot afternoon and took off her frock to cool down in her undies' — an intriguing beginning. 'Then she noticed through the mirror that a man was outside cleaning her window. Did she cover up in confusion? No. She thought to give him a good show, so she removed her slip and primped herself in the mirror, taking surreptitious peeps at the window cleaner to see the effect of her charms. But he went on stolidly cleaning the window. Somewhat piqued, she removed her remaining few garments, but still he got on with his work. Finally, with one last cast, the striptease was complete. She stood naked and turned towards him. Only then did he take any notice. He pulled open the window, popped his head in, and said — "What's the matter with you? Have you never seen a window cleaner before?"

I suppose there was the same bathos in our descending to story-telling while confronted with all the charms of the Dunlossit Estate.

The drive runs for three miles to Dunlossit House above Port Askaig. For almost its entire length it has at least a verge of trees, though in places it traverses woods extending farther on either side.

Everywhere there remains grim evidence of the January hurricane of 1968; trees uprooted by the score, and whole outer rows on the windward side leaning lifeless against the inner rows which they protected from the full force of the storm. But nothing could destroy the beauty of this delectable drive, down which we loitered, enraptured by three more lake views, one of them comparable with Killarney or Glengarriff; resting on banks of primroses and violets and philosophizing on the joys of walking. Norman dug up a root of primroses for Mrs Carmichael's garden. I took her a more material gift, an enormous log which practically filled my pack. It lasted out our second sublimely relaxed evening at the Carmichael's homely hearth, reinforced with a little coal.

'It's cheaper to buy coal than peat,' Mrs Carmichael told us, 'though you'd be better off if you could cut the peat yourself.'

Reluctantly I dragged myself from that log fire for a few moments to visit the graveyard silhouetted against the sunset sky on the brae behind Kiells. The stone to William Hill, who died in 1891, aged 84, and his wife Jane — February 1915, aged 91 — records also the deaths of nine of their family, three in South Africa and one in U.S.A., while the last entry, Flora, 'died at Kiells in 1949 in her 100th year.'

Surprisingly neither Jessie nor Donny Carmichael could tell me anything of the story behind the stone to 'A McDougall, Assistant Keeper, Northern Lighthouse Service, 15 November 1943, aged 29, also his father Alexander McDougall, 29 November 1943, aged 79.' Did the son's untimely death, I wonder, accelerate that of his father?

Everyone seems to know everyone of the 6,000-odd population scattered about Islay's 20 or so square miles. Unlike a city dweller I can't imagine an islander going home to his wife and saying 'Guess whom I saw today.' In the nature of things, despite longish distances, it is no surprise to see anyone. When I mentioned the old 'Lochiel' watchman, for instance, Donny identified him at once as Duncan MacClellan, and added that he had been a prisoner on the notorious Nazi ship, the Altmark. Another titbit of Donny's conversation was his remark: 'About a fortnight ago a helicopter landed in the field opposite to refuel. I talked to the crew, and guess what they were doing. They were counting the deer on Jura.'

As we talked the sun disappeared below the rising ground beyond the Carmichael's western window, but, far away through the eastern window, across the road, the pasture, little Loch Allan on the Dunlossit Estate, and the Sound of Islay, it still shone on Gigha and the Kintyre peninsula beyond it.

'Tomorrow,' I said, 'we'll sail over there. We can get the 'Lochiel' at 8.50 a.m. in Port Ellen, be in Tarbert by 11.40 and sail back with her to Port Askaig for 4.25 p.m., where 'Puss' is picking us up anyhow.'

God's Island with the Goddesses

MAN PROPOSES; woman disposes — in this case 40 women. Donny cycled down to Port Askaig in the morning, picked up his bus and took us aboard at his home, and we were in Port Ellen and aboard the 'Lochiel' in good time. There were lots of women about the ship, obviously in festive mood, and we had barely cleared the little island of Texa, off Laophraig, before I learned that they were members of the Port Ellen Women's Rural Institute bound on their annual excursion — to Gigha, or God's Island. On the Tarbert run the 'Lochiel' normally calls at the pier at the south of Gigha—Gigha rhymes with pier, given two syllables and the initial 'g' being hard. On the afternoon return trip to Craighouse on Jura and Port Askaig it takes on passengers by ferry boat from the north end of Gigha, and my natural caution warned me against this risk less than 20 hours before we were due to fly out of Islay on our way home. So, in my original plan, Gigha would remain unvisited. Now matters were different. The 'Lochiel was calling back at Gigha pier for the W.R.I.— a diversion from its route.

So, for the day, Norman and I were co-opted as members of Port Ellen W.R.I., and an incongruous couple we looked going ashore with them. Again it was a delightfully sunny day, but still with a cold wind from the north-west, despite which the W.R.I. ladies were gay in headscarves or bare-headed; wearing light colourful coats, flimsy sandals or high-heeled shoes, and even a mini-skirt or two, while we clumped along with them like Antarctic explorers, our anorak hoods up against the wind, and carrying full packs where they swung handbags.

Port Askaig, Islay, with the Paps of Jura across the narrow Sound of Islay.

The author lands on the beach in Barra sunshine and meets Miss Kate MacPherson, British European Airways station superintendent.

Throughout our days in the islands the grass and the trees had become steadily greener. Gigha was the greenest yet, almost startling in its verdure, and cuckoos called incessantly from the woodlands which make up much of the southern end of the island, six miles long, not two miles wide, the home of 200, and the property of Sir James Horlick of malted milk.

One of the joys of spring each year is the reunion it brings with wild flowers forgotten since the previous year. Snowdrops, primroses, violets, bluebells — these one remembers; but there are legions of lesser flowers, beloved for a season and then forgotten until the thrill of discovery next spring. Now, on Gigha, my eyes were at once drawn from the sea-lapped skerries, the nearby islands of Gigalum and Cara, and the Kintyre peninsula a bare two miles across the Sound of Gigha, to my first bugle of the year, a dozen blue spikes followed closely by my first red campion and stitchwort, spring's patriotic salute to Britain in our national colours.

We walked nearly a mile to the gates of Achimore House, the W.R.I. footing it sprightly along a road which could have been any-where in the British Isles, with the occasional palm, colourful maples, sycamores, and whitebeams among the more common trees, while white hyacinths and ferns grew in their shade. A visit to Sir James Horlick's famous gardens was laid on at Achimore, and for over an hour we played 'in and out the windows' among the mazy rides and vistas, a kaleidoscope of colour with azaleas, rhododen-drons, camelias, agapanthus, irises, cherries, sorbus, primulas, and many other species. Once through the gate and into the sheltering trees of Achimore, and you have left behind the bleak untamed loveliness of the islands for a sub-tropical suntrap. The walled kitchen garden bore promise of good crops of gooseberries, currants, and raspberries, with all manner of vegetables well advanced for mid-May. A gardener told me they came out of the Great Gale very well. 'We lost only 200 trees,' he said.

I added another to my collection of animal epitaphs at Achimore, a little stone to 'Jack, a working terrier, a faithful and intelligent friend, and a mighty hunter, May 1946-April 1960.'

Past a small area of surprising building development, we came to the Gigha Hotel, a modest pub where the W.R.I. members took lunch in two sittings. Across the road in this island metropolis of Ardminish was the general merchant's shop with a glorious name that has to be seen to be believed, J. and M. McSporran. There we reinforced the remnants of our Islay cheese with apples, bananas, and chocolate, eating them in the churchyard nearby.

Norman and I have been in hundreds of churches together, and procedure in Gigha Church matched all the others. While I wander round windows and memorial tablets with my notebook Norman makes a bee-line for the organ, so that I conduct my researches with my voice raised to join Norman's in our favourite hymns. Soon the strains of Blaenwern, Cwm Rhondda, Crimond and others were floating out across the golden gorse, down to the rocks and the Sound of Gigha, just as they have gone out over all the Midland counties, just as they went out on a snow-streaked Herefordshire landscape from the famous church at Kilpeck on a January day in 1966 from which I returned home to the sad news of the death of my old friend, Dame Edith Pitt, M.P. for the Edgbaston Division of Birmingham.

Gigha Church was the most remote place in which we have made our music; romantic too, being built in 1923-24 on a knoll with a Gaelic name which translates as the Hillock of Music. Here the people of Gigha came years ago to hear the faery music; now they come to sing their hymns and psalms of praise.

Two ministries covering forty years between them are commemorated in two windows at Gigha Church. The one, showing St. Columba kneeling and holding an open book, with seabirds and a ship behind him, commemorates the Rev. Donald MacFarlane, minister for 16 years until his death in 1923, when he was succeeded by his friend who had ministered for eight years in Colonsay and Oronsay, the Rev. Kenneth MacLeod, occupant of the manse at Gigha until his retirement in 1947.

The other memorial window, in the south wall, commemorates MacLeod, 'preacher pastor, poet', best known as the writer of 'The Road to the Isles' which, during the First World War, he set to a pipe-tune he had heard on Barra called 'The Burning Sands of Egypt'. Alasdair Alpin MacGregor tells us that MacLeod made only £5 from this world-famous song. MacLeod's window is a highly-coloured production by William Wilson of Edinburgh, and depicts David the Psalmist with a Celtic harp, St. Columba with the coracle which bore him from Ireland to Iona, St. Bride with a calf, and St. Patrick as a reminder of Columba's Irish origin. The window is completed by a view of the Sound of Gigha with a seagull hovering above, the rainbow of Divine Promise, and a small cross of Gigha. Kenneth MacLeod collaborated with Marjory Kennedy-Fraser in collecting 'The Songs of the Hebrides' and, according to Alasdair Alpin MacGregor she 'deprived Kenneth MacLeod of a fair share of what accrued financially from their collaboration'.

The name, Gigha, is Norse and from an anchorage off the island Haco and his Norse fleet sailed in 1263 to their destruction by the Scots at Largs on the Ayrshire coast. I learned in Gigha of another Irish association with these southern Hebridean islands. To God's Island came many an Irish boat for the exellent potatoes grown there, and with them, often, were the young wives of the sailors, come to pray at the Kneeling Stone in the north of the island, a stone specially venerated by pregnant women.

There seemed some doubt as to what time the 'Lochiel' was calling for us on the return journey, and, delayed by a wait at Tarbert for mail from Glasgow, it was much later than expected. This led to amusing speculation from the ladies gathered on the pier. There is a ferry boat available between Tayinloan in Kintyre and Gigha — a distance of three miles — our funk-hole for a return to Glasgow on the morrow, though no consolation to the ladies. Eventually, however, the 'Lochiel' hove in sight and all was well.

It was an idyllic cruise back to Islay, with one melancholy moment at Craighouse, when a coffin was carried ashore by a party of bearers who had met the boat. On a blue and golden May evening, with the gorse brilliant on the hillsides, and the Paps clear of cloud and serene against the blue, a native had come to his last rest in his island home. As the 'Lochiel' pulled out of Jura, it left behind on the jetty a rainbow carpet of floral tributes that had accompanied the coffin on its homeward journey.

'Puss' and his family awaited us back in Port Askaig, and, as we drove back to Leorin through Ballygrant we asked if they had ever seen that lovely view of the loch. They had not, and when we took them there they were as entranced as we had been on the previous afternoon. Driving on, we saw the one section of Islay under the dead hand of the Forestry Commission; seemingly only one landowner would sell land to them in the belief that forestry work might keep a few more Islay men from leaving the island. We also encountered the Young Farmers' Club engaged in a car treasure hunt, much as their counterparts in England do.

On our last night there was talk into the small hours back at Leorin. Seeing some deer on his mountain skyline led 'Puss' to philosophize on the shooting of them.

'If I shoot a deer,' he said, 'it's in defence of my crop, and I pick the easiest to get so as to scare away the others. If the boys on the farm or from Port Ellen shoot one they choose one with a good carcase, but if a gamekeeper or stalker shoots one he looks for the best horns as a trohpy. A chap once shot a deer up my glen, told me at night, and I went to collect it in the morning, but it had only three legs. Someone had helped himself to a haunch of venison during the night.'

It was unlikely I should ever visit 'Puss' again at Leorin. With his two children approaching secondary school age he faced the prospect as do all island parents, of losing them to a boarding school at Glasgow or Oban. So, in November, he proposed moving to a Welsh hill farm at Cannon, near Newtown, Montgomery.

Next morning, as we drove to the airport, there was a flat calm on Loch Indaal reflecting what few fleecy clouds were loitering in the blue.

'I shall be sad to leave Islay,' 'Puss' told me as we parted. 'When the weather's fine here it's Heaven.'

3   *The Outer Hebrides*

Boot and 'Bus

I NEXT SAW Islay twenty-three days later from a B.E.A. Heron, its northern shore a darker loom in the fine weather haze on a steel-blue sea. Jura's all-pervading Paps were better defined, and below symmetrical Scarba rose domelike from an oily stillness of water which it was hard to believe could be the whirlpool of Corrievreckan.

It did not need the excellent and informative commentary from Captain Starling at the Heron's controls to identify Colonsay for me, and, as we left that little island behind, the beach at Kiloran was sharply etched golden against the darker rock 6,500 feet below.

There were ten passengers aboard our Heron — in which they still call a seat-belt a lap-strap, and where the amount of window space not only gives a surpassing view of the ground, but brings clouds so near that one occasionally flinches away from them. It is more intimate flying, not so much so as in a helicopter, but still near enough the ground, the weather, and the pilot to see what is going on. I remember, while flying back to Glasgow from Barra and Tiree in a Heron in 1963, doing a smartish turn round the skirts of a solid-looking cumulus cloud, and getting, as my side dipped, an unforgettable telescopic view of the sacred green isle of Iona through a hole in the lower murk.

Now, bound immediately for Tiree to begin a scampered five-day foray into the Outer Hebrides, I had palled up across the gangway with Donald Meek, a student of Gaelic in Glasgow, returning, resplendent in a kilt of the Ancient MacDonald tartan, to his home in Tiree, where, he told me, over half of the place names are Norse, and there is no peat.

'My great grandfather used to cross to the Ross of Mull for his peat,' Donald said, adding something which endorsed the droving habits of which I had learned in Islay. 'He was a cattle drover and would take 600 cattle at a time from Tiree to the Ross, drive them across Mull to Craignure, ship them to Kerrara, and finally swim them to Oban.'

Tiree, with its population of about 1,000, recently had a government-sponsored bulb industry which has died out, though I heard that bulbs are being grown in South Uist. Tiree proposes following Islay into the clam industry, and tomato culture has begun in a small way, the sunshine record in Tiree being the best in the Hebrides, though the average wind velocity of 17 m.p.h. is the highest in Britain.

'Our great problem is water,' said Donald. 'The wells are as low now as they were at the end of last September, and we haven't had a substantial splash of rain since winter. I'm going home to help on our farm until October, and in this hot weather I imagine the first job will be shearing the sheep.'

Cattle were paddling on the beaches as we flew low into Tiree, where a hot sun was baking the pancake-flat crisp turf with its thick carpet of daisies and short-stalked buttercups, with yellow irises and kingcups in the ditches. So low is Tiree, some of it actually below sea level and its average height only 18 feet, that it is known as 'The Kingdom whose Summits are beneath the Waves.' It has but three hills, the highest, Hynish, only 460 feet. Yet its houses are almost all tall, built to pattern by a Duke of Argyll, and their gleaming white gables stand above the horizon like sailing ships on a calm sea. Among the Hebrides, Tiree is out on its own, flat, green, and treeless, and throughout my stay I felt I was on the Orkney island of Shapinsay.

Donald Meek invited me to join him in the van with which his father was waiting to drive to the north end of the island, where his home, Coll View, is in the district of Caoles, divided by two miles of sea from the rugged island of Coll. Our road, open to the pasture on either side, took us for two miles alongside Traigh Mhor, a perfect beach of silver sand, and through Scarinish, the island 'capital' where the puffer 'Glenshira' was unloading road metal into lorries at the old pier in a tiny, almost landlocked harbour, where the receding tide had left the puffer high and dry.

After tea and cakes at Coll House I set off back towards Scarinish afoot, a gentle south-east breeze stirring a field of fodder grass stained red with poppies beside me. 'You'll hear the Melba and the Caruso of the larks in Tiree,' Donald Meek had told me, and indeed the afternoon was merry with birdsong; balm to the spirits as it was balm to the feet to tread that short springy turf and the firm white sand of Traigh Mhor. Among the tall gables of Tiree there still stand some of the traditional 'black houses' of the Hebrides, single-storey cabins with the most inadequate of windows. Some are derelict, their thatch mouldering or caved in completely; some are newly-thatched period pieces; most are roofed with utility tarred felt. Among the best dwellings in Scarinish, surrounded by a stout stone wall, is that of the National Commercial Bank manager, William Groat, and there, it being early-closing day at the bank, I went in search of him.

One boisterous day two years earlier, in June 1967, I was bouncing in a small motor boat from the Orkney island of Rousay to its neighbour Egilsay, when a smart cabin cruiser bobbed up on an adjacent wave. 'That,' said my companion, the Orkney historian, Ernest Marwick, 'is 'Otterbank,' the National Commercial Bank boat.' When next it appeared from a trough Ernest and I waved cheerily to the slim man at the wheel, dressed incongruously in a black jacket and striped trousers. 'He's the National Commercial sub-manager for the North Isles of Orkney,' explained Ernest. 'William Groat is his name — mariner, bank clerk, and leading figure in taking the bank to the islands by boat.'

The 'Otterbank' was tied up at Rousay when we called on our return from Egilsay, but Mr Groat was busy in his office-cabin transacting the bank's business with islanders who had congregated from all over Rousay. I had no chance to meet him, but I intended getting the bank boat into this book when I reached Orkney. Now, due to a passing reference to Orkney, Donald Meek had told me that an Orcadian, William Groat, was bank manager in Tiree.

Mr Groat was delighted to meet someone with my interest in Orkney, and I was soon seated before more tea and cakes.

'I had seven years on the bank boat,' Mr Groat told me. 'It operated only from May to September, and when the season finished last year I left it and came to Tiree. Time has marched on and the North Isles bank service has now got wings — it's run by Loganair

88

to the main islands though the 'Otterbank' still does Rousay, Egilsay, Wyre, and Shapinsay. In olden days floating shops served Orkney, Shetland, and the Western Isles, and a bank boat was their natural successor. I suppose you could say the egg was hatching in the minds of three of us; the bank acquired the cabin cruiser 'Otter,' built in Orkney in 1926 for Walter Grant of the Highland Park Distillery, Kirkwall, and I went on the first cruise on May 29, 1962.'

William Groat — he is a descendant of Jan de Groot of John o' Groats — had the right seamanship qualifications for becoming sub-manager of the floating bank. He had sailed his own boat for many years around Orkney shores, including the notorious Pentland Firth, where he had often gone fishing. His interest in boats in general and the bank boat in particular is reflected from the walls of his home where he has a number of evocative pictures of Orkney seascapes, one showing the 'Otterbank' accompanied by the ill-fated Long Hope lifeboat which was lost with its crew of eight in March 1969.

'I had a crew of one boatman on the 'Otterbank,' employed by the bank,' Mr Groat told me. 'We called at nine islands weekly, and at North Ronaldsay once a month, and in seven years we missed Westray, our farthest call, only four times, though I feel we sometimes took risks, and once the lifeboat put out when a coastguard saw us disappear and fail to reappear. It was hard work. We'd leave Kirkwall at 8 a.m. regarding Shapinsay as our point of no return, and arriving at, say, Westray, by 11 a.m. Our official closing time was 8 p.m., but we'd sometimes be open till midnight, with me making up the books until 2 a.m. We'd stay at Pierowall, Westray, for what was left of the night.'

I was told I should get bed and breakfast at the Clachan Guest House at Baugh, a mile from Scarinish, and on that mile I encountered a charming and inspiring group. Alex Cherry, tough, sunburnt instructor from Gairlochead Outdoor Centre, and his wife, Sheena, were on holiday on Tiree with their children, Mark (5) and Alison (2). Their base was a tent at Scarinish, but now they were returning from three days and nights on Barra. The children were seated comfortably on sleeping bags, a tent, and rucksacks deployed about a bogey with four small wheels. Alex was pulling at a forward rein, while Sheena held the bogey back on hills with a rear rein — altogether a splendid example of how to make the most of domesticity, comparable with the chap I once met carrying his small child across the Lairig Ghru in a papoose seat on his back.

The Cherrys had walked right round Barra, and B.E.A., used to unusual characters and cargoes in the isles, had cheerfully carried the bogey, giving Mrs Cherry and the children their first flight.

The Clachan Guest House turned out once to have been the Baptist manse, and while Miss Sinclair prepared an evening meal for me I walked past the chapel, which seemed rooted in the crisp machair, and ascended a bluff to a small obelisk memorial to Dr. Alexander Buchanan, born in 1835 in that Scottish 'Harley Street' of doctors, Callender, Perthshire — the Tannochbrae of 'Dr. Finlay's Casebook' — and died in Tiree in 1911, 'for 51 years the medical officer and loved and valued friend of the islanders.'

The memorial is above one of Tiree's many miniature beaches of silver sand, where grey reefs running to the sea reminded me of the Burren of County Clare as I basked in the sunshine beside the obelisk while yellow ripples came in gently from the haze which cut off Tiree as a world of its own. Another Tiree memorial is a mound near the beach at Crossapoll, said to mark the grave of Lord Ullin's daughter, drowned in Thomas Campbell's poem of our schooldays, her body having reputedly been washed ashore here.

After my meal Mr Sinclair drove me to the village hall at Crossapoll to the annual meeting of the Tiree Council of Social Service, presided over by the Duke of Argyll's factor, Major MacLellan, who described the Council's function as 'to encourage the crofters, to create industry, and to prevent the rapid depopulation of Tiree.' To do this the Council had set up sub-committees on agriculture, social welfare, tourism, industry, and transport. A youth club had been established during the year, improvement of grass had been effected, a block application had been made for the inoculation of cows against brucellosis, and a circular was being sent to Tiree exiles asking if they would return to the island should industry be fostered. At present contact was being made with one firm for the processing of shellfish, and with another producing components for computers.

Then came the big debate during which the identities of several of the 30 present emerged — the doctor, the vet, the storekeeper, the ministers, the meteorological officer, and the postmaster. Havoc, it was said, was being caused among goods coming into Tiree by the cargo boat from Queen's Dock, Glasgow. Fireclay pipes were broken, cement upset, one bag of fertilizer had seventeen stab wounds in it, cans of beer were emptied and replaced upside down in the cartons. Some firms — a minerals manufacturer and a furniture firm, were no longer interested in orders from Tiree. Damage was malicious; MacBrayne's, it was alleged, were not allowed to supervise the dockers. The island was being held to ransom. Finally it was resolved to approach MacBrayne's to consign goods in containers through Oban.

Then came a discussion on the island's dental service. A new resident dentist was too often attending to his practice in Glasgow, but this seemed to me a big improvement on the one visit every three months from the previous non-resident dentist.

Finally came the vexed question of water and a motion that the Argyll Water Board be approached concerning the completion of the Tiree water scheme. Black clouds had appeared during the meeting and, as we dispersed, hopes of a downpour ran high, with me the only person on the island not praying for rain. As we drove back to the Clachan Mr Sinclair stopped his car at a bridge where Tiree's major stream, An Fhaodhail, runs down from the lochs to the beach. We jumped into the almost dry bed, stepped across a brackish trickle, passed beneath the bridge, and came up on the other side quite dry shod. Mr Sinclair told me of Mr MacFadyen, who had sat in front of us at the meeting, and who tries to grow tomatoes commercially. He lost much of his crop in 1968 despite paying £2 per day for water to be specially supplied.

It was, of course, still perfectly light despite the dark clouds, and Mr Sinclair took me to see his own tomato venture in one small conventional glasshouse and another lean-to glasshouse against an outhouse.

'I got 1,600 lbs from 150 plants last year,' he said. 'I've planted the same number this year and I shall need about 9,000 gallons of water on them — 60 gallons to produce 10lb. of tomatoes.' He was also growing parsley, leeks, and cabbages under the glass, but his potatoes outside were doing badly for lack of water. The Great Gale of 1968 had, of course, demolished the glasshouses.

One 'crop' in good shape was Mr Sinclair's 'tangle,' a pile of thick seaweed stalks pulled from the rocks on to the machair and being worth around £20 at £12. 10s. per dry ton, with a bonus of 30s. per ton later in the season. I must say that Mr Sinclair's collection looked a very easy £20-worth. It is collected in a lorry by an islander acting as agent for Alginate Industries, whose boat, the 'Helmsdale,' regularly ships it away to factories for processing.

The Sinclairs, brother and sister, had lived in Tiree for three years, having come from Greenock to this vastly different life. 'I'd never seen the island until I came to look at this house,' Mr Sinclair told me. 'It was in a cold February with snow lying deep in Glasgow and on Mull. But on Tiree I could walk about without my jacket. So we came, and have never regretted the move.'

The rain had not materialized during the night and another sunny day dawned on Tiree, though the fine weather haze had gone, bringing into view from the Clachan garden the Paps of Jura, with Ben More and the other hills of Mull, while sweeping anti-clockwise, the Sgurr of Eigg and the Norse-sounding summits of Rhum, the jagged Cuillins of Skye and the flatter plateau of Canna rose far beyond the seagirt shores of Tiree. If it is correct that the Sinclairs have seen Ireland from their garden then surely St. Columba must have boobed in settling on Iona as the first place in the western isles from which Ireland was no longer visible. Iona is slightly nearer the coast of Ulster than Tiree, and the Sinclair's longshore garden is almost at sea level.

A straight line to Tiree Airport across the greensward known as The Reef saved me a mile, but brought down on my head the raucous imprecations of lapwings, oyster catchers, and worst of all, the terns, those delicate sea swallows, as I disturbed their fluffball chicks. In the airport building I chatted for a while with a young man coming in from Glasgow to pick up his wife from Coll and take her back to his farm in Rhodesia, and when we left for Barra one of my fellow passengers on the Heron was a Roman Catholic priest who had spent twenty-four years in Borneo and was now feeling the cold.

Barra's landing strip, twenty minutes from Tiree, is on the Great Cockle Strand, Northbay; another magnificent beach on the eastern side of a narrow isthmus, washed on the west by the Atlantic. As we flew in low, a van was chasing cows off the beach, so that the Heron had to circle awhile, one moment over the calm emerald shallows on the sheltered beach, the next above the white foam fringe of the ocean. Then, the cows having been removed, we put down gently on the dry sand. I have landed on Barra beach before on wet sand,

and the bow wave flung up to the aircraft windows gave the impression that we had fallen short in the drink. B.E.A. are able to fly to Barra on schedule all but four days a month, when due to tide conditions, the Heron flies in up to two hours before or after scheduled times, with prior notice to intended passengers.

The B.E.A. representative at Barra is the remarkable Miss Kate MacPherson, whose father, John MacPherson, was known universally as The Coddie, from a schoolboy habit of sitting dreaming in class with his mouth open like a codfish. He used to boast that a communication addressed to 'The Coddie, Barra,' would reach him from anywhere in the world. One of the great characters of the Hebrides, The Coddie who died in 1955 was comparable with Paddy the Cope in Donegal — postmaster at Northbay, general merchant and storekeeper there, member of Inverness-shire County Council, and first of his family to represent B.E.A. in Barra, having previously been Scottish Airways agent. His son, Angus, did a spell as B.E.A. station superintendent, being followed by Miss MacPherson, who was awarded the M.B.E. in 1969. Under a broiling sun I posed with Miss MacPherson for a photograph with the Heron, and then set out to walk from Northbay to Castlebay; from north to south of Barra, to catch the steamer 'Claymore' for South Uist at 5 p.m.

As soon as I had passed the shell grit factory on the Great Cockle Strand I began to be enthralled by the wild flowers; the sea pinks, butterwort, orchis, milkwort, bird-foot trefoil, cotton grass — even some late primroses. I had followed primroses up the western coasts from the Dingle peninsula, and I was to learn that had I gone to Eoligarry in northernmost Barra I should still, in mid June, have found whole hillsides of primroses in bloom.

The road winds uphill from Northbay, but the sea keeps creeping into the rugged landscape in creeks of heavenly blue edged with the golden tangle of the isles. Barra is a piece of Connemara broken off and drifted northward round the corner of Donegal. The cuckoo, silent in Tiree, was loud in Barra, following me along the telegraph wires in the absence of trees. Generally the rocky slopes rose on my right to the central hill mass, while from time to time a track went away eastward with signposts pointing to such places as Ardmhore and Ardvinish. After two miles I reached a T-junction with a signpost offering a choice of routes to Castlebay — six miles via the east; eight miles via the west. I ate some bread and cheese and took a swig of water from my plastic bottle while sitting in the welcome shade of a fine sycamore.

That signpost is a snare and a delusion. I had ample time for eight miles, and rather fancied west about, but knowing how powerful the sun can be without the Midlands smog I took the shorter route east, only to find that it ended with a hill up the flank of Heaval, Barra's highest summit, 1,260 feet. This terrible grind more than offset the two extra miles, and would have lost me the boat had I cut it fine on the assumption that I could keep up a leisurely three miles an hour. For the walker's sake some mention should be made of this obstacle on the signpost, but it was as yet unsuspected, and I resumed my walk with a creek on my left and a church ahead, into which I went. Barra has 2,350 Roman Catholics out of a population around 2,500, and this was a Catholic church, a statue of St. Theresa in a window niche and another in the porch of St. Patrick with a snake at his feet. In the interests of truth I must report that the holy water container closely resembled a child's plastic chamber pot. The young priest, jacket off and sleeves rolled up, was helping another man hump a long table around. I told him I was walking from the airport to the seaport through Barra, but when I mentioned that I was writing a book he dropped his end of the table, threw back his head, and laughed immoderately.

'Five hours in Barra,' he said, 'and you're writing a book. Shame on you.'

I explained that I was writing about a journey, that Barra happened to be on my route, and that, anyhow, I had been here before. Somewhat mollified, he told me his church was dedicated to St. Barr, the missionary who converted Barra to Christianity and is now the island's patron saint, of whom there was a statue in the porch. When I said I had seen only St. Patrick, the priest admitted, somewhat crestfallen, that the statue had originally been St. Patrick and that they had removed a shamrock from his hand, but failed to dispose of the snake. In any case, the priest said, St. Barr, too, came from Ireland — and I remembered him as St. Finnbarr of Cork, where the triple-spired Protestant cathedral is dedicated to him as founder of a monastery in the city during the 6th or 7th Century.

'There's a place in Ireland named after St. Barr,' said the priest.

'Gougane Barra — St. Barr's Hollow, a gloomy spot,' I told him.

'It's a black lake, the source of the River Lee, surrounded by hills, with a shrine to the saint.'

The redeeming feature of Gougane Barra is the prolific local occurrence of Irish butterwort, its flower much larger than that along the Barra roadsides, and its petals overlapping.

Continuing up the road from the church I saw several houses with potatoes growing from raised lazy-beds in their gardens. Where Loch Obe pushed the road westward a tall grey school building rose at the head of the loch. Up the ascent on the far side I stopped at a travelling Co-op shop where two women were making their purchases in Gaelic. They told me this was no longer a school, but a spectacle-frame factory, a venture of the Highlands and Islands Development Board, employing at present only seven. To me these small pathetic attempts to stop depopulation seem doomed to failure.

The more elderly shopper told me she knew Stronsay in Orkney and Lerwick in Shetland. The Co-op van and I continued to play leapfrog with one another over two or three lonely miles of peat hags, where great white clouds drifted into the blue from behind the barren hills, and sent their shadows across the heather. Near Skallary Post Office there were trees in a glen, and I heard a corncrake in the pasture. A lovely inlet, Breivig Bay, came in on my left, while ahead was the miniature Matterhorn of Heaval, making me wonder just how the road circumvented it. In fact, it didn't, and I found myself toiling interminably uphill, with a large white Fatima looking down unmoved on my sufferings from near the summit.

At last the road levelled out, and then, suddenly, far below, was Kisimul Castle, lapped all round by the waters of Castlebay, and flying the colourful standard of the MacNeil of Barra. Since 1959 the castle has been habitable again, though a restricted habitation it must be, offshore, no bigger than the rock it stands on, its four-square walls rising direct from the sea with the waves breaking on its front step.

As the castle dominates the harbour at Castlebay so the church dominates the town, the Catholic Church of Our Lady, Star of the Sea, its Stations of the Cross captioned in Gaelic, but, like most Catholic churches, deficient in human interest; no memorials, no graven stories of parishioners dead and gone. Down in the Post Office window was a notice advertising a sponsored walk to Seal Bay and back, twelve miles in all, the proceeds to go to the Shipwrecked Mariners Society, a worthy organisation compared with the beneficiaries from so many of these walks in England — usually Afro-Asian countries whose rampant nationalism makes them the vociferous enemies of Britain. Another link with 'civilisation' in Barra was the pop caterwauling from a teashop near the pier, which lost it my custom thirsty though I was. It was an unhappy reminder of a world I had left only the previous morning, though it seemed much farther away.

There are islands south of Barra in the string of the Outer Hebrides, the nearest, Vatersay, having a population of only 95, reached daily by the post boat in 20 minutes. Sandray, Pabbay, Mingulay, and Berneray are all unpopulated, though Mingulay, with some of Britain's tallest cliffs, is accessible on regular trips from Castlebay. Vatersay, an island of primroses in spring, has a granite memorial to 'three-fourths of the crew and passengers, numbering about 350' lost in the emigrant ship 'Annie Jane' on September 28, 1853. They are buried in a mass grave, with them the bodies of three Chinamen drowned in the wreck of the 'Idomeneus' in September 1917, to whom, however, there is a memorial stone in Cueir graveyard, Barra. These smaller islands are known generally as the Barra Isles, and Barra Head on Berneray in the southernmost point of the Outer Hebrides.

The woman in the Tourist Information Office at Barra told me that though she has been watching them for over 25 years she is still 'mesmerised' by the sunsets, particularly in autumn, from Tangusdale on the west road, where there is another of the ventures to bring industry to the islands, a perfume factory.

'One of the main ingredients in their products is seaweed,' she told me. 'So it isn't surprising they call one perfume Tangle.'

The 'Claymore' came in on time, and while she was loading a high overcast had spread slowly from the west so that when we sailed, around 5.30 p.m. it had reached the zenith. From behind it, however, the sun shone strongly across the Sea of the Hebrides, picking out all the island mountains a slightly different shade of blue from that of the sea and the sky so that they studded the eastern horizon much like a flotilla of jagged icebergs — the Cuillins of Rhum and Skye most prominent, a sight of breath-taking beauty. Ncar at hand on our port side the lesser islands of Fladday, Hellisay, and Gighay gave way to Eriskay of the 'love lilt' and 'Whisky Galore,' where I am assured many bottles still lie in caches forgotten by the islanders in their hurry to hide from the Excisemen their treasure trove from the

Loch Seaforth in the Lews is probably the most magnificent physical feature in the British Isles.

David MacBrayne Ltd.

The Standing Stones of Callanish, Lewis.   *Scottish National Trust.*

wreck of the 'Politician' in the Sound of Eriskay in 1941. A British ship of 12,000 tons, laden with the best Scotch for the United States, the 'Politician' ran aground on the islet of Calvay, which we could see plainly equidistant between Eriskay and South Uist. Eriskay is a Roman Catholic island, and the Angelus is rung at St. Michael's Church on a bell recovered from the battleship 'Derfflinger', one of the German fleet scuppered after the First World War in Scapa Flow, Orkney. It was at Prince's Bay, Eriskay, that Bonnie Prince Charlie, the Young Pretender, landed in 1744, and a blue convolvulus which grows near the beach is said to have sprung originally from seeds which fell from his pocket. Visitors are requested not to remove any roots.

The jetty at Lochboisdale is dominated by the fine hotel. A young married couple of holiday-makers who had been my fellow passengers on the Heron on the previous morning, continuing to Barra when I left it at Tiree, had now left their children with grandad at Castlebay and taken the two-hours cruise to Lochboisdale to dine at the hotel. They would return to Barra on the 'Claymore' after its two-hour turnround, reaching Castlebay again about midnight.

Local buses are always an excellent means of viewing a countryside. Down south, for instance, passengers can see over hedges which restrict the gaze from a car. There are no hedges in the Outer Hebrides; even so, from the elevation of a bus seat the traveller's horizon is a wide one, and it had always been my intention to do the two-hour bus journey from Lochboisdale to Lochmaddy, North Uist. If there is a more unusual bus route in Britain it can be only the 'Overland' in Shetland. Both routes link three islands, but whereas the 'Overland' from Lerwick to Baltasound involves three separate buses, with motor-boat links between Shetland Mainland and Yell, and between Yell and Unst, the Lochboisdale to Lochmaddy service involves only one bus across three islands, South Uist, linked with Benbecula by a bridge, and Benbecula, linked with North Uist by a causeway which the Queen Mother opened in 1960. There is, of course, an Orkney bus which crosses the Churchill Barriers to link the three islands of Orkney Mainland, Burray, and South Ronaldsay, using two smaller islets as stepping stones, Lamb Holm and Glims Holm, but this is not so long a journey as the one I was now beginning.

It was 8.10 p.m. when our bus left Lochboisdale on this 50-mile journey, the single fare being £1. 0s. 9d. South Uist has a population of 2,500 of which 80 per cent is Roman Catholic. Dwellers in Lochboisdale live mainly in pleasant houses lining a road from the harbour, but we were through these 'urban' surroundings in a few minutes and in an open country of many lochs and lochans exotic with large white water-lilies, while from from an island in one of them there bristled — of all things — a tumbledown monkey-puzzle tree. Three miles from Lochboisdale, in the Daliburgh district, we turned north on to the main road through the island and continued across rough boulder-strewn moorland with the peaceful Atlantic nearby on our left, and on our right, farther distant, the rugged mountains of South Uist rising to forbidding summits of 2,000 feet in Helca and Ben More. At intervals minor roads struck off to various communities on the west coast, one to Milton, birthplace of Flora Macdonald who helped Prince Charlie on his escape 'over the sea to Skye'; another to Ormaclete where a ruined castle of Clan Ranald thrust upward with the scattered houses against the serene grey sky, slashed by sunrays like searchlights in reverse from a break in the cloud cover. One large and complicated loch system, Loch Druidibeg, is a Nature Reserve, and its 2,600 acres form the largest natural breeding place in Britain of the greylag goose. On Reuval Hill, seemingly keeping an eye on the rocket range across Loch Bee, stands the massive white statue of the Virgin and Child — Our Lady of the Isles — the largest religious statue ever made in Britain, and contributed to by Roman Catholics all over the world. Another smaller wayside shrine stands not far away, the blue-robed Virgin familiar to any traveller in Ireland.

A bridge across South Ford, nearly a mile long, brought us to Benbecula — and a transformation. Here was a green fertile island with wire fences enclosing small fields, or huge areas of daisy-studded machair rising from fine beaches, and a detour round the west coast gave us a splendid view of the Monach Islands with their lighthouse. As shipping routes have changed this is no longer in use and the islands are now uninhabited, most of the islanders having emigrated to Canada. The Monachs lie just eight miles off the nearest point of Benbecula, and five and a half from North Uist across the Sound of Monach, yet until the 16th Century they were accessible on foot at low tide from North Uist.

Bus journeys are often an excellent way of meeting local people, but this journey was disappointing in that respect. A woman had boarded the bus at Lochboisdale with a chirping cardboard box of day-old chicks; otherwise our casual passengers were youngish men, soberly dressed in their best, who awaited the bus at the junctions where minor roads from their clachans joined the main road, and left us at the next of the two or three hotels we passed. One of these was the Greagorry Hotel on Benbecula, where our detour included Benbecula Airport and a large military hutted camp at Balivanich. A causeway across North Ford took us to North Uist, where, westward of us lay the island of Baleshare, connected to North Uist by a causeway. The name, Baleshare means East Township. There was a West Township, but this was inundated by the changes which rendered the Monachs inaccessible.

North Uist is the most waterlogged of the three islands over which the bus travelled, a bewildering maze of lochans, abounding in trout, now become unruffled silver mirrors among the dark heather as the last vestige of the evening breeze died away, though the sun was still well above the horizon at 10 p.m. The western coast of North Uist is low and fertile, but there are hills in the east. From an unlikely terrain towards them a late cuckoo was calling as the bus dropped down, past the hotel, to Lochmaddy jetty where MacBrayne's car ferry arrived from Uig (Oo-ig, not You-ig) in Skye to lie alongside until sailing back there at 6.45 a.m.

I had had a tough day, unashamedly collected five islands, and was very ready for the shower and comfortable cabin awaiting me in the 'Hebrides,' where I was soon sound asleep.

At Sponish, a mile north of Lochmaddy, there is an alginate factory, one of three in the Outer Hebrides, the others being at Orosay, South Uist; and Kerse in Lewis. The alginate industry — algae, seaweed — seems more valuable to the Hebrides than artificially introduced factories for the manufacture of computer parts or spectacle frames. Not only do the seaweed factories give employment themselves; the collection of the tangle is an important item in the subsistence economy of so many islanders.

Kelp burning was introduced seriously in North Uist in 1735, the seaweed being burned to produce soda and potash for the soap and glass industries. In 1822 the import duty on barilla — an alkali from a maritime plant — from Spain was reduced almost simultaneously with the discovery of a process for producing sodium from salt. The kelp industry folded up, but for a small proportion still used to produce iodine. In 1883 alginic acid was produced from seaweed, and production methods have been developed and improved by Alginate Industries Ltd., who now supply alginate to some 150 varied industries ranging from ice cream to welding electrodes, textile printing, surface sizing of paper, perfume, dental moulding powder, and many others. The properties of the alginate are stabilizing, suspending, gelling, thickening, and film-forming. The Republic of Ireland has its separate alginate company with factories at Kilkerran, Galway; and near Dungloe, Donegal. Alginate Industries Ltd. are 20% shareholders and supply 100% of the customers.

Mountain and Moor

SADLY I HAVE TO ADMIT that my very first journey to Skye was in large part devoted to a succulent pair of kippers at breakfast on the 'Hebrides'. We sailed at 6.45 a.m. passing the three basaltic rocks from which Lochmaddy gets its name. They closely resemble crouching dogs or 'maddies,' a corruption of the Gaelic word for a dog 'madadh.' There comes a time in life when not to have visited a popular place confers something of a distinction. I held out until comparatively late in life against Paris and the Isle of Man. Eventually stories took me to both of them, leaving Skye my one surprise unvisited place; surprising because of the amount of travel I have done in the western islands. In fact, among my walking friends, I kept up a pretence of disbelief at the existence of Skye, claiming never to have seen it, which is almost true, for it has always been shrouded in a great black rain cloud — as on an occasion when I sailed from Mallaig on the Small Isles steamer to Eigg, Rhum, Canna, and Lochboisdale in fine sunny weather. Or it has been hidden in swirling grey mist — as when I lay somewhere off Armadale for a day without a glimpse of the 'Misty Isle.' I have flown over and around Skye, but always above cloud.

On this hurried trip, however, Skye was obviously intent on convincing me of its existence. All the previous day the Cuillins and MacLeod's Tables had been free from cloud, and as the 'Hebrides' cruised into Loch Snizort past the Ascrib Islands the serrated Cuillin ridge again rose unsullied by cloud to southward. Uig Bay is a felicitous place, an enclosing crescent of green hillsides and tree-shaded glens, with substantial white houses scattered about them, concentrated rather more at Uig pier. The 'Hebrides' disgorged its cars and I followed them down the pier where the incoming cars awaited the signal to embark. Though I can no longer claim never to have seen or landed on Skye my acquaintance with the island on my first visit was restricted to once round the uninspiring pillar that marks the visit to Uig on September 1, 1902, of King Edward VII and Queen Alexandra. This must have been the same Hebridean journey on which they crossed the hill road on Colonsay — and later in the day I was to find myself leaning against a plaque on the jetty at Stornaway which also commemorated the same royal visit to Lewis.

In two hours from Uig the 'Hebrides' was back again across the Minch at Tarbert in Harris. Tarbert is a name that occurs often on the coasts of Britain. It has appeared twice before in this book — on the Shannon, and on the Kintyre peninsula. In Harris, as in Kintyre, there is an East Tarbert and a West Tarbert, again only the short width of an isthmus apart, for Tarbert means isthmus.

East Tarbert, Harris, was purple and yellow with lilac and broom in the gardens, and patriotic with a Union Jack and the St. Andrew's flag on MacBrayne's depot. But behind the town light-grey mountains rose forbidding, the highest in the Hebrides, masses of upthrust Archaen gneiss. A quick decision was necessary at Tarbert. It was mid-day on Saturday; I had a seat booked on the aircraft out of Stornaway for Glasgow at 12.20 p.m. on Monday, and I wanted to reach the northernmost point of the Hebrides, the Butt of Lewis. Forty-eight hours may have seemed ample, but the Lewis Sabbath would account for 24 of them, when everything in the island closes down, no public transport, no business motoring, and, if my informants were right, almost no private motoring. Hitching would be precarious. So I caught the bus to Stornaway, 37 miles away, and had soon forsaken East Loch Tarbert for West Loch Tarbert, driving along the most suburban road I had yet seen in the Hebrides, and facing the open Atlantic again round the northern end of the island of Taransay. Across West Loch Tarbert, as our road curved towards Ardhasig Bridge, was Ben Luskentyre, hiding the fine beaches of Luskentyre and Seilibost in South Harris. The coast road which came in from our left at the bridge ran out to Husinish beside West Loch Tarbert, the mountains of Harris Deer Forest frowning to northward of it, one track running among them to Loch Voshimid.

On this mountain loch is Sir James Barrie's 'Island that likes to be Visited,' for he wrote 'Mary Rose' at Amhuinnsuidhe Castle on the Husinish road.

From Ardhasig Bridge our road climbed steeply into the mountains, through a frightening landscape. Clisham, 2,600 feet, highest of Hebridean summits, reared its ugly grey-streaked bulk on our left, while on our other hand Wastwater had nothing on the screes coming down from Skeau Tosal to Loch a'Mhorghain. The more I see of mountain country at close quarters the more it depresses me, and I was glad when the bus emerged from Harris's vertical desolation of unadulterated rock to a splendid northward panorama of Lewis's horizontal desolation of rocky moorland, slashed by the headwaters of magnificent Loch Seaforth. The border between Harris and Lewis runs just north of the mountains, Harris belonging to the Scottish mainland county of Inverness and Lewis to Ross. Harris and Lewis are often spoken of as two islands, in fact they are one, which is correctly known as The Lews, so that the title of my half-inch map 'Harris and the Lews' was wrong. The population of Harris has declined in the past 50 years from 5,000 to 3,500.

It was an exhilarating descent towards Loch Seaforth; the special passing places being essential. From quite a distance over the open country I could see a large assembly of cars and a coach above Ardvourlie Lodge. In my native Midland shires they would have betokened a football match behind a hedge, or, save the coach, cars following a hunt. Neither explanation seemed likely here, but during our manoeuvres to pass the other coach a sombre procession appeared from the lodge — a minister, a couple of women, and sixty or so male mourners bearing a coffin among them.

'They'll may be going as far as Luskentyre,' remarked a woman on the bus, adding that in Glen Laxdale on the road to Luskentyre cemetery there is still a succession of stone cairns where the coffin is rested while the bearers are changed. I reflected that this was the fourth country funeral I had seen on my journey from Dunquin, and remembered, with more pleasure, one wedding seen through the windows of a restaurant at Moate in County Westmeath while driving back to Dublin. Half a dozen cars, dressed overall, hurtled along the main street behind the bride and groom, all tootling merrily on their horns while the passers-by stood and waved.

Loch Seaforth is one of the great geographical features of the

British Isles, a fjord nearly a mile wide and six miles long until it breaks in two round the dome of Seaforth Island, itself a mile and three quarters long. Beyond the island the loch, now half a mile wide, strikes north-eastward through lower country for four more miles, finally turning eastward for another three miles, while a western arm runs for a mile. Our road followed the north-eastern arm, much along the route taken by the fugitive Prince Charlie from Loch Seaforth towards Stornaway, where he was lodged at Arnish, having been met outside the town by one Donald MacLeod with an offering of the brandy which seems to have sustained the prince on his Hebridean wanderings. There is today a large statue of Bonnie Prince Charlie on Arnish Point at the entrance to Stornaway harbour — he should be shown with a brandy glass.

Leaving Loch Seaforth we picked up Loch Erisort, and at Balallan saw the unusual sight hereabouts of hawthorn in flower. Soon we were among the Stornaway turbaries — the peat banks rented by the townspeople, some of whom were busy turning cut peats to dry, or carting them in barrows. The influence of Stornaway reached out along the road too with huge areas of rhododendrons in the policies of Lews Castle, one tiny loch being an exquisite picture with two small purple-clad islets. A large wood shaded the road as we glided into Stornaway, spoilt rather by a quarry, but hawthorn burst into flower again near the great tower which is Stornaway's war memorial.

As I left the bus beside the inner harbour at Stornaway a group of rather obvious tourists were boarding a MacBrayne coach. There were not many places they could be going, and the Butt of Lewis was one possibility. Sure enough that is where they were bound, a round trip, due back in Stornaway in the evening. My day was becoming an unseemly rush, but I wanted to get to the Butt. When I produced my MacBrayne pass the driver was happy enough to take me in one of the empty seats, and off we went across the monotonous Eilean an Fhraoich — the Island of Heather — colourless at this time of year except where blue lochs took their colour from the cloudless sky. We stopped to inspect the Standing Stones of Callanish, old acquaintances of mine, a circle of thirteen pillars enclosing a chambered cairn where remains were found of a human cremation, possibly a megalithic priest-king, with avenues of pillars to north and south, and on either side of the circle, transept-like, an arm of four monoliths. Near the entrance to the burial chamber stands the largest pillar, 15½ feet tall. Surrounded though they are by almost infinite moorland but for the headwaters of Loch Roag coming in from the Atlantic, the stones of Callanish lack for me the eerie hushed atmosphere of the Standing Stones of Stenness in Orkney.

Glimpses of the broch above Loch Carloway, and out to sea of the distant Flannan Isles or Seven Hunters with their lighthouse mystery of three keepers who disappeared in 1901, took us north-eastward passing through the Barvas district, which gave Lewis a murder mystery in 1968, to the community of Ness and beyond it towards the Butt to the long-roofless ruin of St. Moluag's Church, restored in 1912. St. Moluag, a 6th Century contemporary of Columba, operated from the island of Lismore off Oban. He established his church at Europie, probably on a site of pagan worship of the sea-god Shony. Though St. Moluag was accepted in his lifetime and continued down the centuries to be invoked as a healer of wounds and of limb injuries, Shony was also revered, particularly on All Hallows Day when families came from all over Lewis to Europie, bringing malt from which they brewed ale. This done, a delegate was chosen to wade waist deep into the sea at night bearing a cup of ale, and thus to address the old pagan deity: 'Shony, I give you this cup of ale, hoping you will send us plenty of seaware for enriching the ground in the ensuing year.' A candle was now lit for a while in the church and finally extinguished, when, confident that their supply of sea-borne fertiliser was ensured, the Lewismen spent the remaining hours of darkness in revelry.

A red-brick lighthouse on the Butt of Lewis flashes its beam 17 miles into the vast seascape northward. Twice that distance each September the Men of Ness travel in their small boats to the uninhabited rock of Sula Sgeir to find shelter around a primitive hermitage while they catch the gugas, the young gannets, which are preserved for food and considered a great delicacy.

Back in Stornaway I quickly found accommodation with Mrs MacLennan in Kenneth Street, though my room was above an insurance office on the harbour side, and from my dormer window I looked across the basin with its small boats to the cool sycamore woodlands of Lews Castle. After a meal, my conscience not at all happy about a day's travel with no effort on my part, I went for a walk, the sun still high at 9 p.m.

There are, around the coasts of Britain, many memorials to

shipwrecks, some notable, all tragic, but surely none so heart-rending as the small white obelisk on a plinth surrounded by a low railing on the grass above the beach at the northern entrance to Stornaway harbour. Out to sea, a few hundred yards from it, is a red warning post, and at low tide a reef appears between it and the shore, a reef known as the Beast of Holm. Just seaward of it is the green Holm Island, accessible at low water, the verdant grazing place of sheep from Holm Farm as I saw if after a brisk three-mile walk along the Sandwick road, turning right towards the coastguard station.

On my way I had looked, in Sandwick Cemetery, at a row of eleven small gravestones, eight of which bore the same inscription 'A Sailor of the Great War. Royal Navy. H.M. Yacht "Iolaire." 1st January 1919. Known unto God.' The three others bore names of sailors who had been identified. On each stone was carved an anchor with a cross.

Eleven casualties in the same disaster, but eleven of a much greater death roll as the obelisk bears sad witness, for it is inscribed: 'Erected by the people of Lewis and friends in grateful memory of the brave men of the Royal Navy who lost their lives in the 'Iolaire' disaster at the Beast of Holm on the 1st of January 1919. Of the 205 persons lost 175 were natives of the island, and for them and their comrades Lewis still mourns. With gratitude for their service and in sorrow for their loss.' Beneath is a text in Gaelic, and taking Sailm as Psalm, I turned up LXXVII, Verse 19, and read: 'Thy way is in the sea, and thy path in the great waters, and thy footsteps are not known.'

I looked out towards the open sea from the obelisk, past the Shiant Islands to Skye whence the 'Iolaire' had come on that fateful New Year's Morning. The first Hogmanay of peace was at hand after four years of war, and on December 30 and 31 there was a pile-up of Lewis servicemen on leave or demobilised at Kyles of Lochalsh on the Scottish mainland awaiting a ship to Stornaway. The 'Sheila,' the normal boat on the run, could not cope, and when yet another train arrived on New Year's Eve the depot ship from Stornaway, H.M. Yacht 'Iolaire' of 750 tons was sent across to help. So on the afternoon of December 31 the naval ratings awaiting passage were embarked in her while the soldiers boarded the 'Sheila'. When the 'Iolaire' sailed in the evening a fresh southerly wind was increasing to gale force, but for the run across the Minch it was astern and uncomplicated.

The 'Iolaire' made no great speed and New Year In was celebrated aboard about two hours out of Stornaway with a gaiety born of war service that was over and a reunion with loved ones in prospect. The passengers were all sailors so the rough seas left them untroubled, but, it is said, some who knew Stornaway harbour entrance were worried that the 'Iolaire's' course was too far to starboard of Arnish light. Some even approached Captain Mason about this, and, so varying reports have it, were chased off the bridge with a revolver, though others say the captain was holding only a Very pistol. The Stornowegians' fears were well-founded however, and at 1.55 a.m. on New Year's Day, 1919, the 'Iolaire' struck the reef known as the Beast of Holm and heeled over to starboard. Rockets sent up immediately revealed the stern a bare six yards from the shore. John MacLeod, still living at Ness in June 1969, swam ashore with a line from which a hawser was hauled ashore. Along it up to 40 sailors swung to safety. Not many more lived. Through the courtesy of Mr Samuel Longbotham, managing director of the Stornaway Gazette, I was able to see that newspaper's files reporting the disaster, and to read how survivors who could do so walked the three miles into Stornaway whence I had just come, while at 3 a.m. one sailor reached Stoneyfield Farm, near the wreck, 'being hospitably received by Mr and Mrs Anderson Young.' Corpses washed ashore all round Stornaway harbour were taken to the Naval Barracks where they were identified by relatives and friends. Then came what to me is the saddest part of the tragedy. In the words of the newspaper report: 'As the bodies were identified they were handed over to friends and the little processions of carts in groups of two or three, each with its coffin, passed through the barrack gates on their way to some mourning village for interment.'

Among those heart-breaking processions across the barren land of Lewis none would have been more sad than those making for Bragar on the west coast. That village, preparing for Christmas and Hogmanay, had, barely a week earlier, been stricken with the influenza epidemic and ten villagers had died. Now another eight were brought sadly home dead from the 'Iolaire.'

The verdict at the enquiry exonerated the 'Iolaire's' officers of any suggestion of drunkenness, but found that the officer in charge did not exercise sufficient prudence in approaching the harbour, that the boat did not slow down, and that a lookout was not on duty at the time of the accident. Lewis, like all islands, has known many sea tragedies. Almost comparable with the 'Iolaire' disaster in poignancy was the loss of the fishing fleet from the village of Coll one night in 1889, when a sudden gale left 40 widows in this one small community.

Back at my lodging I found my hostess and her son, Ian, friendly and very knowledgeable about Lewis. When I mentioned where I had been, Mrs MacLennan told me that her father had just escaped sailing on the 'Iolaire' that New Year's Eve.

'He was a bit older than most of the young sailors on the 'Iolaire,'' she said, 'and thinking they might be pretty wild on the crossing he had walked instead on to the 'Sheila,' hoping to get more peace.'

Mrs MacLennan was obviously pained that I proposed hitching somewhere on the Sabbath and told me how everything but church-going comes to a full stop.

'I shouldn't like you to have a poor opinion of Lewismen,' she said, 'but if they had to go out in their cars they'd turn away from you tomorrow rather than give you a lift.'

It was nearly midnight when I went up to bed, sitting for a while compiling some notes in my window without any artificial light. There was a knock at my door. It was Mrs MacLennan, with another warning.

'You'll see you're right above the lifeboat shed,' she pointed out. 'I thought I must tell you not to be alarmed at the terrible noise if the maroons go off in the night to call the lifeboat out.'

I couldn't resist it. 'Surely not on the Sabbath,' I said.

My slumbers were undisturbed. All good Stornaway seamen were back in port by Saturday midnight, and the boat that came in as the early church bells were greeting the Sabbath was the 'Battheim' from Maloy in Norway. It was a sunny morning, though inclined to be sultry, and I let Mrs MacLennan talk me into taking it easy with a stroll through the grounds of Lews Castle to the Creed River.

The castle is a monument to the forgiving nature of Lord Leverhulme who, immediately following the First World War, owned both Lewis and Harris, and had far-sighted plans for the development of the island on a farming and fishing rather than a subsistence crofting economy. His schemes, now in part being forced on the Highlands and Islands Development Board with its attempt to bring industry to the Hebrides, cost him a fortune. Among other concrete benefits his farms would have supplied the island's milk, previously brought in at great cost from the east coast of Scotland. At Obbe in South Harris he set up a fishing port, now moribund, known as Leverburgh. Demobilised servicemen returning to Lewis anxious to resume their severely restricted crofting life damaged Lord Leverhulme's new farms, and these saboteurs were supported by the Secretary for Scotland. Eventually Leverhulme abandoned his plans, but, with the islander's interests still at heart, he set up the Leverhulme Trust to administer on their behalf the entire parish of Stornaway including Lews Castle, which is now a college, teaching building along with navigation and textiles, two vital subjects in a community producing so many seamen, and in which the leading manufacture is that of Harris tweed, still a cottage industry, the yarn being distributed to crofters and woven by them into bales of cloth which can be seen awaiting collection outside crofts all over Harris and Lewis.

The shore road through the castle grounds to the Creed River was heavenly, bank upon bank of purple rhododendrons rising with the low cliffs to the moors, a landscape neither wild nor artificially tamed, but incorporating the best of both. It was a photographer's paradise, with trees, usually Scots pines, placed strategically to frame views of Stornaway across the bay. The River Creed tumbles down to the sea in a tiny cove, almost filled by a rocky islet, purple and gold with rhododendrons, broom, and gorse. Trout were leaping, trying frantically to rid themselves of the sea lice which formed grey patches on the backs of fish visible in the pools at the river mouth. The fresh water would kill the sea lice, but the river was so low that the trout were having difficulty leaving the salt water behind.

All morning I sat beneath a beech tree in a natural craggy rock garden set off by Mac an Troineach's Cave, the hideout of an 18th Century murderer who was subsequently hanged at Inverness, not on Gallows Hill rising above the River Creed. In the afternoon I walked farther up the river beyond a drinking fountain with the inconsequential inscription: 'This bird bath and drinking fountain is erected to the memory of Robert Alfred Colby Cubbin, Owner of the Steam Yacht, "Glen Strathallan",' and across a bridge on to the moorland track to Arnish.

During the evening a thunder storm rolled up while Mrs Mac-Lennan was at the Kenneth Street Free Church. There was no rain, and I watched the congregation disperse, 1,500 of them, outdoing any Catholic church. But even Stornaway has its heretic. I was waiting for the airport bus next morning, watching Sammy, the inner harbour's resident seal, being mobbed by gulls, when a middle-aged woman addressed me, apropos of nothing at all — unless it was that I was obviously about to leave Lewis.

'You can say you met one atheist in this benighted Bible-punching community,' she said. 'I'm one, and proud of it.'

Force Eight Off St. Kilda

THE LAST TIME I had been in Stornaway was in September 1965 aboard the British India liner 'Devonia' during the annual cruise of the Scottish National Trust to their remote properties in the western and northern isles. Lewis in general, and Stornaway in particular, had evoked harsh comment in my notebook — 'a dull day in a dull town, and the dullest of coach trips around the dreariest countryside imaginable, visiting the Standing Stones of Callanish, and being lectured at several stops on the amount of reclamation from heather to grass, so that in 1964 on 11,000 reclaimed acres 1,100 cattle and 15,000 sheep were grazing where none was raised eight years earlier.'

Stornaway's Saturday night reputation for drunkenness was obviously known to my fellow passengers. At a Brains Trust aboard the 'Devonia' with visiting Lewismen as speakers one question posed was 'Is the Stornaway Saturday night a fortification against the Sabbath, or is the strict Sabbath a reparation for Saturday night?' The Brains Trust was unanimous that Stornaway's drunkenness is a scurrilous legend, but to the degree that there is noticeable drinking it is because all the pubs in Lewis are concentrated in Stornaway. The speakers did admit, however, in answer to a question about the great number of broken bottles among the bogland, that the Lewisman is inordinately untidy.

The Scottish National Trust cruise offered an astonishing opportunity to see, within eight days, half a dozen of the remotest islands round the sunset coasts of Scotland — St. Kilda, the Flannan Isles, North Rona, Sula Sgeir, and Fair Isle, with a distant glimpse of Foula 25 miles west of Shetland. Five months earlier I had travelled aboard the 'Devonia' to more exotic ports—Tangier, Funchal in Madeira, and Vigo in Spain where the brochure at a sardine-canning factory retailed the interesting titbit that 'the sardine is one of the most important foods for human consummation.' Writing a story about a party of Birmingham schoolgirls on an educational cruise I was a guest of the shipping company, travelling cabin-class. The Scottish National Trust rates journalists lower down the social scale, and a dozen of us shared a dormitory.

We sailed from Greenock on a calm evening, but awoke in the morning round the seaward side of the Mull on Kintyre heading into a gale from the north. Islay, Jura, and Colonsay passed murkily on our starboard side, but things brightened up around Iona, an emerald jewel in the sunshine. This is a stretch of sea I always enjoy under blue skies, with spouting white foam on the Dhu Heartach lighthouse and on Dutchman's Cap. I have gone ashore in Fingal's Cave on Staffa in a flat calm, and I have seen the island through the flying spume of a Force Nine blow. My great memory of the area was of passing, in heavy seas aboard MacBrayne's 'King George V,' among the Torran Rocks off the Ross of Mull where Davie Balfour escaped from the wreck of the brig 'Covenant' in Robert Louis Stevenson's 'Kidnapped.' At times I felt it would have been possible to touch the rocks either to port or starboard.

Our first call on the 'Devonia' was Tobermory 'where the drowned galleons are,' and we went ashore in the ship's launches for an afternoon excursion on Mull. In the evening a party of local artistes was entertaining us aboard when suddenly the concert was cut short. The pipers stopped piping, the fiddler stopped fiddling, and the flashing feet of the girl sword dancer were still. A boat had arrived urgently to take them back to Tobermory. There was no time to spare; wind and water were rising; they must return to their island homes on Mull and we must put out to sea in the gusty cloud-wracked dusk. As the ship turned towards Ardnamucrhan Point and the Sea of the Hebrides, many of the passengers returned to the assembly room to watch the film 'Goldfinger.' It was after midnight when it ended and already we were taking a dusting. Major Iain Campbell of Arduaine, the cruise leader, addressed us briefly before we dispersed to our bunks. 'I told you yesterday as we sailed from Greenock that this was an adventure cruise. Well, the adventure's begun.'

The gannets of St. Kilda. In the background are the outlines of Hirta, the main island, Soay, and, on the right, the tip of Boreray.

Scottish National Trust.

Leafy Kirkwall — confounding the suggestion that the Orkney Islands are treeless.

All night the 'Devonia' pitched ceaselessly and I lay sleepless. Next morning from the spindrift-swept deck St. Kilda was visible, Britain's loneliest island group, the Tristan da Cunha of the Northern Hemisphere, 40 miles west of the Outer Hebrides in the open Atlantic. Hirta, the main island, evacuated in 1930 but re-occupied in 1956 by an Army rocket-training unit, was barely visible through a squall, but Boreray's fantastic pinnacles rose clearly ahead, as menacing as the roaring combers bearing down on us from the north. The gale blew harder, clearing the squall from Hirta, and the entire archipelago was visible in the heaving sea.

Aboard the 'Devonia' was a British Council party of students, among them Chung Chai Tsang from Mauritius, with whom I watched the quarter-mile high cliffs of St. Kilda. Mauritius was the home of the extinct dodo and, as the ship pitched beneath Stac an Arnim, at 627 feet the highest sea stack in Britain, a commentary from the bridge reminded us that 120 years ago the last great auk seen in the British Isles was killed on Stac an Arnim.

Our passengers included many bird watchers, and those of us who were not were converted by the bewildering display put on by the gannets of St. Kilda, 37 per cent of the world total, some 45,000 pairs who unleashed a mad flying snowstorm in the ship's wake. We leaned on the rail in awe, forgetful of the weather, as they plummeted down like wave after wave of dive-bombers, plunging deep into the water leaving bubbling jade tracks behind them. These noble white birds with the dark wingtips have a six-feet span, and their dive-bombing could be fatal if those javelin-like beaks struck the skull, as was seen in 'The Brothers' a stark film about feuding on Skye.

St. Kilda faded astern as we set course for the Flannans. Passing them we rounded the Butt of Lewis and dusk found us off Sula Sgeir, normally an uninhabited rock, but now sending torch flashes to greet us from the Men of Ness, ashore there for their annual September slaughter of the 'gugas.' Twelve miles from Sula Sgeir, and also uninhabited, North Rona is visited each year by shepherds from Ness to inspect 150 Cheviot sheep which share the island with 7,000 grey seals. Aboard the 'Devonia' were experts on these islands, their bird and animal life, and the economy of inhabited islands like Fair Isle between Orkney and Shetland, which we circumnavigated next morning in better weather to a commentary from men who knew the island well.

From Fair Isle we could see Fitful Head and Sumburgh Head, the southernmost capes of Shetland, and as we drew nearer to cruise up the east coast of Shetland Mainland the famous bird cliff of Noss loomed east of the island of Bressay. Soon we were anchored off Lerwick, capital of Shetland, bringing back memories of having sailed south from there in the 'simmer dim' of a May night in 1951, with a torch flashing a farewell from the windows of Lystena House where I had been staying. The 'simmer dim' — summer dim — is the name in these isles of nightless summer for the short period of sundown.

Going ashore in launches we were taken by coach across the island to Scalloway on the west coast, a felicitously-placed township dominated by its castle. Turning northward we drove to 'Kergord' a fine house set among planted tree glades with a monkey puzzle tree on the lawn, which was marked out for clock golf. There was, too, a large greenhouse. The trees were first introduced 70 years ago. Our Lerwegian guide told us that during the morning he had seen a fire-crest, only the second on record in Shetland, and among the birds we saw were redshanks, three ruffs, a raven, and a family of red-breasted merganser.

We sailed from Lerwick at night and were off Cape Wrath by morning in pleasant weather with magnificent views of the grotesque hills of Sutherland — isolated mountains, Quinag, Canisp, Ben Stack, Stack Polly, and the amazing Suilven, cone, double peak, or ridge as we moved past it out at sea. To such a majestic landward panorama were added distance views of Sula Sgeir, North Rona, and the hills of Harris. Southward past Handa and the Summer Isles we came to an anchorage in Loch Ewe, going ashore in Inverewe Gardens. While some passengers were content to roam the gardens eighty of us did a ten-mile walk with an impressive background of the Torridon Hills, through Inveran with a glimpse of Loch Maree, to Kersary, returning across the boggy moors on the northern shore of Loch Kersary.

During the night we crossed the Minch for our day at Stornaway, and thereafter the weather took a hand. The following day should have provided the high spot of the cruise, a landing on Rhum for our climbers to try conclusions with Hallivall and and Askival, while I intended doing the Kilmory Walk across the centre of the island and up to the north-west coast, but a gale and low rain cloud made a landing by small boat hazardous, with the additional hazard of marooning 1,000 passengers among a population of only 40, with dire effect on the subsistance of the natives. So the 'Devonia' moved eastward to explore the possibility of landing us in Loch Scavaig, Skye, for a walk round Loch Coruisk, but this, too, had to be abandoned, so we nosed into Loch Hourn and Loch Nevis, finally anchoring in the shelter of Armadale Bay.

Early next morning it was still apparent that both Rhum and Skye still remained inhospitable, so we cruised instead down the Sound of Mull into the Firth of Lorne in improving weather, past the Garvelloch Isles and Scarba to a distant view of Corrievreckan Whirlpool. Continuing down the west coast of Jura we had splendid views of many stags and wild goats feeding on its raised shingle beach. On our starboard side the bracken and heather clad hillsides of Islay were glorious with a tweedy mixture of rust, purple, and green as we approached Port Askaig.

Passing Duart Castle, Mull, our siren had saluted a good friend of the Scottish National Trust, Sir Donald MacLean, the Chief Scout, who came out and waved to us. Now, on his little island of Gigha, we accorded a similar sonorous salute to Sir James Horlick as we continued southward to circumnavigate the gigantic rock of Ailsa Craig, 'Paddy's Milestone' as it is called, off the Ayrshire coast. This enormous dome, rising to 1,100 feet, was our last birdwatchers' benefit, another vast gannet colony. Here, maybe because conditions were calmer, we saw many gugas, baby gannets, like fluff balls on the sea. They are abandoned by their parents early, and when first they leave the nest they are too plump to fly and must bob about on the waves for a fortnight or so until sufficiently streamlined to become airborne.

Most interesting to me on Ailsa Craig was the tiny quarry clinging precariously to the cliff where the rock was cut for curling stones. Like the Men of Ness on their annual visit to Sula Sgeir, the quarry workers came to Ailsa Craig from the mainland, and in several weeks hewed out a year's supply of stone. I am told that, since 1965, the quarry has closed and curling stones are produced from other rock.

From Ailsa Craig we cruised northward again, and that night we lay in Brodick Bay encircled by the lovely hills of Arran. In the morning, the weather making a deathbed repentance for our last day of the 'Island Run,' a group of us climbed Goatfell. Through drifting cloud from the summit I looked down at the white 'Devonia' lying serenely in Brodick Bay, just as 140 days earlier I had looked down on her from a mountain behind Funchal in Madeira.

4   *Orkney*

Kirkwall Starlings

MY FIRST ARRIVAL IN Orkney, aboard the S.S. 'Archangel' on April 17, 1941, as a gunner in the 59th Searchlight Regiment R.A., was inauspicious. Bad luck had dogged my journey north from Warwickshire where we had spent a sleepless winter opposing the blitz on Birmingham and Coventry. At Aberdeen a slap-up meal awaited us after 24 hours on haversack rations, but I had somehow got to the rear of our thousand-strong column. Nevertheless, I was nearly in the hall where the food was laid when the Regimental Sergeant Major thrust out a detaining hand.

'Last four ranks back to the docks as baggage party,' he said. More haversack rations eventually reached me in the 'Archangel's' hold.

I was still carrying the last two sandwiches in the morning as we came to anchor in Scapa Flow, debating whether to eat them or feed them to the seagulls — only the seagulls were missing, as scared as I was at the heavy gunfire from a couple of cruisers bursting round an aircraft above. My conjecture as to whether this was practice or the real thing was disturbed by the order 'On Parade.' Hurriedly I joined the ranks on deck, having first popped the tattered sandwich packet on my bunk.

It was the wrong thing to do. Apparently the parade was to get us out of the way while our cabins were inspected, and that blasted R.S.M. put me on a charge in that I 'W.O.A.S. did leave my cabin in an untidy condition contrary to discipline.' I was subsequently admonished for this crime.

On a dark night in December 1910 two Germans had made an equally inauspicious, if lucky, landing in Orkney. Knocking at the door of Park Cottage, near Kirkwall, they asked what country they were in. They had ascended from Munich in a balloon on the previous afternoon, hoping to reach Switzerland. After 30 hours aloft a chance glimpse of the lights of Kirkwall through the murk of a winter's night had saved them from watery oblivion in the Atlantic.

They were the first to travel by air to Orkney. Now here was I in the skies above the islands yet again, returning for the sixth time since my wartime service. Compared with the 30 hours from Birmingham by the notorious 'Jellicoe' train to Thurso, and a crossing of the Pentland Firth aboard the 'Morialta,' 'St. Ninian,' or 'Earl of Zetland,' a five hours flight from Birmingham in a comfortable B.E.A. Viscount is an impressive achievement.

Yet on this occasion Aberdeen still had a kick at me, and the fine weather benediction of the Cashel cross which had so far favoured me along the sunset coasts finally ran out 121 days later on August 1 at Dyce Airport — on the sunrise coast — during the last of my four journeys for this book.

'Owing to adverse weather in Wick and Orkney, B.E.A. flight 8192 will be delayed one hour. There will be another announcement at 12 o'clock.' Thus the public address system at the airport. Weatherbound among the 30 or so passengers with us was an Edinburgh woman with three children travelling to the Orkney island of Hoy.

'We go there on holiday every year at this time to my parents,' she said. 'They grow strawberries and they'll be at their best now.'

My wife was travelling with me to Orkney, but the suggestion that the climate of these northern isles allows strawberries to grow, startling as it was, scarcely mollified her against the North Sea haar that was delaying our flight. Eventually we were airborne, to duck and dive, dip and accelerate among the cotton wool cloud over Wick and Orkney. At last the captain addressed us: 'Ladies and gentlemen. It's just not our day. It's too thick to get down so we're returning to Aberdeen.'

At Dyce, B.E.A. packed us into a coach for the Imperial Hotel, Aberdeen. In the Granite City I saw, painted on a derelict building, advertisements for a 'Woodchoppers' Ball,' the 'Poor Man's Ball,' and the 'Virgins' Ball!'

Denied a night in Orkney I still got more than my share of Orkney material. Apart from two Canadians going to Orkney to visit the island of Eday, all of our companions were Orcadians, among them Mrs Bob Wylie, who had lived on the island of Burray when I was there with 428 (Shirley) Searchlight Battery in 1941, and whose late husband had owned the uninhabited island of Hunda, west of Burray but joined to it by a causeway. I once wrote of Hunda — a mass of dead heather in winter — as being 'black as a bat's wing.' Colonel Rowse, who bought Hunda from the Wylies, now has much of it under grass as grazing for his cattle. The night prior to our arrival in Orkney, in a thunderstorm which had raged round our Aberdeen Hotel, Colonel Rowse's prize white shorthorn bull was killed by lightning.

There was with us, too, at the Imperial in that storm, Mr George Walker of Strathyre, Birsay, in the far north-west of Orkney Mainland. I pulled his leg about the headstones in Birsay churchyard, which suggest strange goings-on in the neighbourhood. One records the death of Andrew Spence, 'lawfull son of Magnus Spence.' A reclining stone bears the inscription, 'In memory of John Spence, died June 30, 1847, aged 29. Done by his wife, Mary Sabiston.' A third was 'Erected by John Merriman in memory of Marion Spence, his mother, spouse of his father, William Merriman.'

Miss Meta Muir, librarian at Edinburgh College of Art, came of a North Ronaldsay family. She talked of the high intelligence of the people of that island, and of the important positions they have come to occupy. Miss Muir it was who introduced a subject which led to a lot of laughing reminiscence in our circle.

'They used to call us North Ronaldsay "selkies" or seals,' she said. This rang a bell with a man from Dunbar going home to his native South Ronaldsay.

'When I was a boy the Burray "bogglers" or "boggies" used to call those of us who lived across Water Sound in St. Margaret's Hope the "hop scooties." '

'In Birsay parish,' volunteered Mr Walker, 'we were known as the Birsay "dogs" because so many dogfish were caught among the rocks around the Brough of Birsay.'

Kirkwall 'starlings' and Shapinsay 'sheep' were two other names remembered among our company who had bandied them derisively in the Orkney past. Finally the inhabitants of the parish of Firth around Finstown in West Mainland were known as Firth 'oysters' — and someone remembered that for many years it was an Orkney stock-rearing tradition that the prize cow at all shows was reared on one of the two islets in the Bay of Firth, Damsay or the Holm of Grimbister.

Miss Pauline Wishart, a nurse in Edinburgh going home to Kirkwall, introduced the 'uppies' and the 'doonies' into the conversation. Kirkwall has its annual ball game like Atherstone, Warwickshire, or Ashbourne, Derbyshire, when a free-for-all is contested between the 'uppies' born uphill of the Mercat Cross, and the 'doonies' born below it.

'The ball is thrown from the cross,' Pauline told us, 'and the doonies' objective is to get it into the harbour basin preferably with half a dozen or so of themselves. The uppies have to try to get the ball to a point on the Scapa Road.'

'They have a boys' game before the men get going,' added Mrs Wylie, 'and for some years there was a women's match, but they were downright wicked and tore one another about something awful, so it had to be stopped.'

We flew north from Aberdeen on August 2, 28 hours late, but with all the Orkney companionship and with B.E.A. paying for our stay at the Imperial, the delay had been pleasant enough. After a direct flight of 40 minutes we touched down at Grimsetter, Kirkwall's airport, to find Orkney enveloped in a love-in-the-mist fret borne in from the North Sea on a bounding breeze. It could have been worse; it could have been better. I would wish any air traveller reaching Orkney for the first time to land under blue skies and sun which turn the shallow waters of Inganess Bay into emerald and jade.

Convenient the air may be, but Orkney should be approached as Eric Linklater, the writer, himself an Orcadian, approaches it in his autobiography, 'The Man on my Back' — though not necessarily at the same time of year.

'In the morning I stumbled along a frozen ice-roughened road, and looked north over the Pictland Firth to the great island of Hoy. Often I had seen it as black as peat, as red as clover, and in the early morning the colour of a pigeon's breast. But now, beyond the dark sea, it was all unbroken white. It lay on the horizon like a white lion couchant, like a watch-dog for the hard-weather islands beyond, and the sky above it was the soft and faded blue of an old battle-flag.'

I, too, have seen Hoy like that on the road from Thurso, marching back from leave to the tiny port of Scrabster — though snow never lies long in Orkney. Back in his islands that night Linklater wrote:

'Though half the sky was dark enough, the north was lighted by the long stiff petals of a flower that was rooted at the Pole. The Northern Lights were up; the Merry Dancers were afoot.'

Many a time during my war service in Orkney I saw the Aurora Borealis, the Northern Lights; often when I had left my bed reluctantly to shiver my way to the bucket just outside the door of the hut. Annoyance at nature's call was forgotten, and I would stand entranced in my pyjamas, oblivious to the cold, while the sky flamed and shimmered overhead. One Aurora I recorded in my Orkney diary on my birthday, October 31, 1941, spent on the island of Burray:

'With Pat and Penny I walked along the muddy road eastward to Ness Headland. There was a soft breeze, but the night was full of the rushing of breakers and the occasional cry of a lapwing which we disturbed. Around us stretched a vast horizon of moonlit sea on which the darker capes of South Ronaldsay loomed black to southward. Fleecy clouds clustered round the moon, while from the north to the zenith the sky was alight with the weird glow of the Aurora Borealis. Grotesque cumulus clouds were silhouetted against a scintillating background of slowly-revolving rays and rainbow arcs, while from time to time glistening waterfalls of yellow, pink, or lilac light seemed spilled from the heavens to reflect on the heaving, tumbling seas almost surrounding our headland.'

Orkney's history thrusts itself on your notice on that road above Kirkwall as you travel in from the airport to the island metropolis. St. Magnus Cathedral you will have been led to expect, its green copper spire rising above a cruciform mass of reddish sandstone. The ruined Bishop's Palace and Earl's Palace across the road from St. Magnus will be more unexpected, as certainly will the leafy sycamores above their well-cut lawns. Two islands in the mazy northward expanse beyond Kirkwall Bay you may not even see if the mist is virulent. If conditions are favourable they are there, the round dome of Gairsay with its lower eastward protuberance, the Hen of Gairsay, and to right of it, passing the low island of Wyre superimposed on hilly Rousay, is Egilsay, and faintly seen on it something like a factory chimney, the decapitated round tower of another St. Magnus Church, on the spot where the saint was killed.

The ancient history of Orkney is a complicated chronicle of Viking and Scottish skullduggery, featuring heroic villains with picturesque names like Magnus Barelegs, Sweyn Breastrope, Thorfinn the Mighty, Olaf the Fat, Harald Fairhair, Sigurd the Stout, Erik Bloody-axe, and Thorfinn Skullsplitter. Anyone bold enough to delve into the intricate relationships of these characters can best do so through Eric Linklater's book, "The Ultimate Viking" — Sweyn Asleifson of that island of Gairsay.

St. Magnus, whose name cannot help but impinge on a visit to Orkney, was a man of doubtful saintliness. In fact, Linklater wrote 'much of Magnus's recorded behaviour smacks of political irresponsibility rather than saintliness, until death with much nobility resolves all discord.' Early in the 12th Century Magnus shared the earldom of Orkney with his cousin Haakon. After an absence in Scotland, Magnus's return to Orkney with five battle ships was seen as a threat to Haakon, but the Orkney parliament, the Althing, anxious to avoid warfare, ordered the two earls to reach some compromise, to which end they agreed to confer on Egilsay at Easter 1117, each to take an equal number of ships and men. Magnus, arriving first, counted eight ships in Haakon's approaching fleet — more than the agreed number. He anticipated trouble, and got it. After a night of prayer in a church Magnus parleyed with Haakon, offering to accept exile, imprisonment, maiming, or blindness if his life were spared — understandable, but scarcely noble. His life was not spared. He was dispatched with blows to the skull from the axe of Haakon's cook. His body was taken to Birsay in northwest Orkney Mainland for burial, and miracles occurred at his grave, continuing when his bones were moved to a church in Kirkwall. When his nephew Rognvald became Earl of Orkney and built a cathedral in Kirkwall at the suggestion of his father, he dedicated it to St. Magnus, whose 'martyrdom,' and the miracles, had brought him canonisation. The holy bones were encoffined in the choir of the cathedral, and when, in 1919, the coffin was opened, sure enough it revealed a skeleton with a skull hacked about just as the cook's axe was said to have cleaved the skull of Magnus.

Orkney continued under the dominion of Norse kings until 1468 when Christian I of Denmark was also ruler of Norway. To patch up a protracted quarrel between him and King James II of Scotland a marriage was arranged between Christian's daughter, Margaret, and

James's son, later James III. A dowry of 60,000 Rhenish florins was to go with Margaret, for 50,000 of which Christian was to pawn the Orkney Islands, redeemable like any pledge, on payment of that sum. It has never been forthcoming, so Orkney has the ignominy of being in pawn to Scotland, though it can take consolation in the even less dignified case of its northern neighbour, Shetland. Only 2,000 of the remaining 10,000 florins being available in cash, Christian was allowed to throw in Shetland for the other 8,000, a paltry valuation beside Orkney's 50,000 florins.

St. Magnus is an uncongenial cathedral, too narrow for its massive pillars, gloomy and sepulchral with more 'memento mori' of skulls, crossbones, scythes, spades, and hour-glasses to the square yard than any church I know, and with little of interest on what is left of its walls by the impeccably-carved but monotonous stones of local worthies. One hatchment-like board hangs in the north aisle, decorated in grisly fashion on one side with a monkey-like skull protruding from a shroud, a spade over the shoulder, and the inevitable hour-glass. On the reverse are these lines:

> Below doeth lye, if ye would trye,
>   Come read upon this brod,
> The corps of one Robert Nicolsone
>   Whose soul's above with God.
> He being 70 years of age, ended this mortal life,
>   And 50 of that he was married to Jeanne Davidson, his
>   wife.
>
> Betwixt them 2, 12 children had
>   Whereof 5 left behind,
> The other 7 with him in Heaven
>   Whose joy shall never end.

The windows are not striking and are difficult to see, some depicting the heroes of Orkney's past, including Turf Einer, an Earl of Orkney who, in North Ronaldsay, took revenge on Halfdan Longlegs for the murder of his father by severing his ribs and withdrawing his lungs through the gap. Perhaps he gets his place in the cathedral from his more useful contribution to Orkney's welfare, for he is said to have taught the islanders the use of peat for their fires.

Headstones cluster thick in St. Magnus churchyard, most of them testifying to the enlightened Orkney custom of using a woman's maiden name after her marriage, thus: 'Erected by John M. Sinclair in memory of his father James Sinclair, 1882, and his mother Agnes Eunson, 1881.' Another way of doing this is at first confusing, the woman being described as, for instance, 'Mary Ann Delahay or Mooney.' In Stromness the public library flaunts a large inscription: 'The Gift of the late Marjory Skea or Corrigall' — the first surname usually being the maiden name, the second her married name.

Two Chelsea pensioners lie in St. Magnus Churchyard, one of them James Haltow, with his 'beloved wife, Margaret Copland.' He died in 1869, aged 39 — which seems young for a pensioner of any kind. Two stones side by side commemorate seamen who 'fell from aloft', another a sailor killed while 'coaling ship,' and there is one to Captain Robert Mainland who died aboard the 'Loch Troon' and was buried at sea near St. Helena.

Kirkwall's three narrow main streets, Bridge Street leading from the harbour, Albert Street, and Victoria Street — the two latter divided by Broad Street where the road widens in front of St. Magnus — now form a one-way traffic system to their great detriment. None of them has pavement and roadway, and in the past the pedestrian ambled along safely among cars which crawled at walking pace because they met others head on. Now, given right of way in one direction, and confronted with nothing more lethal than humans, they hurtle along far too fast, while the walker goes to the wall or the shop window. There is a marked increase in tourist cars on Orkney roads, and the peaceful quality of the islands will deteriorate even more if the projected short ferry crossing of Pentland Firth eventuates, from near John o' Groats to Burwick in the extreme south of South Ronaldsay — eight miles only against the present 30 of the car ferry passenger route from Scrabster to Stromness. The new route would bring streams of cars both ways through Burray, thus destroying the last vestige of its island peace before the Second World War brought the Churchill Barriers.

Upper storeys with crow-footed gables lean confidentially towards one another across Kirkwall's bustle, the beautiful garden behind Tankerness House, Broad Street, providing a tranquil and colourful retreat. One mid-day during our visit a single drumbeat drew our attention to a red-coated Scots soldier wearing a bearskin, serenading the town's halberdier, Mr Robert Sclater, as he strode to the harbour, there to proclaim the Lammas Fair, a picturesque figure himself in cocked hat, yellow and black gown, and white gloves. Time was, when for the period of the Lammas Fair in Kirkwall, young couples of opposite sex were allowed to associate together as Lammas brother and sister. No such excuse is needed nowadays.

Kirkwall pier is always lively, an open book on island life with little craft coming and going from and to the North Isles. Pride of place goes to the 'Orcadia' and the 'Islander,' which ply the North Isles for the Orkney Islands Shipping Company. Often one of the North of Scotland, Orkney and Shetland Steamship Company passenger ships is in — the 'St. Ninian,' perhaps, or one of the cargo ships like the 'St. Magnus.' Fishing boats from Norway and Denmark are there. One evening we watched the Grimsby trawler 'Ross Zebra' come in. Next morning a uniformed charter pilot was having breakfast at the next table to us in the Royal Hotel. He had flown up from Norwich the previous day with a replacement for the skipper who was going into hospital for observation.

But most evocative to me are the drifters. During the war the drifters from the Cromarty Firth, Nairn, Lossiemouth, Buckie, Banff, Fraserburgh, were commandeered to provide a water bus service round the islands of Scapa Flow, free alike to servicemen and civilians, sturdy little craft flaunting a storm sternsail at almost the worst winds of an Orkney winter, and carrying us safely, if adventurously, about our business or pleasure.

There was one jarring note on the pier during the week of our stay; the evenings were rendered hideous by a team of evangelists bawling their half-baked nonsense through loud-speakers for two hours at a time, interspersed by some execrable hymn-singing. One night we could hear them from over a mile away up the Carness road, and what the management of the Kirkwall Hotel was doing to allow this dreadful racket right into its dining-room windows I can't imagine. It was a shocking disturbance of the peace. Ever since she has known me Edith has had continually to pull at my coat tails in places where two or three are gathered together to keep me out of verbal trouble, or worse. Now here was she, heckling vociferously, telling them what she thought of them and not mincing her words.

Kirkwall stands on the north of an isthmus not two miles wide. Its situation in relation to Orkney is ideal, a half-way house between East and West Mainland, and between the north and south isles. The wartime soldier, returning to Orkney 25 years after will have two major surprises. He will find the islands green, with cultivation where they were black and brown with heather, and he will find a shift in activity from the south isles to the north. It is difficult for the visitor to Kirkwall these days to visit Hoy and Flotta, once spilling over with servicemen, while Scapa Flow, that wartime scene of seething activity, is deserted but for a pleasure boat or two plying from Stromness to Flotta, Lyness, and Graemsay at times inconvenient to holiday-makers in Kirkwall.

We walked out along the old road across the isthmus and found not a soul on Scapa Pier in August 1969, while tied up there were just two vessels, the 'Three Boys' fishing boat, and the 'Hilton Briggs' lifeboat — 'provided out of a legacy left by Mrs Emily Annie Briggs of Southport, Lancs, 1951.' In a window of a grey building at the pierhead was an aneroid barometer, and inscribed around it the words: 'There is sorrow on the sea.' I looked out over the white-caps advancing up the Flow, directly between Flotta and Fara into the deep inlet of Long Hope, and, remembering the recent fate of its lifeboat crew, re-echoed those words. While we were on the empty pier a car drew up and decanted three men on to the 'Three Boys.' Within minutes they had put to sea; divers bound for the Tarf of Swona in Pentland Firth to continue diving for the cargo of copper from a Finnish ship 'Joanna Thorden,' sunk in 1937 returning with copper from her maiden voyage to America. The divers had only recently located her, and were salvaging three tons of copper a day.

One December morning in 1941 I sailed to Scapa Pier through a blizzard aboard a large drifter 'Humility.' On our decks was an astonishing assortment of the rubbish carried around by an army unit even in wartime, for we were moving from Burray to Borrowstone Hill, near Kirkwall. Waves breaking across our bows slopped indiscriminately over an upright piano, the wooden posts of a boxing ring, an old settee, and many equally unmilitary items which should surely have been fixtures in service camps. Arriving at Scapa Pier we found we should lie about twelfth boat out wherever we tied up, and that our junk would have to be manhandled across a dozen bucking decks, the usual situation at this busy spot. So we put to sea again and made for St. Mary's Holm and an easier landing if a longer journey on land. We suffered one exceptionally loud-mouthed staff sergeant who was superintending the landing of our goods and chattels. A little naval rating popped his head out of the hatch of a nearby vessel. 'Blimey, mate,' he said. 'They call us the Silent Service. What do they call you?'

Up above the New Scapa Road many houses have been built recently. Kirkwall's population, around 5,000 of Orkney's 18,000 total, has increased since the war at the expense of the outer islands. But in the 100 years from the 1861 census to 1961 the population of Orkney was nearly halved — from 32,225 to 18,650, though this is due, not to failure, but to success, as so many Orcadians have taken larger farms in Scotland. In Orkney itself the tendency is for more mechanisation on farms so that, even if they grow above the 45-acre average, they can be maintained by one family without hired hands. Edith was soon intrigued in Orkney by the well-grown bullocks still sucking from their mothers. The answer is that Orkney produces beef cattle almost exclusively, black Aberdeen Angus, so there is no need to conserve the milk. Bull calves have a longer life in a beef economy than in milk herds, and veal is almost unknown in Orkney though the steak puts to shame any I have tasted elsewhere.

A street in Stromness, Orkney.

The ruined church of St. Magnus on Egilsay, Orkney, where the saint was murdered.

Stromness and West Mainland

THE DIRECT ROAD from Kirkwall to Stromness is the most travelled in Orkney, and on week-days there is a two-hourly bus service in each direction. It was so well patronised when we did the journey that a relief bus had to be put on for our standing passengers. For a microcosm of Orkney's bland charms the journey is unsurpassable.

Kirkwall has an inland 'sea,' the Peerie Sea, called the 'Peedie' Sea, which, in either pronunciation, means the Little Sea. A causeway divides it from Kirkwall Bay, and from the bus on this road can be seen Kirkwall's power station on the town side of the Peerie Sea, while on the other a white flock of gulls scavenges on rubbish tips which are steadily cutting down the area of what might well have been developed as a marina.

Immediately beyond the Peerie Sea is the grey building pile of the Ayre Egg Grading Station. In 1941 the Orkney Egg Producers Ltd. was formed, a farmers' co-operative embracing 90% of the egg producers in Orkney. Eggs and Orkney were synonymous in those days, and no soldier ever went south on leave without a box of eggs carried inconveniently among all the belligerent junk we had to take with us. Up to about 1951 all went well, but a slump came along. Two great gales in 1952 and 1953 wrecked many hen houses and killed thousands of hens. With capital and feeding costs rising as the battery system became generally adopted, it was uneconomic to keep fewer than 2,000 birds. The decline continues — 1965-6 production was down 14.3%, 1966-7 down 15%, and 1967-8 down 22.7% on the previous years. From 580 producers of eggs in Orkney today there comes a weekly total around 400,000.

On the right of the hill out of Kirkwall the huts of the wartime Naval Air Station at Hatston, looking much as they did 25 years ago, are now taken over as council dwellings by Kirkwall. Among them is one much older residence, an earth house, possibly 2nd Century; one of the antiquities in which Orkney abounds. Don't be misled by the Ministry sign 'Grain Earth House' — Grain is the name of the area, and Grain Farm opposite Hatston has one of the thickest shelter belts of gnarled wind-blown sycamores in Orkney.

The earth house, fenced off beside a carpenter's workshop in the shadow of a Hatston hangar, was first discovered in 1827, and is of a construction found only in Orkney and Shetland, consisting of an entrance stair and a low passage to a bean-shaped chamber 12 feet long, 6 feet wide, and 5 feet 6 inches high, its roof supported by four free-standing pillars. The roof is seven feet below ground, and the Ministry of Works notice suggests that such places were dwellings, stores, workshops, or hiding holes — which, barring tombs, just about exhausts every possibility, unless in a windy place like Orkney you credit its 2nd Century inhabitants with more sagacity than their 20th Century successors in ensuring themselves subterranean safety from winter hurricanes.

One of the most striking features of Orkney in August is its gardens gay with flowers, of which the nemesia and mesembryanthemums merit special praise. Many of the houses on the outskirts of Kirkwall have little greenhouses or conservatory porches in which roses, sweet peas, geraniums, and tomatoes are grown. If the greenhouses are put to no particular winter use, and I doubt if the short Orkney winter sunshine merits this, it might be well worth someone's trouble to put a collapsible greenhouse on the market which can be taken down and tucked away safely during the winter gales, when greenhouse mortality must be heavy.

Across the Stromness road from Hatston, Wideford Hill rises beyond the golf course, its summit a mere 741 feet, but providing a magnificent viewpoint when it is free from the cloud cap it so often puts on and Orkney horizons are free from haze. On four consecutive April evenings I toiled through the heather up Wideford in 1942 hoping to see Fair Isle, and there, on the fourth, it was, the Sheep Craig thrusting above the sea directly over Balfour Castle on Shapinsay.

The fields to seaward of the road are opulent with black cattle for the six miles to Finstown. Away beyond them and the Bay of Firth rise the gentle hills of the Mainland parishes of Rendall and Evie. On the left cultivation creeps ever farther up the heather on Wideford Hill, and where the slopes have levelled out is the white house, the Old Manse, where Jo Grimond, M.P. for Orkney and Shetland lives, a popular figure often to be seen clumping about Kirkwall in gum boots. The Bay of Firth, where a good potential trade in oysters was killed by the introduction of a foreign strain among the natives, is one of Orkney's most felicitous scenes, though its peace was disturbed at Yuletide 1154 when Erland, joint Earl of Orkney with Sweyn Asleifson, was killed on the islet of Damsay as he celebrated, in a moonlight attack by Earl Rognvald, Orkney's other saint of doubtful saintliness, whose name is remembered in the island's history second only to that of Magnus. The Holm of Grimbister, Damsay's twin island in the bay can be reached on foot at low tide.

Finstown is as unexpected a sight as you will see in Orkney, a tree-shaded village of neat cottages and colourful gardens which might be anywhere in Britain out of the red brick belts. Its name derives from an Irishman, one Phin, who opened a pub, the Toddy Hole there in 1822. To this pub came regularly in later years two Orcadians who lived in the locality for an evening's drinking. They paid with the pension one received monthly for having fought in the Federal Army during the American Civil War; his friend had been in the defeated Confederate ranks, and received no pension. At each meeting they toasted a soldier famous both in the Civil War and in the American frontier wars with the Indians, the hero of the famous 'last stand' against the Sioux at Little Big Horn, General George Custer — or Cursiter, for he was of Orkney descent. The name is much respected in Orkney today through Stanley Cursiter who portrays island scenes so faithfully as a leading painter.

The Toddy Hole has changed its name to the Pomona Inn. Pomona is a name occasionally given to Orkney Mainland, though Orkneymen will look at you askance if you use it today. It arose from a misuse of a capital 'P' for the Latin word 'pomona' (fruitful) in a mediaeval manuscript, so that it translated that 'The island is Pomona' instead of 'The island is fruitful.' The erroneous name found its way on to Lily's map of Britain in 1546 and has stuck to a limited and resented extent — though it cannot be gainsaid that Orkney is very fertile. Today, in addition to the Pomona Inn at Finstown, there is a Pomona Cafe in Kirkwall, and Pomona

Potato Crisps, where the alliteration may excuse the word.

There is grand walking from Finstown into the hills both north and south, and one excursion is unique. Part way up the hill out of Finstown on the Stromness road a tubular gate gives access to a track across a pleasant field into the Wood of Binscarth, Orkney's largest woodland. A strong wind was threshing the trees when we walked the quarter-mile path through the wood, listing a dozen different trees, brambles, and a wild raspberry. Emerging from the plantation we continued beneath a tunnel of trees until the road turned right for Binscarth House, the splendid home of the Scarth family. The Scarth who built the house planted twelve flagstaffs each with a flag on various sites and left them through the rigours of an Orkney winter. In the spring he visited them all and subsequently built on the spot where the flag was least ravaged by the winter gales.

The next landmark on the right of the Stromness road might well be missed in the traveller's interest in picturesque Tormiston Mill on the left, one of Orkney's many corn mills now no longer used, but in a good state of repair, their streams marked by kingcups in spring and hidden in summer by creamy masses of meadowsweet, their scent overpowering even the white clover sown widespread as a fodder crop. At Tormiston Farm they keep the key for Maeshowe, a symmetrical grassy dome one field distant across the road.

For 36 feet the curious, and that includes all who come to Orkney, shuffle in an undignified stoop along a passage four feet high into a burial chamber of priest kings who died 3,000 years ago, a sepulchre 15 feet square, the most impressive megalithic tomb in Britain. Drystone walls rise to a domed roof, and in three of them are funerary recesses for bones and ashes of the dead. It is, however, more modern additions that bring spice to Maeshowe — time turning vandalism into history. Runic inscriptions tell that pilgrims to Jerusalem broke in to Maeshowe around 1153 and that 'Thorny was bedded. Helgi says so.' Maybe their pilgrimage was necessary in penance. Some Runic misogynist wrote: 'Many a woman, for all her airs and dignity, has had to stoop to get in here,' and of them all, another recorded 'Ingigerd is the best.'

From Maeshowe there is a fine panorama of the two great lochs, the Loch of Stenness and the Loch of Harray, with the mountains of Hoy now looming far behind and to the left across Hoy Sound which cannot be seen. An isthmus not 20 yards wide carries a road between these two lochs from the Standing Stones of Stenness to the Ring of Brogar, a circle of 27 vertical slabs seven feet tall, though there were once sixty of them. Archaeologists differ as to their significance; burial, sacrificial, sun worship, or calendrical. Whatever their original use they are pregnant with atmosphere, surrounded by so much space on a brooding Orkney day when a flotilla of Stenness swans glides round the bluff on which the stones stand, like vestal virgins coming to the sacrifice. Loch Harray is almost six miles long with an average width of well over a mile. Loch Stenness, not much smaller, drains into the sea at the Bay of Ireland through the Bridge of Waithe, between which, and the Standing Stones Hotel, a new cottage occupies a historic site. At its predecessor the first man in Britain was killed during an enemy air raid of World War Two — the first, unhappily, of more than a few.

Stromness has beaten Kirkwall to an indoor swimming bath, and 20 or so children who had paid their fare from Kirkwall, jumped off the bus and hurried in for a costly swim while the bus dropped downhill to Stromness. Home of some 1,400 Orcadians, and terminus of the sea passage to Orkney from Scrabster aboard the 'St. Ola,' Stromness is a proud little place, and a lamp rising from a fountain at the pierhead tells of its successful fight against subservience to Kirkwall, for it is a memorial to Alexander Graham, an 18th Century resident of Stromness who 'at great pecuniary sacrifice' strove to free Stromness from paying cess to Kirkwall. Before 1693 royal burghs were allowed to trade with foreign countries, but then the Scottish Parliament granted a similar right to burghs without royal dignity, provided they paid a tax — which in the case of Stromness relieved Kirkwall of one third of its duty. In 1743 Stromness protested, and in 1754 the Court of Session ruled that Kirkwall should no longer be permitted to levy the tax on Stromness trade. When the House of Lords upheld this decision in 1758 the freedom from such tax was granted to all other lesser burghs.

With Stromness the spot where most visitors arrive in Orkney, it was appropriate that notices giving a timely warning should be posted prominently on the Custom House and the shipping company office. 'Old Man of Hoy' they were headed, and continued 'Climbers are hereby warned that there is neither suitable rescue equipment nor experienced rock climbers in the vicinity. Climbers therefore proceed at their own risk.' The television exploit of Joe Brown and his colleagues on this 450 feet high sea stack in Pentland Firth in 1968 apparently attracted some tyros to the Old Man.

One of its exports which bears the name of Orkney is Robertson's Fudge. My nose almost ran it to earth in Stromness, but it was Edith who saw the toffee trays through a slit of window in a most un-fudge like building in Victoria Street, more resembling an Edwardian block of solicitors' offices. Mr James Robertson greeted us cheerily and was delighted that Edith could name the shop near our home where she buys Orkney fudge. Had he any secret formula for fudge I asked him. He had not.

'It began in my bakery,' he said. 'It was sweet rationing time and it seemed a good idea to make something sweet and sticky. Visitors liked it and asked for it to be sent south to them. So I began making it commercially and now supply it widespread in the south, among other places to the big stores in London and Birmingham. The one real Orkney product in its manufacture is milk.'

Mr Robertson employs fourteen and is so busy that he has not had a holiday for four years — but then he has no wife to force his hand. We fell to mentioning Gerry Meyer, Editor of the 'Orcadian' with whom I worked during the war on the 'Orkney Blast,' the Forces eight-page weekly, for the production of which we took over the 'Orcadian' offices and printing works for two days each week. Gerry, a Fleet Street journalist before the war, married a Stromness girl and became editor of the 'Orcadian' in 1947. He lives happily in Stromness, counting Fleet Street well lost for life in the islands.

'Yes,' said Mr Robertson. 'Wartime servicemen married so many Orkney girls that there were none left for us natives.' It was a fact that we ran a regular feature in the 'Blast' entitled 'Romance in Orcadia,' in which we reported weddings between servicemen and local girls — and the column was usually full. The 'Orkney Blast' took its apt name from the winds of Orkney and a quotation from 'Othello' — 'A fuller blast n'er shook our battlements.' Thursday nights, when we put the paper to bed, were happy occasions, with interludes for tea in a Kirkwall cafe, and a supper of fish and chips at Smoky Joe's in Junction Road.

Not far beyond the fudge factory, but on the seaward side of the narrow pavement-less street, is the Orkney Fishermen's Society where we looked in at crab being processed. In the harbour barely 50 yards from the benches in the process room 12,000 lbs. of lobsters were confined in submerged boxes awaiting the next charter flight to Norway. Lobsters are also sent live to the Continent, and we were told that the supply comes from a dozen Stromness boats, reinforced by boats from the North Isles of Orkney.

The serpentine wriggle of Stromness's succession of main streets — Victoria Street, Dundas Street, and Alfred Street, with picturesque wynd and court names like Khyber Pass and Hellihole, ends in South End with Login's Well, the name above a red door in a wall which presumably shuts off the well. An inscription tells of the importance of Stromness as a watering place for ships: 'There watered here the Hudson Bay Company's Ships 1670-1891; Captain Cook's vessels 'Resolution' and 'Discovery' 1780; Sir John Franklin's ships 'Erebus' and 'Terror' on Arctic exploration 1845; also the merchant vessels of former days. Well sealed off 1931.'

Stromness was, in fact, the last port at which Franklin's ill-fated ships touched before disappearing into the Arctic ice, but Orkney retains its interest in their tragic story with the memorial in St. Magnus Cathedral to John Rae, who lies in effigy in his sleeping bag south of the altar, hands clasped behind his head, his gun beside him. He died in 1893, and his memorial proclaims his 'intrepid discovery of the fate of Sir John Franklin.'

Stromness continued to water British naval vessels in Scapa Flow, and on June 21, 1919, one of the water boats, the 'Flying Kestrel,' was involved in a bizarre adventure. Two hundred children, boys and girls of 13 and 14, from Stromness Academy boarded her for an excursion on Scapa Flow among the captured ships of the German Navy, 74 of them including seven battleships, which lay at anchor there. Their headmaster had warned the children neither to cheer nor jeer at any German sailors they may see on the ships, but the party was surprised that seemingly the entire crew of each ship was mustered on deck as the 'Flying Kestrel' passed. The water boat called at the naval depot ship at the end of its outer journey and turned back for Stromness. The story of what followed was vividly recounted to me by Mrs Rosetta Groundwater at her home in Deerness Road one evening as damp summer mists enveloped Kirkwall.

On that historic June day 50 years earlier, as a teenager at Stromness Academy, then Rosetta Bain, she was one of the party aboard the 'Flying Kestrel'. 'As we turned back from the depot ship,' she told me in that soft Orkney voice which is so much kinder to the English language than is the Scots tongue, 'there seemed a strange stir in the air, and the German ships were all lower in the water. Then suddenly the battleship 'Sedlitz' turned turtle, and we saw holes in the bottom of it, the open water-cocks with jets spouting from them. We realised by this that the German sailors from the 'Sedlitz' and the other vessels were all in small boats, standing with their hands held up, some waving white flags. We were still wondering whether this was some kind of show put on specially for us when two British cruisers came along at full speed, either to chase the Germans back on to their ships or to prevent their landing on shore. I heard a British naval officer shout something at a boatload of Germans. At once those who were not already holding their hands above their heads put them up — except one man. The British officer shot him. As he toppled out of the boat I realised for the first time that this was real. I was only 13; the war hadn't impinged on us much in Orkney — and anyhow, it was over. I heard a megaphone ordering the 'Flying Kestrel' to return to the depot ship. All round us by now ships were keeling over or sinking by the stern. We were right in the centre of it all.'

'We were kept some time at the depot ship and then sent home through the boom at Houton. People were crowding to the shore wanting to know what was happening out in the Flow, and I heard our captain shout that the Germans were scuttling their fleet. Back at Stromness the whole town turned out to meet us, anxious for our safety. It was dawning on me that we'd been present on an historic occasion, and inevitably, I suppose, we had soon to write essays on what we'd seen.'

While Mrs Groundwater was talking her husband, William Groundwater, had come into the room, a room decorated like so many on the islands, with paintings of Orkney scenes by local artists. Mr Groundwater, too, was on the 'Flying Kestrel' as a pupil at Stromness Academy when the German fleet went down. Ultimately he became headmaster of his old school, from which post he had only recently retired, marking his retirement by becoming one of the three joint editors of 'The New Orkney Book' (Nelson, 1968, 30s.)

The holiday-maker in Kirkwall is at considerable travel disadvantage, at least on Orkney Mainland. Having a car on hire for a week or longer is impracticable and costly when the visitor may want to spend frequent days off the island. Bus routes, however, with the exception of Kirkwall-Stromness, are naturally more concerned with Orcadians intent on spending a day in Kirkwall than with visitors wanting to make a day's excursion from the island metropolis. Consequently there are morning buses in from Evie, Dounby, and Deerness, returning to those places in the afternoon, while even the South Ronaldsay and Burray service is more for the convenience of Ronaldsay people and Burravians.

There are, fortunately, frequent half-day coach tours, including Sunday, eastward across the Churchill Barriers, or westward around the tourist attractions of West Mainland. One of these, out via the Scapa coast through Orphir and Houton, is excellent value at 7s. 6d., though coach travel is rendered less pleasant by the filthy anti-social habits of smokers puffing pompously at their pipes or nervously flicking their cigarettes.

For a moment as the coach leaves for Orphir, with the Highland Park Distillery beyond Scapa Bay and another on the near side, Kirkwall seems to rival Port Ellen in Islay. A good story is told of Magnus Eunson, beadle of the U.P. Church in Kirkwall, who kept illicit whisky under the pulpit. Hearing that Excisemen proposed searching the church he removed all the kegs to his home, placed a coffin board on top of them, and draped the pile with a white sheet. When the Excisemen called a wake was in progress with Eunson at the head of the 'coffin,' Bible in hand. Waving his disengaged hand at the 'coffin' he whispered something about smallpox, and the Excisemen decamped hastily.

The Orphir road, high above the cliffs through Greenigo and Hobbister, gives spacious views of Scapa Flow with the submarine-like reef called the Barrel of Butter, and beyond through Hoxa Sound to Duncansby Head and the Scottish coast. From other vantage points on East Mainland, Ben Hope and Ben Loyal can be seen on clear days, deep in Caithness.

It was a glorious afternoon for our tour, Ward Hill and the other hills of West Mainland even more inviting tramping country than ever under pastel-tinted skies. Orkney was in its smiling mood. Waulkmill Bay, a deep inlet with firm sands, is one of the beauty spots near Orphir. Almost opposite, on the inland side of the road, is Loch Kirbister, Kirkwall's water supply, with the Germiston road skirting it and striking five miles through a valley odorous with meadowsweet, to join the Finstown-Stromness road. In this valley, at Summerdale in June 1529, was fought Orkney's one land battle, the opposing leaders being cousins. One William Sinclair had become Earl of Orkney and occupied Kirkwall Castle when he was attacked and driven from it by his cousins James and Edward Sinclair. William fled to Caithness and appealed to James V, King of Scotland, in whose gift the earldom of Orkney lay. The king ordered James and Edward to restore Kirkwall Castle to William, but they gaoled the royal messenger. So William sought help of his relative, the Earl of Caithness, and they landed near Waulkmill Bay with an army. The two usurping brothers confronted them with an Orkney force in Summerdale. Caithness was killed and his men driven back, up to 500 perishing by sword or drowning. It is said that St. Magnus himself came down from Heaven to fight alongside James and Edward — a strange act of discrimination.

An obliging coach driver made a detour for the sake of anti-quarians in our party to the ruins of the round church of the Holy Sepulchre at Orphir, little more than an apse, though it was written in the Orkney Saga of 1135 that 'a maginficent church stood facing the hall door.' Even less remains of the drinking hall, merely the foundations and another murder story. One Christmas Earl Paul was entertaining Sweyn Asleifson at Orphir, a young man with a couple of chips on his shoulder — his father recently killed in Caithness and his brother drowned in Stronsay. Another Sweyn was of the company, the Earl's champion, Sweyn Breastrope, gloomily drunk, who kept repeating a sinister threat that 'Sweyn must be the death of Sweyn'. Thus forewarned, Sweyn Asleifson waited in hiding in a dark corner, axe in hand, and when Breastrope came along, his sword drawn to fulfil his maudlin prophecy, Asleifson split his skull.

Morose thoughts were soon put out of our minds by a pause at the postman's garden above the shore at Houton. I doubt if more colour is compressed into so small a space anywhere in the British Isles, a tribute not only to the postman, but to the length of Orkney summer sunlight — the sun is above the horizon for 18 hours and 16 minutes on the longest day. And from the intimacy of the postman's garden to the immensity of a view over the Lochs of Stenness and Harray the coach took a by-road down to the Standing Stones and the Ring of Brogar, and then on skirting the attractive smaller Loch of Skaill and passing the formidable Skaill House to reach the Atlantic coast at one of Orkney's best beaches, the Bay of Skaill, conveniently handy for the major tourist attraction of Skara Brae.

What Maeshowe reveals of dying in ancient Orkney, Skara Brae reveals of living in the Stone Age period. Many centuries ago a village beside Skaill Bay was overwhelmed by sand. There it lay, with the Atlantic washing the white beach beside it, until one day in 1850 that western ocean rose in fury and sent high tides swirling up the dunes to wash away the piled-up sand of thousands of years and to expose again a stone wall. Although there was conjecture that something exciting might lie just beneath the surface, it was not until 1927 that serious digging began and Professor Gordon Childe eventually unearthed a prehistoric village where even the furniture remained in the dwellings.

Skara Brae, as the village is called, comprises ten stone huts, some nine feet tall, sunk into the sand and connected by stone-built passages, also subterranean. Each house has vestiges of an individual door. In the absence of wood in Orkney the furniture is of stone — dressers, beds, wall cupboards, seats near the hearth in the centre of the rooms, and boxes thought to be for keeping shellfish. Limpet shells, rotting fish bones, and the bones of sheep and cattle indicate the diet of the Stone Age inhabitants, though there was no evidence of grain. Because of the absence of winter feeding most of the animals would be slaughtered in autumn. Tools made among other things from deer antlers and pins of walrus ivory testified that deer and walrus thrived in Stone Age Orkney.

The half-mile walk to Skara Brae along crisp turf leads alongside an old water mill, with a reed-grown mill pond above it. Somehow my imagination remains unmoved by thoughts of the Stone Age people of Skara Brae, but I was intrigued by the thought of a miller living out his working life so close a neighbour to the Atlantic waves that the water which turned his wheel escaped directly on to the beach. Many a time in winter storms the miller must have trembled for the safety of his walls, stout though they still are, though the woodwork in the building is in chaos.

Three miles north of the Bay of Skaill the Kitchener Memorial was visible away to the left, a tower on Marwick Head. Thus 120 days after visiting his birthplace in Co. Kerry, I was near the spot where Kitchener of Khartoum met his death when H.M.S. 'Hampshire' was sunk by a mine on June 5, 1916 while taking the Secretary of State for War to Russia. The tragedy is still shrouded in mystery. Why did the escorting destroyers turn back shortly before the 'Hampshire' struck the mine? The weather was rough, but the wind was said to be north-east, which would have given shelter up the coast of West Mainland. Why were local people discouraged from rescue attempts on the grounds of security? Why were the half dozen or so survivors dispersed to distant stations away from enquiring journalists? The questions are still asked.

One of the most remarkable 'memorials' in my native Warwickshire is to Kitchener. In June 1916, a soldier, Ernest Ivens, home on leave near Long Compton in the south of Warwickshire, went into Whichford Wood with friends who were felling trees. There he first heard of Kitchener's death, and idly cut on the trunk of a beech tree, 'K. of K., drowned 6 - 6 - 1916, R.I.P.' — one day late. As the tree has grown so have the letters, until today they are a foot or so tall.

The Barony of Birsay in the north-west of West Mainland has much to attract the tourist, both in interest and, maybe, excitement — the excitement of being marooned on its offshore island, the Brough of Birsay. A concrete path has been made among the tangle-covered rocks to facilitate access at low water, but one eye must be kept on the advancing tide unless you intend one or two crowded hours of glorious Robinson Crusoe existence. While we were at Birsay a young woman was cut off, inadvertently. She had left her sandwiches in her car. To divert her she had the large remnants of a Viking village, St. Peter's Chapel on the site of an earlier Celtic church, and the foundations of a monastery.

Birsay always reminds me of a wartime 'mishap' of my own. One fine April afternoon I took the heavy old bicycle from battery headquarters at Borrowstone Hill, two miles south of Kirkwall, cycled through Kirkwall, on to Finstown, between the big lochs and up to Birsay. Insofar as it is so flat Orkney Mainland is excellent cycling country, and I reached Birsay in double quick time on the wings of the wind — literally. When I turned south-east round Loch Swannay it was another matter. The wind was in no way violent, merely a strong breeze. But Orkney has nothing to temper a strong breeze, no hedgerows, trees, built-up areas. In eight miles through Evie and Rendall I cycled one mile, pushing the seven afoot. Night was falling, so was I, when a searchlight was exposed down near the shore. I went and threw myself on the mercies of the detachment for the night, and, the wind still blowing, got a lift from them for me and the bike into Kirkwall next morning. It was one of the only two occasions in $5\frac{1}{2}$ years of war service that I went A.W.O.L. — the other, as you will read, was also through stress of weather in Orkney — and the charge was dismissed, the wind being an Act of God.

Edith and I were decanted from our coach for tea at Birsay, but I preferred to look over the ruins of the great palace raised in the 16th Century by Robert Stewart, the illegitimate half-brother of Mary, Queen of Scots, who bestowed on him the Crown estates in Orkney and Shetland. Later, when Mary was a prisoner of Elizabeth in England, Robert became Earl of Orkney and gave his subjects a thoroughly bad time, taking what lands and estates he wanted and expropriating the previous owners. Although Earl Robert seemed the ultimate in oppressive rule he left Orkney a son who was even more iniquitous and hated, Earl Patrick, known as 'Black Pate,' builder of the Earl's Palace in Kirkwall and of the castle at Scalloway in Shetland.

In Birsay I also renewed acquaintance with the churchyard, where our coach driver was mystified by a series of recumbent 18th and 19th Century stones to members of a Johnston family. Much of a pattern, these elaborate memorials all featured a coffin, a spade, a skull, and bells. The driver felt there must be some significance in the different position of these emblems of death on the various stones. I did not.

Two years earlier, in this far-flung but populous corner of Orkney, I had visited Swannay Farm. The milk from a herd of Ayrshires goes to the making of cheese, the whey being fed to pigs. Liquid manure from the pigs and the cows is piped from the farm buildings and sprayed on the pastures to produce abundant grass in a never-ending circle of model husbandry.

The coast road from Costa Head through Evie and Rendall back to Finstown — my wartime via dolorosa on the bike — is perhaps the finest panoramic road in Orkney, with glimpses of almost every one of the North Isles in good visibility as we saw it. Noup Head with its lighthouse, and the western cliffs of Westray were suspended between a blue sky and a blue Atlantic. The benign hills of Rousay rose across the sound which danced and surged around the green isle of Eynhallow, uninhabited, sacred, mystic, and once thought to have that fey Celtic quality of disappearing at will. Having watched it from above Evie Sands on a day of Orkney sea mist, now there, now gone, I can well appreciate how the legend grew in more credulous days. It was said that not until a warrior pinned Eynhallow to the sea bed with his sword would it stay there, and this eventually happened. As Eynhallow and Rousay fell behind and peat cuttings came up to the road on the lower slopes of the hills inland, the view to seaward was breathtaking with distant glimpses of each island north of Mainland with the possible exception of North Ronaldsay.

The North Isles of Orkney

SOME YEARS AGO A Birmingham journalist wrote lightly that he must have been the only man to have walked to Builth Wells (Radnorshire) and Blubberhouses (Yorkshire) during the same week. Capping him, I remarked in my own article that within four days that week I had walked across Water Sound in Orkney — by the Churchill Barrier — and crossed Radnor Forest in Wales to Water-break-its-Neck, a waterfall near New Radnor.

I am something of a connoisseur of the silly circumstance, and I was no end tickled at the strange chance which led, on the afternoon of August 6, 1939, to my being on North Ronaldsay while my wife was on South Ronaldsay. We had both intended going to the South Ronaldsay and Burray Show at St. Margaret's Hope when a sudden invitation came to me from Loganair to fly their round trip to Stronsay, Sanday, and North Ronaldsay. The first two islands I had visited before, but North Ronaldsay, always the Orkney odd man out, had previously eluded me.

The Britten-Norman Islander, a twin-engined, high-wing, nine-seater monoplane waiting on the tarmac at Grimsetter was aptly named 'Captain E. E. Fresson, O.B.E.' The pioneer of air services between Inverness and Orkney in 1933, Captain Fresson was still flying during the war, and I went south with him once on leave. Not only did his Rapide from Orkney to Inverness enable me to reach Birmingham early in the morning instead of late in the afternoon, it also ensured that I retained my leave date instead of slipping back a day whenever the leave boat failed to cross Pentland Firth in winter gales. During wartime, at reveille in every billet in Orkney, anxious eyes would be cast on the weather and the question asked by someone: 'Any fear of the leave boat not sailing?' Once only do I remember a variant on the question, from my pal Dick Bradberry on a morning when he was due to go on leave. A terrific gale had rocked the hut all night, enough to deter the stoutest sailor. Dick took one look at the wicked white smother of the North Sea beyond Water Sound, and asked: 'Any fear of the leave boat sailing?' On that stormy day it didn't.

Nothing stopped Captain Fresson. In addition to his link with Scotland he had opened up inter-island air services in Orkney, but these ceased when war began. His Highland Airways was taken over by British European Airways after the war, and internal services in Orkney were not revived until Loganair came on the scene in 1967 under charter to the Orkney Islands Shipping Company to do regular scheduled daytime flights to Westray, Papa Westray, Stronsay, Sanday, and North Ronaldsay. Evening flights off schedule are Loganair's own affair, and by the summer of 1969 there were two pilots, one flying the daytime schedule, the other taking over on evening flights.

My pilot, Captain Andrew Alsop, turned out to be a Midlander from Kenilworth and an old boy of Warwick School, where he began his flying with an R.A.F. scholarship, actually learning to fly at Wolverhampton Flying Club. After a short flying commission with the Navy, he now, at 28, had been with Loganair in Orkney for one year. 'Andy' Alsop was an answer to my prayer for a Midlander in the islands as my subject for an article to take back to my newspaper in Birmingham.

Strapped in the Islander beside him I was one of five passengers as we took off over the blue waters of Inganess Bay, and, flying low across Shapinsay, the island just north of East Mainland, I realised that this was the perfect way to see Orkney. Nothing is hidden by trees in the islands; there are few spots where a bird's eye view cannot penetrate, and our flight had all the intimacy I previously associated only with helicopter flying — five white ducks on a pond, a wave from a man driving a tractor on Shapinsay's dead straight road, and a peep inside a ruined broch on the Ness of Ork.

Stronsay Firth soon lay steel blue and slumberous below us, broken only by our own shadow and the wake of the 'Orcadia' returning from the North Isles to Kirkwall. We could almost shake

144

Aftermath of a tragedy. Ashore at Grimness, South Ronaldsay, Orkney, is the "Irene", for which the Long Hope lifeboat was searching when it was lost with its crew of eight on March 17, 1969.

An exciting day for Lerwick, Shetland, as a British India liner calls on the Scottish National Trust Annual "Island Run". Across the sound is the island of Bressay. *Scottish National Trust.*

Captain Harcus's hand as he raised it in salute from his bridge. Farther to starboard the 'St. Ninian' was making its unruffled way to Shetland. The fantastic sprawl of Sanday was now ahead, a low fertile island like a starfish embedded in the sand of the magnificent beaches from which it gets its name. The grey toy farms with their encircling walls grew larger, the white dots on the pastures assumed the identity of sheep, the black dots became Aberdeen Angus cattle. Then a yellow windsock came into sight near a grey wooden shed at the edge of a field. Captain Alsop lined up the aircraft on two sets of three boards striped yellow and white, flew low over the first, dropped down into the grass, and with the suspension knocking and complaining, hurtled astonishingly smoothly towards the second, pulling up short and taxi-ing back towards the small group of people outside the shed.

Three of our passengers left us, Captain Alsop looked in the shed and emerged with a large cardboard box. 'Bread for North Ronaldsay', he said as he stowed it in the aircraft. Within five minutes of landing we were airborne again, heading low over the jade shallows of Otterswick Bay, fringed with brown seaweed, northward for North Ronaldsay. A tiny jetty jutted into the sands of Otterwick — the starting point for the small boat crossing from Sanday to North Ronaldsay when it was Orkney's most inaccessible and least visited island.

North Ronaldsay has its own breed of sheep, unhappy scrawny creatures they seemed, foraging on the beach among the seaweed which is their food, for they are kept out of the pastures by a wall encircling the island. Their peculiar diet is said to impart a delicate flavour to their mutton, but Captain Alsop told me they taste of kippers. Several of them shared an offshore skerry with thirty or so somnolent seals as we crossed the wall to land near the church at Hollandstoun. As we rushed among the buttercups, clover, and yarrow, three snipe jinked away, a number of indignant tern took to the air screeching, and large black missiles assaulted the aircraft.

'Your cows have got got diarrhoea again, Hugh,' said Captain Alsop to the owner of the airfield as he ruefully surveyed the Islander, converted in one fell swoop into a flying cow-pat. Over two miles from the airstrip rose the tall tower of Dennis Head lighthouse which I remembered from a cruise to Iceland blinking out of the darkness as we set a north-east course between Orkney and Fair Isle.

We were now aground barely five minutes before taking off again for Sanday, flying low over the calm lagoon of Otterwick. Most of the Orkney farms look alike from the air, but Sanday had one different feature, an obelisk war memorial at a crossroads. So low in the sea is Sanday that many ships have been wrecked on its shores, and it shares the unenviable distinction with several other seagirt places of supposedly having a parson who prayed that if ships had to be wrecked, the good Lord might ensure that they be wrecked on Sanday, where the wood and other loot would be put to good use. Five minutes or so on Sanday again and off we went for Stronsay, where the airfield is at Huip. Whitehall, the settlement on Stronsay, is a closely-knit row of buildings, not scattered like most of the island 'ports.' This is a legacy of the days when a herring fleet operated from Stronsay and Papa Stronsay, the former having five and the latter fifteen fish curing stations. There was a seasonal influx of 1,500 women to gut the fish from the holds of 300 boats.

Our last passenger, picked up at Huip, was Mr Andrew Duncan, deputy county surveyor of Orkney. He is a regular traveller by Loganair, as are various other local government officers. The Orkney banks book their island visits three months in advance. A vet from Sanday flies to some island or other almost every day. In term time sixteen itinerant specialist teachers fly around the islands. Three or four new babies are flown home most weeks. The Scapa Knitting Association sends wool to women knitters in the North Isles, and the completed products are returned to Kirkwall by the plane. Machinery spares, tractor and garage parts, are flown to farmers and motor mechanics, and it is often cheaper and certainly quicker to have a motor engineer flown out to one of the islands than it is to bring a vehicle in to Kirkwall by boat. A refrigerator engineer flies regularly to do services at Westray Processors Ltd., where fish, fishcakes, crab, and chips are prepared. One fact about Loganair has slightly confounded the Orkney Isles Shipping Company — the North Isles residents have become better and more regular passengers than the commercial travellers and businessmen, and the best Orkney travel story I heard was of the girl from Rhodesia who took a job as nanny with a family spending the summer on Eday. She was warned Eday was remote. How remote she discovered when she had toothache.

She made an evening appointment with a dentist in Kirkwall and boarded the 'Orcadia' at Backaland on a day when Eday was the first call on its North Isles cruise — Eday has no airstrip. Round the islands she went — Westray, Papa Westray, Stronsay, Sanday, and so to Kirkwall, in a half gale, arriving that evening in time to keep her painful appointment. Next morning she flew by Loganair to Sanday in a few minutes, finishing on a tempestuous trip in a small boat across Eday Sound back to Eday.

Another man, from Stronsay, staying a night in Kirkwall before travelling 'sooth', found he had forgotten his spectacles. He phoned his wife on Stronsay, had her put them on the Loganair plane next morning, and picked them up at Grimsetter as he went for his southbound flight — the cost, 2s. 6d.

Fifteen minutes after landing at Grimsetter we were in the air again flying Mr and Mrs Jack Scott back to Westray with their new daughter who was blissfully oblivious to the proceedings in her kari-cot. The flight to this northern island — 2½ hours by sea — took thirteen minutes. Mr Scott owns the airfield at Westray, and his home, Skaill Farm, is so close that, as we took off, he was back there handing the precious kari-cot from the car that met him to his three older daughters. We gave them a wave and got a concerted wave in return. As soon as we were airborne from Westray we could see the windsock on Papa Westray — 'The shortest scheduled flight in Europe,' said Captain Alsop, 'two minutes — and we do it in one and a half, flying to 300 feet. Papa Westray has only four miles of road and three road signs. One says 'School;' the other two, where the road passes the airstrip, 'Danger, Low-flying aircraft.'

'Have you ever seen the west coast of Westray?' Captain Alsop asked me.

'Only Noup Head from Mainland and Rousay,' I answered.

'Then we'll go and have a look. It's better than West Mainland around Yesnaby,' he said, and we were soon flying along this awesome coast with its bird-haunted ledges and arches of rock. Crossing Westray Firth we flew over Rousay, where negotiations are afoot for a landing strip. Rousay always captured my imagination during my war service, a hilly island but not grim like Hoy, green rather than black though much is uncultivated moorland. I first landed there in June 1967 to be driven round the perimeter road, and to know the poignancy of those deserted crofts scattered about the western Atlantic-facing slopes. A population of 1,000 in 1831 has dropped now to around 250.

Rousay's central hills, unpenetrated by roads, have always seemed to me the true secret heart of Orkney. Now that heart was laid bare to me as we flew low over Muckle Water and Peerie Water, well nigh collided with a great skua, and watched a hen harrier quartering the heather. We flew on over two famous Orkney buildings, their age separated by 700 years. Trumland House, Rousay, a splendid mansion sheltered by one of Orkney's largest woods with an ornamental stream, was built during the late 19th Century by General Burroughs and bought by Walter Grant of the Highland Park Distillery which rears its pagodas above Kirkwall. Half a minute's flight away we were looking down on Cubbie Roo's Castle in Wyre.

Cubbie Roo or Kilbein Hruga was a Viking pirate who built his castle on Wyre and somehow became the 'bogey man' of Orkney, with whom mothers threatened their naughty children rather like English mothers did with 'Boney' — Napoleon Bonaparte. From the air the castle looks a small concentric spiral of ruined walls.

Captain Alsop's working day was over when we landed at Grimsetter. He and his colleague, Captain Lee, fly the daytime schedule alternately, the other doing any evening charter work. Already a wedding party, resplendent in carnations, was gathering for the short charter flight to Stronsay, after which Captain Lee had to fly to Sumburgh for a plane load of police from Wick, loaned to Shetland for the Queen's visit that day.

Back in the Royal Hotel, Edith had returned from St. Margaret's Hope with a suspicion of thunderclouds on her brow. Had she enjoyed her afternoon? Yes — but guess what?

'Those damned evangelists were there bawling their guts out through their loud-speakers in that lovely little bay, absolutely ruining the peace one expects in Orkney. I gave them a piece of my mind.'

Three days after my Loganair flights I did the round of the North Isles aboard the Orkney Islands Shipping Company's 'Orcadia' in the traditional way. Traditional; but this was a special kind of cruise, taking the islanders back home after their day at the annual Orkney Show in Bignold Park, Kirkwall. I was warned to expect alcoholic mayhem, but we were a sober enough crew as we sailed at 6 p.m. into the light mist of Kirkwall Bay after a day of mixed cloud, rain, and thunder. Inevitably my mind went back to the glorious sunny day in May 1942 when first I did the trip on the 'Orcadia's' predecessor 'Earl Sigurd.' My companions were two of my 'Orkney Blast' colleagues, and for some reason we were under the influence of Beethoven's Seventh Symphony, whistling and other-wise murdering all four movements all day, so that I never hear them but I think of that memorable occasion among my 'blue days at sea.'

Now, 27 years later, Wideford Hill and the capes of Mainland had already disappeared into the mists as we passed Thieves Holm, the islet off Carness to which felons were sent on the understanding that they would go free could they swim ashore. The distance was not great, but now, off Loch Vasa, Shapinsay, I saw the dread hazards of Orkney waters as the 'Orcadia' nipped through a narrow channel between a skerry and the shore, drawing the water away so that a tide race left a wall of water out from an angle of the shore.

I got into conversation with John Kent, a retired Westray school-master in his seventies.

'Westray's main export is gold braid,' he told me, pointing to the rings round the First Officer's sleeve. 'Sea captains are our speciality. I pulled the ears of Captain Harcus up on the bridge there, of Captain Brown the First Officer, and of Captain Stevenson of the 'St Ola,' but they don't bear me any grudge.'

Mr Kent taught in Westray when it had three schools, one with four teachers and 150 pupils, the others with two teachers and maybe 50 children each. Now there is one school only with fewer than 100 children. Westray children passing their eleven-plus examination go to Kirkwall Grammar School and live there in approved lodgings or hostels.

The shortest way between two points in Orkney seas is not necessarily a straight line but a zigzag course according to the tides. We ran close up the east coast of Egilsay and saw St. Magnus tower looming through the mist, but then turned to starboard to run between North Fara and Eday, the former now deserted, its buildings raising roofless gables to the grey skies. Mr Kent pointed out the one-time school and said he could remember when there were up to a dozen inhabited crofts on North Fara.

'One moved and then another until the island was no longer a viable proposition,' he told me. 'There weren't enough men to round up the sheep or to ship the cattle or to man a boat. After the island was depopulated an Eday farmer put cattle on it but they reverted to a wild state and were unmanageable, so he gave it up.'

So Fara, lonely and lifeless, its Calf to northward, slipped into the mists as the 'Orcadia' continued towards Westray, where we tied up at Pierowall two hours and ten minutes out of Kirkwall. Unfortunately for Westray this excellent harbour is in the far north of the island, much of its excellence coming from the shelter afforded by Papa Westray from north-east and east winds. Grey houses are spaced out fairly evenly round a wide semi-circular bay, the white stones in the graveyard being particularly prominent. Sixty or more people and half a hundred cars were at the pier to meet us. The gentle Orkney voice of Captain Harcus from the bridge eased the 'Orcadia' in, the First Officer handing over a child's cycle and getting a parcel in return almost before we were fast. A sector of the setting sun was soon obliterated by mist, and down came the rain as we crossed to Papa Westray, where half a dozen of our passengers were transferred to a small boat. The 'papa' in an island name signifies a priest's island — there are Papa Stronsay in Orkney and Papa Stour in Shetland. Papa Westray has even a saint, in the remains of a church dedicated to St. Tredwall. She was an abbess of the 8th Century with whom a King of the Picts fell in love, acclaiming in particular the beauty of her eyes. So she plucked them out, impaled them on a thorn twig, and sent them to him; a hard way of retaining her virtue.

The most spectacular feature of a North Isles cruise is the passage into Calf Sound between Red Head, Eday and Grey Head on the Calf of Eday, both of which raised themselves perpendicularly into the murk as the 'Orcadia' ploughed between them — the Scylla and Charybdis of Orkney. Fulmars were prolific here, white heads, and quick wing beats.

It was at Calf Sound, a tiny village on Eday, and at Carrick House nearby, that Sir Walter Scott found stirring material for his novel 'The Pirate,' badly neglected but one of the most readable of the Waverley Novels. John Gow, whose father had come to Orkney from Caithness, was second mate aboard a ship off North Africa in November 1724 when the captain was murdered. Gow assumed command, renamed the ship 'Revenge,' and took to piracy. He sailed back to Britain and, anchoring off Stromness, attacked Clestrain House overlooking the Bay of Ireland. After other adventures in Scapa Flow the 'Revenge' sailed north and fell foul of the roosts in Calf Sound, so put ashore on Eday where the pirates were outwitted and captured by James Fea of Carrick House. Gow was hanged with seven of his crew in February 1725, but is immortalised as Cleveland in 'The Pirate.'

Friendly lights were beginning to twinkle from farms on Eday, each with its boat, but seeing them on this uncongenial evening from the sinister tide race of Eday Sound was to realise how grim life can be in Orkney.

Backaland, Eday; Whitehall, Stronsay; and Kettletoft, Sanday, came out of the darkness and went back into the darkness in that order, and by 11.30 p.m. the 'Orcadia' was headed back for Kirkwall, rolling in Sanday Sound exposed to the North Sea weather until we reached the shelter of Shapinsay. Somewhere before Kettletoft, where he left us, I got talking with Mr John D. Mackay, another of the editors of 'The New Orkney Book.' Discussing the birds of Orkney he told me: 'My great grandfather, William Foulis, committed a shocking ornithological sin in 1831 on Papa Westray. He killed the last great auk in Orkney. When the Duchess of Bedford visited Papa Westray and heard of this she said she would provide a memorial stone, jointly for my great grandfather and the great auk, but she was lost flying, well over 70, before she did anything about it.'

Mr Mackay is himself something of a storm petrel. 'I'm the chap,' he told me, 'who suggested in a letter to the national press that the one-time Scandinavian colonies around Britain should revert to Danish rule. I've had support from the Isle of Man, some people in the Western Isles, and others in Orkney and Shetland.'

I also met Mrs Robertson, wife of Mr George Robertson who, with Mr Jack Sykes, has set up on Sanday the firm of Sykes-Robertson Electronics. She explained how her husband had answered an advertisement in a trade journal from Mr Sykes and joined him in the venture. They had installed the firm in an old school at Sellbister on Sanday and now employed ten. They make language laboratories, and from remote Sanday one of these has gone as far as Hong Kong.

'We beat the Japs to it,' said Mrs Robertson, adding, 'The general idea is to keep some young folk employed in Sanday. We tend to lose them when the harvest has to be got in — must make hay while the sun shines. But they come back.'

I was not yet quite done with the North Isles. Edith is no sailor, and the 'Orcadia' round trip can be boisterous. But the O.I.S.C. has a smaller boat, the 'Islander,' with accommodation for twelve passengers, which does a journey to Egilsay, Rousay, Wyre and back in about five hours. Surely on such a sheltered passage nothing could go amiss.

So at 6.40 a.m., after an early breakfast cheerfully volunteered by the Royal Hotel when all I had hoped was some overnight tea in a flask, we stole through the quiet streets of Kirkwall to the harbour and went aboard. Passenger accommodation on the 'Islander' is excellent, a cosy saloon with six front-facing seats in pairs rather like an aircraft in two blocks of six side by side; press-button reclining seats at that. Breakfast was available had we missed ours, and cups of tea, coffee, and biscuits at other times.

We had our nearest view of Balfour Castle, the Victorian pile on Shapinsay, from the 'Islander.' Now the home of a Polish lancer who came to Orkney and prospered after the war, it has a sizeable woodland around it. I was sorry not to visit Shapinsay this time, fairly easy of access though it is, with a small boat doing the 25-minute journey at 11 a.m. most mornings from Kirkwall, returning usually at 4 p.m. It is a pleasant island with some historic farm names — Inkerman, Balaclava, Lucknow. I remember a wartime walk I did around it, a glorious breezy experience. I was striding smartly back to Balfour Pier when I overtook and passed an ancient horse-drawn farm cart driven by an even more ancient man half asleep. As I passed he bestirred himself. 'D'you want a hurrl?' he asked. I knew enough of Orcadian terms to know that a 'hurl' was a lift, and, as I had time to spare, I waited for the cart to catch me up and climbed up beside the driver.

Shapinsay has a tenuous link with my own Birmingham. It was the birthplace of Washington Irving's father. The American writer had relatives, the Van Warts, who lived in Birmingham, the head of their family being Alderman Henry Van Wart. In 1819 Washington Irving was staying with the Van Warts in Birmingham, depressed because he was going through a spell of being unable to write. One evening literary inspiration came; the Van Warts went to bed but Irving sat on, writing. In the morning he was still there when the family came downstairs, and over breakfast he read to them the product of his night's labours — 'Rip Van Winkle.'

I was sorry the 'Islander' did not repeat the 'Orcadia's' spectacular passage of Vasa Sound. Instead we passed farther west, between Taing Skerry and the Holm of Boray, close to the Hen of Gairsay, and reached Egilsay after an hour's cruise to tie up alongside the little grey jetty, set off by yellow tangle on the rocks beyond. This, at last, was authentic island-going — a calm morning with the sun struggling through high cloud, a Landrover, a tractor, a car, five people and six black cattle awaiting the 'Islander.' Another tractor was lumbering down the road towards us, half hidden by a crop of barley waving high. Two drums of petrol were put ashore and a crate of chickens; a dozen bags of cement and a container of assorted groceries. A woman and a boy left us on a visit; they had moved from Egilsay two years earlier to live near Perth. The woman preferred Perth; the boy Egilsay. A gangplank was fixed forward, linking with a ramp into the hold. Two of the Egilsay men started rounding up the cattle, pushing, prodding, tail-tweaking. The cows themselves played ring-a-roses in ever decreasing circles. Two other men joined in, and at last the cows were manoeuvred on to the gangplank and coaxed aboard, the last one moving on backwards and having to be turned. At last all six were in the hold, impounded in groups of three in portable pens while the stink of cow manure pervaded the ship. We gained one passenger, an islandwoman going on holiday.

The 'Islander' had been forty minutes at Egilsay, with the truncated round tower of St. Magnus's ruined church above the fields which were loud with corncrakes when last I was in Egilsay two years earlier. The island suffered a drop of population from a maximum of 228 in 1831 to 54 in 1961, and the trend is still downward.

Moving round to Rousay pier we passed two churches on the shore at one point not 100 yards apart. Perhaps one was older and disused. On the pier stood a large case ungrammatically marked 'Rev. Tulloch, Manse of Ronaldsay.' Our crane, fixed amidships, soon had it down in the hold with the cattle followed by a huge red crate containing the furniture of a teacher who was quitting Rousay. The inevitable tractor could be seen winding its way down the island roads towards us, the truck it was towing containing two armchairs, in one of which a young man was seated. These, too, came aboard. A man with a heliotrope shirt and an important manner busied himself with some documents ashore as a wooden shed in sections was slung aboard.

Then the galley boy provided Rousay with its best entertainment in weeks. Slinging the gash into the sea he forgot to keep hold of the bucket, and boathooks, grappling irons, and goodness knows what else were employed to recover it.

While in Rousay in 1967 I had lunch at the home of Mrs Alice Logie, just up the road from the pier. In her dining room was a picture which has haunted me ever since in a vague way — vague because though I remembered it to be a period battle scene of dead and dying men and horses, with an heroic figure dominant in the foreground, I couldn't be quite sure of the subject. So now I popped up the road, knocked her door, reminded Mrs Logie of the occasion when we met, and asked to see the picture again.

'Oh dear,' she said. 'I'm so sorry, it's gone to Glendevon in Clackmannan. I gave it to my daughter. It depicted the handing over of the flag after some battle or other.'

However my call was not wasted. Apart from the pleasure of seeing Mrs Logie again I begged some cuttings of carnations so that Rousay may be represented in my carnation garden which harbours plants brought back from my travels as far away as Cyprus and Malta.

I went back aboard with two more black bullocks and we put across towards the jetty on Wyre, not a mile away, which had long shown signs of activity. We lay offshore and a pair of boats chugged to us, breasted up, one a cabin cruiser the other an open boat carrying two men and one large pig. A door was opened just above water level in the 'Islander's' side, and with one strong heave the pig shot into the hold. The boats returned to the jetty and back to us with two more bullocks which were hoisted adeptly into the air on a sling and deposited in the hold by our crane.

I had been wondering about the member of the 'Islander's' crew who was wearing some heavy earphones. Not at all tecnhically-minded, I still felt there should be a lead to them, which there was not; nor could I comprehend from where, wandering about so small a ship, he was receiving messages. He answered my unasked questions as we stood off Wyre. Raising the 'earphones' from his ears he said 'Did you ever hear such a noisy ship? I don't know what the designers were thinking of.'

He was, it seemed, the engineer, and the 'earphones' were an ear muff. Chatting about Rousay, with a retired civil servant from the south of England who now has a house there, on the trip back to Kirkwall, I learned that as short a while as eight years ago a new school was opened on Rousay with thirty pupils — it now has only a dozen. And a pub has recently been opened on the island.

'No,' he said, 'it hasn't got a name. You just call it The Pub, and show whether you approve or no by the inflexion of your voice.'

Burray and the Barriers

The rotund G. K. Chesterton once told us in an ode
The rolling English drunkard made the rolling English road;
If that be so, then sure it is the dead straight road to Holm
Was made by some dry sober Scot who never drained a dram.

THIS WAS A FILLER for an empty space in the 'Orkney Blast' perpetrated by me one night at a moment's notice. It really isn't so bad as it appears. For instance, the last two lines rhyme.

Six miles south of Kirkwall, in East Mainland, the settlement of St. Mary's Holm straggles along Holm Sound through which Lt. Com. Prien brought the U.47 on the night of October 13, 1939, to sink the battleship 'Royal Oak' in Scapa Flow early next morning with the loss of 888 men according to the tiny brass plaque in St. Magnus Cathedral. A 'holm', of which there are many in Orkney, is an islet with some grass still uncovered at high tide, as distinct from a 'skerry' which is a rock submerged at high tide. But St. Mary's Holm is not an islet. It is a harbour, a 'hamn' in the old Norse, and though I don't know how it came to be anglicised in St. Mary's case as 'holm,' it is still pronounced 'ham.'

That six-mile road, dominated in wartime and now by the tall wireless masts at Netherbutton, was not popular with servicemen from St. Mary's and points eastward, or from Burray, who had to hitch it for the fleshpots of Kirkwall on short leave. Its monotony was matched only by roads across the heather in Lewis, but today much of that dark heather has gone and green pasture taken its place. Gone, too, are the Army slums, the huts bought up by Orkney farmers or blown down by Orkney hurricanes. By 1961 I had difficulty in identifying the site of my old battery headquarters at Borrowstone Hill, immediately to the right of the road from Kirkwall and almost above Deepdale where the 'Royal Oak' was sunk and the Scapasaurus was washed ashore in 1941.

This was a strange sea monster in a state of partial decay, which the Orkney Blast christened the Scapasaurus, in which name it made national news. I saw it, and can vouch for the following description given by Inspector Cheyne of Kirkwall Police and reprinted in Douglas Sutherland's book 'Against the Wind' (Heinemann, 1966, 30s).

'From head to tail it is 24 feet eight inches long, but it must have been larger than that because part of the head is torn away and some of the tail appears to be broken off. The hair on the body resembles coconut fibre in texture and colour. The monster has a head like a cow only flatter. The eye sockets are three inches in diameter and very deep. The neck, which is triangular, is ten feet long and two feet round, and at the base of the neck there is a bone, shaped like a horse collar and about four feet thick. Across the back is a fin which is ten inches thick at the base and tapers. The fin is two feet six inches high. Four flappers with bone structures like hands, each three feet eight inches long were apparently the monster's means of propulsion. The tail is pointed. There is at least a ton of flesh still on the body.'

The Scapasaurus mystery was never solved satisfactorily to my knowledge. Incidentally, 'Against the Wind,' described as 'An Orkney Idyll' is excellent, but one of those irritating books which do not give place names, though identification of 'the Island' as Stronsay is quickly possible from reference to its seven miles length and its earlier great fishing importance, while the isthmus where the family house was built seems to be that between St. Catherine's Bay and the Bay of Holland. Having done this much detective work one finds it un-necessary — but correct — by a single reference to Rothiesholm Head.

St. Mary's is the Mainland end of the Churchill Barriers, laid down across the four eastern entrances into Scapa Flow during the war to prevent a repetition of the 'Royal Oak' tragedy. During 1941–42 I saw only the preparations by the firm of Balfour Beatty and Co. Ltd. One outstanding evening of my wartime sojourn in Orkney was spent in their large hutted camp at St. Mary's Holm playing against their women's table tennis team, a reminder of feminine softness for which we all craved in an Orkney winter.

157

Of the four sections of the Barrier the longest is nearly half a mile, and the greatest depth of sea crossed by them is 54 feet. Concrete blocks of five and ten tons are staggered on either side of the unrailed road to break the waves, and it is very rarely indeed that the roadway becomes impassable.

During the war a malady known as 'Orkneyitis' was rampant among troops of all the services stationed around Scapa Flow. Its manifestations ranged from eccentric behaviour to deep melancholia brought on by the different environment Orkney provided from that normally known to town dwellers. Possibly it had something in it of agorophobia — fear of the great open spaces, of all the light pressing in from all angles. More frequently it stemmed from an inability to adapt to one's surroundings; to utter soul-destroying boredom. I alleviated this, assuming it was ever a problem, by identifying wild flowers, and, to a lesser extent, birds. On the little island of Burray alone in the spring and summer of 1941 I listed 160 wild flowers, including such rarities as the aromatic lovage on Bu' dunes, and sea lungwort, mertensia, or oyster plant — a fleshy forget-me-not of the shingle which occurs scarcely anywhere but on the beach at Burray, just eastward now of the Churchill Barrier, and on the Pentland shores of Caithness.

On Lamb Holm, the first of the Barrier's stepping stones out from St. Mary's Holm, there stands a building which is a reproach to all the servicemen who were bored in Orkney. They, at least, still had some freedom, even the precious boon of two weeks' leave every four months. On Lamb Holm, and at Bu' on Burray, were several hundred men who could not expect leave, men farther from their own native land than we were. They were Italian prisoners of war captured in North Africa, some maybe from northern Italy, but many of them from sunny Mediterranean lands, to whom the windswept, sea-wracked desolation of Orkney must have seemed fearful when they arrived in the winter of 1941–42; defeated men, men without hope, torn perhaps for ever from their homes and their loved ones. I saw their coming and was deeply sorry for them. They were put to work on the construction of the Churchill Barriers. Four sounds had to be closed — the half-mile channel between St. Mary's and Lamb Holm and between Lamb Holm and Glims Holm; Weddel Sound, only a quarter of a mile between Glims Holm and Burray; and Water Sound between Burray and South Ronaldsay — a total of about 1½ miles of causeway in all. The Italians joined Balfour Beatty's work-men on the job, and with what energy they had to spare they ren-dered their camps habitable.

Around a dozen or so bare huts on Lamb Holm they made paths, grew flowers, created a theatre and scenery for it, even constructed a concrete billiard table in their recreation hut. Then, Domenico Chiocchetti, an artist, mocked up a figure of St. George with cement on a barbed wire skeleton. His slaying of the dragon symbolised the Italian prisoners' victory over loneliness and despair in their Orkney captivity, and the statue rears itself today above the bare skyline of Lamb Holm; bare, that is, but for the other exquisite labour of love of these men from the warm south, men whom I always thought to be reluctant allies of the arrogant Germans.

In 1943 and 1944, at the insistence of the War Office Inspector of Prisoner-of-War Camps, and with the benediction of a new com-mandant, the padre Father Giacabazzi, and the artist Chiocchetti, led their fellow-prisoners in the conversion of two Nissen huts into a chapel. A cement worker, a smith, electricians and others of the prisoners added their skills to Chiocchetti's art. The original artistic conception was just a chancel. Plaster board hid the curved cor-rugations of the Nissen. Central above the sanctuary Chiocchetti painted the symbol of the Holy Spirit, a White Dove. Then, sur-rounded by frescoes, he painted two Cherubim and two Seraphim, but the reredos was his masterpiece. From a religious picture which he had carried throughout the war he copied a Madonna and Child with the words 'Regina pacis ora pro nobis' — 'Queen of Peace, pray for us.' One of six encircling Cherubim holds a shield with the arms of Chiocchetti's home town, Moena in the Italian Dolomites, a ship moving from storm into calm weather. Stained glass windows of St. Catherine of Siena and St. Francis of Assisi flank the Madonna. Wood from a wreck was fashioned into the Tabernacle, brass and iron candelabra were made, and from their welfare fund the prisoners bought gold curtains for the sanctuary hangings. Finally, a four-months job, a prisoner who had worked with wrought iron in America added a beautiful rood screen.

So the initial conception was complete, but the contrast between the chancel and the bare body of the chapel did not please the meticulous Chiocchetti. On a plaster board lining, helped by a painter from another camp, he painted imitation brickwork and a dado beneath it simulating carved stone. Now an exterior had to be fashioned worthy of the interior. A porch was added, surmounted by a pediment with a thorn-crowned head of Christ moulded in red clay. Above this was a belfry and on either side a Gothic pinnacle. A final coat of cement all over the exterior, and the chapel was complete.

When the Italians left Lamb Holm in the spring of 1945 a pledge was given them by the Lord Lieutenant of Orkney, Mr P. N. Sutherland Graeme, that their chapel would be cherished lovingly by the Orcadians, and in 1958 deterioration of the fabric necessitated the formation of a preservation committee. In 1960 Chiocchetti returned for three weeks to Orkney as a guest of the committee, his travelling expenses being paid by the B.B.C. During his stay he effected many renovations and was the first to receive Communion at a service to mark the restoration. In 1961 the town of Moena donated a crucifix which stands as a shrine beside the chapel, and inside, with Chiocchetti's home marked, is a large photograph of Moena, its sharp Dolomite pinnacles in striking contrast to the bare grassy dome of Lamb Holm. The Italian Chapel has become a sight which all visitors to Orkney must see, and its bulging visitors' book contains tens of thousands of names. The volume I signed in June 1967 had been replaced by the present one in the spring of 1968, so that I added my signature to the current book.

Two names before mine was an undecipherable one, though it was easy enough to read the address entry — 'No fixed abode.' This had been written by a long-haired black-bearded young man who, as we approached the chapel, appeared over the skyline of Lamb Holm mobbed by a flock of terns whose nesting place he had obviously violated. He left the chapel before us, and as we went back to our car he was breasting the hill whence he came, still harried by the screeching terns. A strange place, Orkney, for one of no fixed abode; islands so homely that even the Italian prisoners-of-war left their own bit of Italy behind them.

I did hear that one Italian managed to escape from Orkney in a rowing boat but was very relieved to be recaptured as he tried conclusions with the turbulent Pentland Firth in so frail a craft.

The next stepping stone for the Barrier is Glims Holm, another uninhabited islet, whence a third section leaps across to Burray which I knew so well in wartime when it was an island. Although the drifter service from the north pier of Burray at Warebanks took only 20 minutes to St. Mary's Holm, dodging west of Glims Holm and Lamb Holm, this was the north-east corner of Scapa Flow where big seas kicked up in dangerous straits whenever a gale blew from the south-west across the vast expanse of the Flow. Then this quick and convenient service was suspended and a long roundabout journey became necessary. On November 5, 1941, my fellow searchlight-waggler Dick Bradberry, and I crossed by the short Warebanks ferry on a 24-hour leave to Kirkwall, which we spent in the customary way there, dozing, reading, and playing table tennis at Toc H, seeing a film in the Albert Cinema at night, and sleeping on comfortable Toc H beds. A gale blew up during the night and interfered with our sleep. Now read on from my diary, written at the time:

'We managed a good breakfast of bacon, egg, rolls and toasted buns at the Albert Cafe before hitch-hiking back to St. Mary's in an Army 'pneumonia wagon' which spouted boiling water on the radiator to temper the biting wind as we tore along the Holm Road. At St. Mary's however, as I had begun to suspect, we were told that the drifter 'Stockdove' had tried to make Burray on an earlier trip, but had been forced by stress of weather to abandon the attempt for the day. Our alternative was to return to Scapa Pier, near Kirkwall, which we did at breakneck speed in a closed Army van, and make a tedious and roundabout journey. This involved a cold wait of nearly two hours for the 'Sir Richard Grenville' which we boarded from a smaller boat after hazardous exertions. In a comfortable saloon we cruised from north to south of Scapa Flow getting some shelter from the hills of West Mainland. At Lyness on Hoy we got the small drifter for Burray South Pier. The wind was at its highest by this time, and we pitched and rolled tremendously. Our call at Flotta was risky, drawing alongside with waves leaping over the jetty. Then on, hanging grimly to a handrail on the lee side, poised a foot or so above the sea with each roll, and at other times almost catapulted over the deckhouse as our side went aloft. In flying spray we turned eastward through the boom, and with a following sea our acrobatics were considerably diminished except for some heavy broadsides as we rounded the bar of St. Margaret's Hope, South Ronaldsay. Then another twenty minutes to Burray, which we reached after about 30

161

miles of detour, instead of the straight cruise of about three miles, arriving at 4.30 p.m. instead of 11.50 a.m.'

As with my bicycle misadventure, although we were four and a half hours A.W.O.L. it was deemed to be an Act of God and no action was taken. During our night at Toc H the wind had reached hurricane force in parts of Orkney, and as usual the barrage balloons were casualties, 22 of the 50 round the fleet anchorage being destroyed, one of which we saw from the drifter, a billowing mass on the Calf of Flotta. The gale abated for a day on November 8. My diary takes up the story again on Sunday, November 9.

'After a respite of less than 24 hours the gale has returned, this time from the south-east. I have been awaiting an opportunity of seeing the breakers at Ness with such a wind, so this afternoon I struggled out along the cliffs, leaning on the wind and becoming wet through with perspiration from the effort of making headway. The reward was well worth the fight. Hill upon hill of imposing combers of the North Sea were hurling themselves against the cliffs. Spume and spray were flung high in the air and across the island in clouds. The breakers curved over in translucent jade-green bows before bursting in an explosion of white. In clefts of rock great heaps of dirty foam were piled high, and, as gusts of wind caught them they were whirled high like thistledown. Five of us lay full length on a flat slab of cliff and watched the advancing seas frothing below. Now, after tea, as I write in battery office, the gale is shaking the hut so much that at times it interferes with writing. It seems only a matter of minutes before the whole show goes over.

Tuesday, November 11: Just 48 hours since my last entry, and the gale has blown — increased to hurricane strength at times — without a moment's respite. But still, miraculously, nearly everything is standing, battered and torn, but four-square to the solid walls of wind. There is an incessant roar and whistle inescapable anywhere. In the two nights I have not slept a wink, but lain miserable and tired in our resonant Nissen hut, thankful that it has a surrounding wall of sandbags. The office shakes like a sapling, lights dance up and down, and tables rock to and fro. From all quarters in camp comes news of roofs lifting, doors blown off their hinges, and sections of huts nearly stove in. Everything moveable went long ago — cowls, aerials, signs, dustbins, buckets. No one can remain on a roof for many minutes, so all the felting is long since gone from several, and rain pours in during the frequent squalls. The windmill which pumps up water on the foreshore has been wrecked. Strangely-clad figures are borne about on the wind, protected by oilskins and wearing balaclavas, scarves, and gas eyeshields against the cutting sand. It is possible to lean on the wind, and difficult to make any headway against it. Beyond the blockships the entrance to the sound is one lather of foam, though the roar of the sea is lost in that of the wind.

No boat has reached Burray since Sunday mid-day. We are unable to receive or send post, and in the absence of rations are reduced to biscuits and bully-beef. Last night I took the negative side in a debate 'That Life is Worth Living.' Every other minute the roof of the Jane hut lifted a foot or so and flurries of the snow that was now falling scattered about the heads of the forty who were present. Despite everything, when a vote was taken the audience decided almost unanimously that life is worth living though I had done my utmost to convince them to the contrary.

Wednesday, November 12: At 12.30 p.m. today, after a morning of heavy rain, the first drifter since Sunday arrived at Burray pier and left safely. I was aboard, en route for St. Margaret's Hope. The wind had dropped, though not completely, nor had it shifted its direction a single point from south-east. Beyond the bar heavy seas were still crashing, but Water Sound was quiet. I heard that a wind velocity of 97 m.p.h. was recorded at Brough Ness, South Ronaldsay, yesterday, and some camps have had huts completely demolished. Now that the roar of the wind has died the thunder of the sea can be heard everywhere. It seems that no gale last winter in Orkney approached this one in ferocity.

I was picked up in a Utility Van at the pier at St. Margaret's, and decanted at 399 Battery above Widewalls Bay for lunch. Thence I was driven out to 'B' Troop HQ, where I addressed a lugubrious-looking gathering on the Baltic, on which I am supposed to be an authority, in a cheerless cold hut with sad rain drizzling outside. I was glad to escape back to Burray to pick up letters from home, the mail having reached the island as I left it at mid-day.

Friday, November 14: At last, by mid-day today, the gale appeared to have died and the sun shone for the first time in a week. I now hear that 104 m.p.h. was recorded on Hoy.'

Burray, with a population in 1961 of 262, fallen from an 1881 maximum of 685, is roughly anchor-shaped, some two and a half miles down the haft and four miles from hook to hook — Hunda in the west to Ness headland which protrudes into the North Sea. Scapa Flow penetrates the island from the west in Echnaloch Bay, where a gravel bar has built up, substantial enough to carry the main road and effectively damming the brackish Echna Loch. Just beyond Echna Loch a road goes eastward to Bu', and, alighting here from the St. Margaret's Hope bus one morning, Edith and I walked this road towards Bu' Farm and the North Sea.

Bu' farmhouse is Burray's most striking building, rearing its three gaunt storeys from the dunes behind the extensive strand of Bu' Bay. The name occurs elsewhere in Orkney, in Wyre and Orphir for instance, and identifies the main farm of several under the same ownership. The Bu' of Burray belonged in the 17th and 18th Centuries to a Stewart family. In 1725 the incumbent was a Sir James Stewart whose brother, Alexander, was enjoying an affair with the wife of a Captain Moodie of Melsetter in Hoy, a retired naval officer. Surprising the couple together one day Moodie gave Stewart a thorough hiding. Not much later the Stewart brothers encountered Moodie in Broad Street, Kirkwall. Words gave way to blows, blows to firearms, and Captain Moodie was shot dead. The two Stewarts fled from Orkney, Alexander to die abroad, Sir James to be pardoned and return to Bu'.

In 1745 Sir James Stewart was out of Orkney again, following Bonnie Prince Charlie at Culloden. He survived the battle and again came back to Bu'. Here he was run to earth by Government forces, led, it is said by some strange interposition of justice, by the son of Captain Moodie. He was captured while trying to hide near Bu' house, and died in a London prison.

On Stygian nights of wind and rain in the winter of 1941–42 I used to stumble back to camp from Bu' after evenings with the Kennedys, a much-travelled family where talk was often of New Zealand, South Africa, and Canada. Old Mrs Kennedy, aged 93, once told me that her last ambition was to rear peacocks at Bu'. My first postwar return to Burray was in 1951, and off to Bu' I went to meet, not the

Kennedys but John Dass, a South Ronaldsay man who had bought Bu' Farm in 1945. One other change was the inscription on a wall — 'P.O.W. Campo. Disumma Gino, 1943' — a memory of the Italians. Mr Dass was rightly proud of his home, and asked me if I had ever seen the Stewart coat-of-arms on the inside wall of the large barn. I had not, so I was taken there, and told to climb on an old table while Mr Dass caught the sunrays falling through an open door in a large mirror and shone their reflected light on to the coat-of-arms, dark beneath the roof. As I stretched up to see the shield something brushed my ear. I pushed it away, but it tickled me again, and I turned to find a peacock's feather in a wall bracket.

'Does this mean Mrs Kennedy reared peacocks at Bu' ' I asked excitedly.

'No,' said John Dass, 'I picked that up at Balfour Castle, Shapinsay. They keep peacocks there.'

I have visited John Dass several times since 1951, and now here he was again, coming from his gate with recognition in his eyes, hand outstretched, and an enthusiastic greeting in his high-pitched sing-song Orkney voice. I was telling Edith the story of the Moodie murder and Stewart's capture, so I appealed to John.

'It's right, isn't it, that grass never grows where they captured Stewart?'

'Yes, yes, yes, yes,' said John, 'down there among the segs.'

The segs are wild yellow irises which were waving in their usual profusion beyond the battered wall of the one-time fruit garden at Bu'.

'I've tried growing hundreds of trees here,' John told me, 'but it's no good. I like the trees doon sooth. Yes, yes, the trees is very bonny — but you can't see anything else for them.'

Generally Orcadians who go to England distrust the trees. 'I daren't go under them in the dark,' one Kirkwall girl told me. She is a nurse in London. Yet Kirkwall has an abundance of sycamores. Whoever put an iron railing round the tree in Albert Street started the legend of the treeless isles. Wartime servicemen used to write home jocularly that they had only one tree in Orkney so they put a railing round it.

Of 246 acres at Bu' Farm 109 are arable, and on them John grows oats and other fodder for his 132 head of Aberdeen-Shorthorn crosses.

'They're usually sold at the Kirkwall auction to dealers who ship them to Aberdeen,' John told me, and added, 'Sheep is not profitable here.'

It is, in fact, Bu's least likely acres that yield the best return. A constant string of lorries take sand from the Bu' dunes for building at points all over Orkney Mainland, and John gets the royalties. This I remember being done at Sandside Bay, Deerness, in 1963 when I camped there two nights with a party of Birmingham University archaeologists who were doing a dig on a Danish drinking hall, nights rendered memorable by my doubts as to whether we were camped above the high tide mark, and by the constant bellowing of the foghorn on Copinsay island. One of the more recondite tourist possibilities in Orkney today is a small boat trip from Skaill Farm, Sandside, to Copinsay, and to the Gloup on the Deerness coastline just north of Sandside. The Gloup is a deep sea cave where the upper ground has fallen in at the interior extremity leaving a wide bridge of land between the hole thus formed and the clifftop. Into the cave, and up this shaft the waves rush with a sound not unlike 'gloup.' The much more common 'geo' on Orkney coasts is a narrow inlet caused by the falling in of all of a cave roof.

Since my last visit to Bu' John had lost his wife and married again. Margaret, the second Mrs Dass, soon had us embarrassed at a table groaning with Orkney hospitality at the unlikely hour of 10.30 a.m., and while her husband went out to speak with a lorry driver she proudly showed us round the great house. Margaret wasn't sure how many rooms there were, but John produced an inventory dated 1710 which listed 16 rooms. It was drawn up when Dame Margaret Stewart, widow of Sir Archibald Stewart, was about to marry Lord Lindores and was 'no longer qualified to manage her son's affairs' which obviously included Bu'.

John's latter-day Margaret seems highly capable of managing Bu' and of opening up new worlds to her husband. They had spent their honeymoon in the Channel Islands, where John found time to admire the cattle. Then, earlier this year, they had been for a cruise on the 'Oriana' to such exotic places as Capri, Athens, Izmir, and Istanbul. Over the teacups photographs were produced of John Dass at the captain's cocktail party, or going ashore in Mediterranean sunshine, an unfamiliar figure without the cloth cap and dungarees in which I know him. With this wider awareness John has not forgotten his native Orkney, and when the photographs were put away he took down from a wall a brightly-polished metal object for my inspection.

'It's a cruise,' I said, 'the old Orkney oil lamp,' and I went up in John's estimation for being able to put a name and use to it.

Orkney hospitality, such as we were accorded by John and Margaret Dass is outstanding, and proved one of the happiest features of her holiday to Edith. We spent two evenings with Mrs Wylie whom we had met in Aberdeen and her daughter and son-in-law, Sheila and Tom, and in addition to the inevitable spread Tom got out his car and drove us round a fair chunk of Orphir and Firth. In the O.I.S.C. office, where he is now chief clerk, I met again Reg Bates, a Sheffield man who had married an Orkney girl and tried his hand at egg farming. Our first meeting had been in 1951, when I had hitched a lift in Reg's van and was promptly invited to his home for an evening. Now he at once asked us along for a meal, and what a magnificent repast his wife set before us at an hour when normally we have long finished eating for the day

Then there was our Deerness adventure. Noticing that a bus left Kirkwall for Deerness at 8.55 a.m. on a Saturday, returning from Deerness at 12 noon, we dashed for it without looking at the weather. We had travelled only two miles when rain began teeming down and thunder rolled over the wide spaces of East Mainland. It was still pouring relentlessly when we reached the end of the journey in the garage of the driver, Mr Laughton.

'You can't go walking in this,' he said above the tattoo on the corrugated roof, his arm rotating to embrace a waterlogged landscape which disappeared into the thunderous murk within fifty yards.

'Can we shelter in your garage for a while?' I asked.

'Certainly. Make yourselves comfortable in the bus,' he said, and went into his house alongside. Within two minutes he was back.

'My wife says you are to come into our lounge,' he said, and in we went to be met by a smiling Mrs Laughton with the inevitable question: 'Do you take tea or coffee?' We sat reading on a comfortable settee before an electric fire and with cakes, buns, and biscuits on the table until 12 noon, when we boarded the bus again and returned with Mr Laughton to Kirkwall.

When I mentioned to John Dass that Edith and I proposed walking across the Barrier to South Ronaldsay to see the wrecked

167

'Irene' in Grimness Bay, it was the work of a moment for him to get his car, and off we drove, across Water Sound past the old block ship 'Carron' whose mast had fallen since last I saw her. The effect of the Barrier is to prevent the daily scouring of Water Sound by North Sea and Atlantic tides so that sand has now built up from the shore to the 'Carron' on the North Sea side of the Barrier, while on the westward side tides from Scapa Flow pile up higher than before and have spoiled the pleasant little beach at Westermill. Goodness knows what a rubbish hole this would be if Scapa Flow was as full of ships as in wartime.

A couple of miles in South Ronaldsay, passing a house which had misspelled its name as Honeygoe instead of Honeygeo, and we came to Mrs Bichan's cottage above the bay south of Grimness. Her resplendent flower garden behind its sheltering walls, a kaleido-scopic carpet of mesembryanthemum, nemesia, dianthus and many other blooms, was lucky to survive the fateful night of March 17, 1969, when it was trampled by many urgent feet in the stormy darkness.

The 'Irene' (2,600 tons) now standing bolt upright and seemingly undamaged on the rocks below the cliffs, was the Liberian ship which caused the tragic loss of the Long Hope, Orkney, lifeboat with a crew of eight, including the father and two sons each of two families, on the very day when one of the fathers, Coxswain Daniel Kirkpatrick, was awarded the R.N.L.I. silver medal for the bravest lifesaving act of 1968.

'Why couldn't she stand out to sea?' I asked in amazement at the astounding sight of the 'Irene,' comfortable as in a dry dock.

Mr Bichan gave me a long look.

'She tried,' he said, 'but the sea were so heavy and broken that her screw was racing most of the time and she made no way. She was blown in here broadside on.'

The crew of seventeen, Greeks and coloured sailors, were brought ashore by breeches buoy and taken first into the Bichan's cottage which was almost bulging with coastguards, police, rescue personnel, and Orcadians from far and wide.

'The hoose was practically confiscated,' Mrs Bichan told me, 'and the poor garden was trampled all over. The satisfaction of saving the crew of the 'Irene' began to give way to concern and then dismay as no word came from the Long Hope lifeboat, and by midnight we'd begun to suspect the worst.'

Driving back to Burray John told us that the outline of Grimness on South Ronaldsay was so similar to that of Roseness on East Mainland that the prominent beacon tower had been erected on the latter to enable mariners to distinguish between the two. Farther north round the coast of East Mainland in Deerness, and facing north towards Eday away up Stronsay Firth, stands another tower, a memorial to the Covenanters who lost their lives in the wreck of the 'Crown' on December 10, 1679. They were members of the force defeated at Bothwell Brig, 250 of them, shipped from Leith for either the West Indies or Virginia, though sinister suggestions have been made that they were never intended to complete the voyage. When storms caused the 'Crown' to seek shelter towards Deer Sound the prisoners, fearful for their lives, asked to be put ashore. Instead they were battened below hatches. As the vessel struck the crew escaped along a mast which they cut down as a bridge, leaving the prisoners to perish.

Back on Burray we walked up the brae to the lonely home of Mrs Ara Swanney who, depite her solitary widowhood, says she loves her home and Burray, though she deplores the fact that with so many Burravians owning cars she, without one, is at a disadvantage because the bus to Kirkwall has been cut accordingly. Yet, while Burray was really an island, and before war brought life to it, Ara knew an even more restricted girlhood in the croft among the heather at Blinkbonny looking across Water Sound to St. Margaret's Hope, or down the slope of wild lupins towards Hunda. There, in 1939, Ara Taylor lived with her wrinkled old mother, and to Blinkbonny, so appropriately named, came a searchlight detachment, a dozen young men in two huts alongside the low croft. Ara became very popular, many soldiers proclaiming her the Belle of Burray. With them she went to dances, to parties, to cinema and Ensa shows, revelling in a new social life brought to Burray by war.

But, war over, loneliness again descended on Burray. As the huts decayed Ara was left with only a few house bricks from a fireplace in one of them, inscribed with the initials of the detachment which built the fireplace, including those of Norman Williams, my companion on Islay earlier in this book. In 1951 I visited Ara and her mother, more wrinkled than ever. Ten years later when next I was on Burray old Liza Taylor had been taken to the little churchyard above Bu' Bay, the croft at Blinkbonny was empty, and Ara had married — a man in his seventies — and was living with him in his house high on the brae with a terrific North Sea horizon which must be intimidating in winter gales. Two more years, and on my next visit in 1963 Ara's husband was dead, leaving her alone in that exposed house.

War brought life to Ara; peace snatched it away. But she says she is contented up there with her view — and contented and bonny she still is in a quiet Burray way.

When he was on the Blinkbonny site next to Ara's home in the summer of 1941 my friend Arthur Webb tamed a young hooded crow, and a most remarkable bird it was, remembered by Ara, Mrs Wylie, and her daughter Sheila. A rough road over a mile long stretched from Blinkbonny to the village hall at Westermill where we held our cinema shows. I often walked up there for exercise and for the pleasure of Arthur's company walking back to a show. We would set out from Blinkbonny with the crow on Arthur's shoulder. A single telegraph wire ran with the road to the village, and the crow would fly up to the top of a telegraph pole ahead of us, wait for us to pass, and fly down on to Arthur's shoulder, repeating this antic all the way to the village hall. There it would perch on the roof throughout the show, and when we came out, a hundred or more soldiers all dressed alike, the crow would glide unerringly down on to Arthur's shoulder.

At this time I was on site at Westermill alongside Burray village and the delightful little beach that has been spoilt by the Churchill Barrier. Dick Bradberry looked after our searchlight projector, and several times he had grumbled that someone was putting seashells in its gleaming bowl. We all pleaded not guilty — and wouldn't have known how to anyhow.

One fine evening Arthur had called to see us. We had enjoyed a swim and were sitting on the dunes when Dick burst out:

'Just look at your blasted crow, Arthur.'

The crow was perched atop Dick's projector busily pushing a seashell through the fan. This done successfully it swooped down to the beach, picked up another shell in its beak, and flew again to the top of the projector.

Whenever I return to Burray certain memories crowd back into my mind. Two of my Army friends there were Tom Heath Robinson, son of the eccentric cartoonist, who would walk up and down our hut in deep contemplation for an hour at a time, and Neville Masterman, son of the Rt. Hon. C. F. G. Masterman, a famous Liberal M.P. and a member of governments between 1908 and 1915. Neville was a grand chap, but even less military than I. The Army, with its penchant for putting square pegs in round holes, called up Neville from the useful job of teaching English to Czech soldiers, and made him a useless unit in a searchlight crew — useless that is, unless you count the good humour he generated wherever he went. On Burray he found a job to his liking, as barman in the wet canteen — not that Neville was a drinker. Efforts were made from time to time by his family to get the gangling good-humoured Neville into something more consistent with his upbringing and education, and a year or so after we left Orkney he would disappear occasionally on strange interviews. These normally proved abortive, until after one of them came an astonishing recommendation 'that a quiet academic backwater' be found for Gunner Masterman. Eventually he went into the Intelligence Corps, his initial reaction being a mild annoyance that this necessitated his putting up some stripes.

Shortly after the battery's arrival on Burray our sergeants bought an enormous boat, a whaler or some such thing, and had the carpenters hard at work making it seaworthy. Its maiden voyage came one lovely calm June night when Water Sound was an opalescent mirror. The itinerant cinema operator and his girl friend had been entertained in the sergeants' mess and missed the last drifter to St. Margaret's Hope. The sergeants decided to launch the boat and take them across, about a mile and a half of a narrow sound barely a half mile wide.

'Row along the shore of Burray until you're past St. Margaret's,' advised Jock Wylie, the Burray baker, who knew Water Sound intimately, 'then you'll drift across on the tide.'

Even so the sergeants got too far out, into midstream as it were, and from Westermill site we had the happy experience of watching eight sergeants rowing like galley slaves towards Scapa Flow and the west, but drifting inexorably eastward to the North Sea. They managed to pull ashore on the tip of South Ronaldsay, the last bit of land before Norway.

It was on Burray that I blew up the Battery Sergeant Major. I had been walking one fine winter mid-day along the beach where I found a sea cucumber, a leathery waterlogged object about half the length of a garden cucumber. It is, in fact, an animal, and had I known this

171

the outcome of my picking it up would have been less spectacular. I took it to battery office and showed it round. Then — what does one do with a sea cucumber one no longer wants? With a poker I removed the round lid of the roaring stove in the centre of the hut, dropped the sea cucumber into the flames, and replaced the lid. Just on that the sergeant major came in, took up the traditional English-man's stance, backside to the stove, rubbed his hands vigorously together, and said 'By Jove, it's jolly cold.' Hardly had he spoken than there was an explosion. The lid shot up and hit the sergeant major on the back of the head as he disappeared in a cloud of smoke, soot, and water vapour. B.S.M. Jim Alford was the best sergeant major in the Army, but he looked pretty cross as he retrieved his hat and the smother cleared.

'What idiot put a round in the stove?' he demanded.

'Sorry sir,' I said. 'It wasn't a round, it was my sea cucumber.'

But my two great Burray memories are of Orkney atmosphere. There were the November dawns when the sun flamed crimson out of a turbulent North Sea above the white foaming bar where Water Sound merged with the ocean, and the patrol vessel rose and fell dizzily as it kept watch and ward on the eastern approaches to Orkney. Such dawns I often saw from my bed as a shrewd wind blew in through the open door of the Nissen hut. More tranquil were the June nights, the afterglow bright long after midnight; sheep and cattle preternaturally large on the brae against the turquoise sky still flecked with pink from a sun loth to sink far below the Orkney horizon. Tin hat clamped firmly on my head, greatcoat collar turned up comfortably against the chill breeze filtering in with the soft sighing of the North Sea, I clumped around the dunes on guard, or did a bit of surreptitious reading or writing in the gunpit in the wee small hours by the light of what, in the farther north Shetlands, they call the 'simmer dim.'

5   *Shetland*

Sumburgh to Scalloway

THE YOUNG WOMAN seated beside me in the Viscount on the last lap of my journey was returning to Shetland from a commerce course at the University of Warwick.

'Does this mean you'll be leaving the islands to pursue a career in commerce?' I enquired of her.

'No,' she said. 'I'm employed by the Shetland Education Authority in administration. There was a shortage of teachers of commerce in the county so they sent me on the course intending that I teach commerce in Shetland schools.'

I was flying north, Edith was flying south and home on the same afternoon. The Viscount is a lordly aircraft, fly in it where you will. In the south an air trip is an 'occasion,' bringing out in a woman her most cherished clothes, crowned by a suitably decorative hat, and rounded off by quality luggage cases. In the northern isles, flight as a means of transport has a different quality. Another young woman flying out of Orkney to Shetland was clutching a half drunk bottle of pop when she joined the airport coach in Kirkwall, and she took swigs at it on the flight to Shetland.

Fair Isle, riding the seas alone half way between Orkney and Shetland, is a collector's piece, if only to have seen it. Normally it will be in view from the starboard windows flying from Orkney to Shetland, and from the port windows on the return. If, however, you are on a direct flight between Aberdeen and Shetland the reverse is usually the case; Fair Isle is to port flying north, starboard returning south, a stern rugged outpost with a lace-fringe of sea foam. On December 8, 1941, a German plane swooped over Fair Isle, its machine guns blazing, to kill Catherine Sutherland, aged 23, the wife of a lighthouse keeper. She lies buried fifty miles to northward in Bressay's little churchyard across the Sound from Lerwick, Shetland's capital.

The Loganair Islander from Orkney gives Fair Isle much more rapid and convenient communications than previously it had. A Birmingham man, Gordon Barnes, who went there for a spell at the bird observatory, enjoyed island life so much that he has settled down permanently in a croft called Setter at the north end of the island. Prior to Loganair his annual journey to Birmingham began dishearteningly with 25 miles in the wrong direction on the 50-foot Fair Isle boat, the 'Good Shepherd,' a converted fishing craft, across the violent Sumburgh Roost to Grutness in the south of Shetland, only a mile or so from Sumburgh Airport. Often the 'Good Shepherd' lies stormbound in North Haven on Fair Isle, and there is also a waiting list for places aboard. A few minutes after flying out of Shetland Mr Barnes would see his starting point in Fair Isle down below. Now he can fly out of Fair Isle with Loganair to Orkney and join B.E.A. there, but he pays for the convenience. The cost of chartering the Islander from Fair Isle to Orkney is £35, a matter of £5 single per person if seven passengers share it. As against this the return fare by B.E.A. from Orkney to Shetland is £7. 10s.

Not so lucky in communications is the island visible to north-westward as the Viscount approaches Sumburgh — Foula, home of only 30; the most inaccessible of all Britain's islands, in fact as tantalisingly inaccessible as any island on earth. Only 20 miles from Walls in Shetland, and 25 from Scalloway, Foula has a 'weekly' service from the former, but this is much at the mercy of the weather. Visitors risk being marooned for long spells even in summer. The complete film unit which made 'The Edge of the World' on Foula was weatherbound there for a month after completion of the filming. A dark loom on the sea as we saw it from the Viscount, it dominates the western horizon from much of Shetland Mainland, with several dips and scarps like the teeth of a gigantic saw rising from the ocean.

Thirty minutes from Grimsetter we went in over Sumburgh Head, surely the most spectacular, not to say hair-raising, landing approach in Britain — to touch down at Sumburgh Airport, a beautiful place as I now saw it, washed by the inlets of Grutness, the Pool of Virkie, and West Voe, the sea a darker blue than in Orkney from its greater depth and the absence of large white beaches. To give credit where credit is due, I must add that my two previous visits to Sumburgh had also been in cloudless halcyon weather.

The name on the buses had changed from Peace in Orkney to Leask in Shetland, and I boarded one of these for Lerwick, a journey of 25 miles which gives an introductory insight into Shetland as a starker, more angular, less comfortable place than Orkney, the sea beating its shores more urgently so that the Shetlander has been described as a fisherman with a farm where the Orkneyman is a farmer with a boat. The man beside me in the bus was spending a third holiday in Shetland pursuing his ancestry. His surname was Fea — same as the man who captured Gow on Eday, and this reminded me that Scott sets much of 'The Pirate' in the south of Shetland. On Fitful Head he established the ancient sibyl Norna who sold favourable winds to mariners, basing her activities on those of one Bessie Miller whom he met in Stromness in 1814, and of whom he wrote that few sailors, never sure whether in jest or earnest, would dare leave Stromness without paying sixpence for her intercession and spells. Scott also made the 17th Century 'Laird's House' at Jarlshof the home of Mr Mertoun, while Magnus Troil with his lovely daughters Minna and Brenda lived at Burra-Westra, 20 miles away off the coast of Shetland Mainland.

Our road northward was more adventurous than Orkney roads, now high on a headland with fulmars racing the bus, now on sea level skirting a bay, as at Channerwick. To right and left tracks left the main highway, to places named Quarff, Gord, Sandwick, and Fladdabister. From above Sandwick there was a view, across a mile-wide channel, of Mousa, with its famous broch clearly visible, an Iron Age tower, 40 feet tall, kiln-like in construction, which Eric Linklater thinks was a defensive position armed with a catapult of sorts. One of the stories Shetlanders like to tell is of the piling up of the 'St. Sunniva' on Mousa one foggy night on her passage from Aberdeen to Lerwick. At Cunningsburgh post office the driver delivered a large parcel. A man leading a bull stood on the grass verge as we passed; shaggy sheep cropped at the roadside, each with a well-grown lamb. Amid a desolation of heather and peaty hillside the bus stopped and a young man in R.A.F. uniform alighted and made off with his grip towards an outcrop of rock but without any habitation in sight.

176

'They must live in caves here,' said a woman tourist behind me to her companion.

Ahead as the bus pursued its way could be seen the Ward Hill of Bressay and the bold Noup of Noss, described by the Nature Conservancy as 'one of the most spectacular islands in Europe, 774 acres where gannets, guillemots, shags, kittiwakes, puffins, eider duck, and great and Arctic skuas nest.' Houses became more frequent as we approached Lerwick, and I remembered that in 1951 they were building near Clickimin Broch as fast as possible from an enormous pile of red house bricks brought in from Belgium. If Mousa is inaccessible you can see all you want of a broch at Clickimin only a mile or so from the centre of Lerwick which seemed to be enjoying its siesta as the bus arrived, the hard shadows in brilliant sunlight accentuating the Spanish effect. Anxious to use such fine weather to advantage I booked in at a hotel and made straight for the ferry which regularly crosses the sound to Bressay, the island guarding Lerwick from the east and making its harbour a comparatively snug place. Bressay Sound has seen many stirring sights including two ill-fated Norse fleets — that of Harald Hardrada which lay there in 1066 before sailing for England where Hardrada was slain by the army of King Harold at Stamford Bridge, Yorkshire, and in 1263 the ships of King Haakon before they left for defeat at Largs in the Firth of Clyde.

From the village which faces Lerwick across less than a mile of water a road crosses Bressay towards Noss, the Mecca of all bird-lovers who land on Bressay. I stepped out along this road, a desolate road stretching across a gentle valley falling away to the sea in the north, and continued between Brough Loch, with a colony of greater black-back gulls cruising around, and Setter Loch lower down on the seaward side. I was preceded along this road by a sturdy freckle-faced girl who ultimately made off across the fields towards a huddle of farm buildings beneath a hill. She patted the cattle as she passed, and, collecting a man and a horse from some ploughland, disappeared with them into the farmhouse. Yet another loch, Ullin's Water, lay on my right as I reached the height of land and looked towards Noss.

Bressay once turned its inhabited face east towards the North Sea, and the deserted village still clings to the crisp turf of the hillside. I passed a number of sheep pens made of dry stone, and made across the heather to a croft without a roof whose gables stood skyward like a bishop's mitre. My intrusion into their domain seemed to worry the fulmars who dived very close to me, soon being joined by a pair of skuas. The ruin consisted substantially of one room with a low door now open for ever to the solitude and the winds of the North Sea. Enclosed by a dry-stone wall at the rear was 70 yards of the loveliest turf, where babies could play without any of the hazards of more sophisticated communities. Even so, life must have been hard in this lonely croft. Birds may find sanctuary in such places; not so human beings. I always thought Amiens wrong to consider the 'winter wind' less unkind than 'man's ingratitude.' As I speculated on the earlier occupants of the croft the bleating of sheep came to me down the wind like voices from the past.

Below the highest tide mark on the shore of Noss Sound were the apple-green rosettes of butterwort leaves. The breakers running in from the north were magnificent, quite fifteen feet high and turning over in beautiful jade and bottle-green to become a smother of the purest white which swept on down the narrowing bottleneck between the two islands. Cormorants were diving beneath these combers as they broke, to emerge, long-necked, in their concave wake. Terns were prolific, and two skuas, those pirates of the northern skies, chased a terrified gull which took refuge in the chimney of an empty croft. Access to Noss is by boat, arranged with the warden at Gumista, Bressay, though I believe the boat is kept at the farm on Noss.

Back in the village and with some time to spare before the ferry left I explored the churchyard. It has a memorial to the 16 men of Bressay who died in the 1914–18 war. A gravestone commemorated Noss farmer Joseph Booth, who died on February 15, 1847, aged 81; and the more recent addition to another stone was the name of Catherine Sutherland, who I have already mentioned as being killed by a German aircraft on Fair Isle.

With Shetland's 'simmer dim' there was plenty of daylight left after the high tea preferred to dinner in these parts, so I set off to walk inland on the Scalloway road. As often happens low cloud had succeeded the unbroken blue of the day and was scurrying in from the North Sea with a shrewd wind rustling the heather sloping gently upward on either hand, a monotonous landscape peopled by groups working at the peat cuttings. All were townsfolk of Lerwick, who pay an annual rent for a peat bank and obtain fuel limited only by their time, energy, and car space in carrying it back to their homes. Most of the cutting is done earlier in the year and the peat stacked to dry throughout the summer. Urged on by a friendly couple I found the 'tushker,' the peat cutting spade, easy enough to push into the peat, and, with a little experience I could stack the peats in that open-wall fashion which gives a maximum draught for drying.

I accepted a lift into Scalloway. The Burras and Trondra, the islands off this pleasant little township, have no peat, unusual in Shetland where all distant hillside views feature the black zigzags of the walls of cut peat. Scalloway is Shetland's ancient capital, contemptuous of its upstart rival, Lerwick, and proclaiming this contempt in a jingle:

Scalloway was Scalloway when Lerwick was nane;
Scalloway will be Scalloway when Lerwick is gane.

The 'way' is not accentuated in Scalloway, the final syllable being a quick 'wa,' and Lerwick is two separate syllables unlike Berwick — Ler-wick.

From the road above it Scalloway is one of the sights of the northern and western isles, straggling round an almost landlocked bay and frowned upon by the ruins of the castle built by the hated 'Black Pate,' who is said to have mixed the mortar with the blood of his tenants. During the war Scalloway was a Norwegian base, the 'free' terminus of the 'Shetland bus,' that intrepid service of small boats that braved the North Sea to bring Norwegians out of German thralldom. Some were lost, but most landed their gallant passengers safely on the Olaf Slipway, named in 1942 by Prince Olaf of Norway in person. Norway is, of course, only 200 miles away, and Norwegians and Shetlanders claim a common ancestry. Today Norwegian shark hunters lie in Scalloway, narrow boats with a small barrel for a masthead lookout.

The evening was wearing on and I had time only for a fleeting glimpse of Scalloway before setting out to hitch the six miles back to Lerwick. Even so I tried the door in a stout grey wall that led to West Shore Garden as I knew it eighteen years ago. The door was locked, which is perhaps as well because it left me with one of my most felicitous memories of travel.

In May 1951 I pushed open that heavy green door in the grey wall and stepped inside to an experience I have never forgotten. I had been attracted by the trees which flaunted their unexpected branches high above the wall, and within its shelter I found their slim trunks rising from a riot of daffodils. Snug in this sylvan paradise, sheltered by the wall from Atlantic gales which howl up South Channel beside Burra and Trondra, was a bungalow, and I was most kindly received when I asked permission of the occupant, Mrs Younson, to photograph her garden. I mentioned that I was staying in Lerwick.

'Ah, Lerwick's a cruel place in a north-east wind,' she said. 'Now Scalloway . . .'

Scalloway was speaking for itself, a blue secluded haven in encircling hills, and Mrs Younson's garden a haven within a haven. Several varieties of daffodil dappled the well-trimmed lawns. Tulips, honesty, aubretia, auriculas, poppies, and a huge orange globe-flower were in bloom, while the wild lesser celandine found a place among these grander neighbours. The trees were mainly sycamore, and lying on the ground was a crow's nest, torn only that morning from the boughs, pieces of rope and small bones lying among its debris of twigs and rushes.

'Young crows are such a nuisance,' Mrs Younson explained.

A sundial, possibly the northernmost in Britain, stood on a small lawn, recording much longer sunshine in the summer days of Shetland than those in more formal southern surroundings.

Mrs Younson was a widow, her husband having been gathered to the Valhalla of ancient mariners only six months before. At sea as a boy of 16 he had sailed on several famous ships of the past — three years on the 'Dumfriesshire;' dismasted with the 'Loch Katrine;' and shipwrecked on the Friendly Islands on his 21st birthday. His last voyage in sail was on the 'Pamir' in 1913 when German members of the crew would drink to 'Der Tag.' Wounds in the First World War deprived him of his legs and confined him to a wheel chair which stood vacant in his room. He continued to sail a boat however, a pleasure in which Mrs Younson joined him. A fine library of books on sailing, navigation, and sea adventure, with models in bottles kept green the memory of this 'sailor home from sea.' His small boat 'Norseman' lay dry ashore, but a treasured photograph recorded its last outing before Mr Younson's death.

The roses rambling round a trellis had received a bad setback in the late frosts in 1951 — Mrs Younson's chief regret in having been no farther south than Scotland was in not having seen the rose-gardens of England. But no Shetlander was better blessed with flowers than those blooming behind the grey garden wall in Scalloway. Islandmen, unused to trees, used to ask Mrs Younson why she did not cut them down, but though she mistrusted her sycamores in the early days — expecting them to jump out of the earth — she now loved them as part of her garden of memories. They were, too, part of history; the plantation and the surrounding wall being mentioned by Hibbert in 1822 in his 'Description of the Shetland Islands.'

Another memory of my 1951 visit concerns the remains of a corpse unearthed in the Delting district of Shetland Mainland by two men digging peats. The body was practically disintegrated, though the hair, dark and perfectly preserved, was intact in a curious skull cap. The clothing, too, had deteriorated very little, and I was allowed to see it in Lerwick Police Station. It consisted of a short jacket with a long skirted coat beneath it; a pair of shorts, and long knitted stockings with cloth smocks fitted on to them. Also in the grave was a pair of gloves; a spare cap in one of the pockets; an inkhorn with a quill; a horn spoon; a leather belt with a small metal buckle; the handle of a knife; a purse or small leather bag; a small oak bucket; and a knitted purse with a pattern containing a piece of silk ribbon and three coins. These coins were in fairly good condition, the date 1683 being decipherable on one of them. All the garments were khaki-coloured, but this may be due to staining by the peat. The whole outfit might have been a uniform. Certainly the material was extremely good thick woollen cloth and showed no ravages of time.

Twenty-five cloth-covered buttons ran down the front of the skirted coat, and there were seven buttons on either side corresponding to the position of the pocket flaps on a man's jacket today. The short jacket had three buttons on each cuff, much as a jacket has today. It was made from a different material from the coat and the pants. The long stockings were beautifully knitted, and the gauntlet gloves were perfect examples of their kind.

The preservative qualities of peat are, of course, well known. Early during the Second World War a searchlight detachment, engaged in its perpetual digging on Hoy in Orkney, dug up a well-preserved female body. Having taken a good look they buried her again, but on being relieved by a new detachment they told them of this 'Old Lady of Hoy' as they had named her. Her slumbers were disturbed a second time, and a third, a fourth, and so on, as curiosity proved too strong for each new detachment occupying the site. With the coming of peace she too, presumably, regained her peace. It is said that this Old Lady of Hoy was one Dettie Corrigal, originally denied a proper burial for being no better than she should be. One of the soldiers who saw Dettie's body was a boyhood friend of mine from Birmingham, John Boland. John was an aspiring writer, and she was good copy for him, so he wrote her story and sold it to the World Wide Magazine — his very first success. One of John's subsequent successes was far more resounding. He wrote the thriller 'The League of Gentlemen' from which the famous film was made, bringing him a respectable fortune.

Skerries and Sixareens

MY OBJECTIVE IN SHETLAND, and the end of my journey north by west up the sunset coasts of the British Isles was Hermaness, the northernmost headland of all on the island of Unst. There are two ways of reaching Unst and the one I travelled in 1951 is still in operation. This is the North Isles cruise aboard the 'Earl of Zetland' of which I kept an account in my diary at the time, worth putting on record, I think, as the journey is little changed and travellers today see much the same things that I did 18 years earlier from the same deck.

* * * *

The 'Earl of Zetland' was an old friend. With 'St. Ninian,' 'St. Ola,' and 'Morialta' she carried Orkney servicemen to and from leave across Pentland Firth during the Second World War. Her antics were bearable going south; on the return she was called all the names under the sun — by those who could still speak. Never was such a rolling-pin. I remember one roll off the Old Man of Hoy from which I never expected us to recover. But recover we did, and here she was, all 548 tons of her, straining at her ropes to be off and playing among the rollers around Shetland's northern shores. As the Town Hall clock struck 9 a.m. our bells replied and we cast off. Slap-happy waves were splashing the quayside, and a singing of the north-easter in our ropes and spars was suggestive of fun to come — a point of view reinforced by glimpses of breakers northward beyond Bressay Sound.

Out of the Sound the 'Earl' began to show her paces — confound all ships with masculine names and titles which nevertheless have to be referred to as 'she.' We were meeting a north-east swell head on,

183

and whatever her detractors may say, the 'Earl' is a dry ship, being built very high out of the water. Most of the people aboard were Shetlanders using a day's holiday to visit friends and relatives at Whalsay. I don't know why of quite a number I picked on Mrs Teale to speak to — possibly it was little flaxen-haired Jeanette reminding me of my little twin daughters. Mrs Teale was a Whalsay girl, now living in Lerwick, who was going to spend the day on her native island, and she was married to a Birmingham man. I received an invitation to visit their home on the following night before we had to interrupt our conversation and attend to Jeanette who was seasick. Mrs Teale, of Shetland seafaring stock or no, did not like the sea, and was glad of the shelter of Whalsay's pleasant little harbour, where she disembarked into a motor-boat or 'flit-boat' which put out to us. Also among the exodus into the Whalsay flit boat was a superior-looking gentleman incongruously wearing a grey homburg and carrying a walking stick. In return we got three men with attache cases and tushkers. After taking the passengers ashore the flit boat returned for cargo — sacks of sugar, sacks of coal, boxes of groceries, tins of pineapple and beans, drums of marine oil, a consignment of wooden doors, a roll of linoleum, and a stretcher.

As we dipped across to the Out Skerries, Shetland's eastern outposts, I chatted with a lighthouse keeper, an Unst man, who was returning to Skerries lighthouse from leave. Three men always man the light, a fourth being on two weeks' leave, thus the sequence of duty is six weeks on and two off. I met, too, a Ministry of Health planning officer from Inverness, a pleasant man very interested in seabirds, who was bringing his chief on a tour of the North Isles. Doubtless his chief was equally pleasant, but at the moment he was preoccupied, as so many travellers on the 'Earl' are apt to become.

The Out Skerries as we drew near were a lather of foam and spouting breakers around a small archipelago. We found some shelter in a narrow sound and lay off a rocky island which showed several well-built modern houses through gaps in the cliffs. A blast was sounded on our hooter to attract attention from the island, and it met with flattering success. Not one boat but a flotilla put out, and while a motor-boat came alongside the others circled around some way off, one of them towing a large heavily-laden boat which contained, among otherwise inanimate cargo, a dejected white cow. As the rise and fall of the small boats when lying alongside was about ten feet the business of transferring the cow, on a sling, was rather tricky. I saw it successfully accomplished and went below to lunch — price 4s. 6d. Sitting beside me was a plump young woman who had been staying with her grandparents on the Out Skerries, having reached them by fishing boat four days earlier. From her I learned that the Skerries population was about 100 and, what I had guessed, they make their own amusement. Dances are generated spontaneously; whenever anyone feels like a dance he seeks out sufficient like-minded people and one is arranged, with music from a fiddle.

We had reached thus far in our conversation when my companion was precipitated across my knees by a prodigious roll as we turned broadside on to the weather to make back for Mid Yell. All the crockery on the tables on the port side was piled against the bulkhead of the saloon. That on the starboard side, with nothing but the inadequate fiddles to arrest its headlong career, crashed to the floor. I took my sweet course holding tightly to the plate. Other diners elected against further courses and went elsewhere. So we continued, rolling merrily, until in the lee of Fetlar. There was plenty of blue sky between the drifting cloud, a soft marine blue, and over Unst a delectable 'window in the North' remained open all afternoon.

Bird life in these waters was most fascinating. Fulmars glided restlessly over the waves and along our rail, birds which always seem ill at ease, never resting, interminably searching, their powerful grey bodies hurtling through the air without perceptible wing motion. The kittiwake was plentiful — a more composed bird, able to rest on the waves, his black wing tips folded gracefully and pointing upwards. A solitary passing gannet was a great thrill, snow-white but for the brown wing-tips. Terns, closer identification is beyond me, graceful swallow-like birds but with uncertain and even laboured flight, dived frequently, submerging completely.

Many people deplore the increase in Shetland of the great skua or 'bonxie,' a powerful brown bird flecked with white, because of his ferocious habits. At one time reduced to two known pairs on Hermaness, the bonxie has taken possession in Bressay, Noss, and Foula, and breeds readily. He is in evidence, usually chasing a kittiwake, his wing and tail feathers spread fearfully whenever he approaches his victim. The skua's intention is not murder under these circumstances so much as to make the kittiwake regurgitate undigested food, on which the skua then pounces. I saw several of the more graceful and dart-like Richardon's skuas.

The imagery of folk-lorists and poets who see in these seabirds the ghosts of ancient mariners is easy to understand. I wonder had Norah Holland been watching fulmars when she wrote:

> Spirits of old mariners
> Drifting down the restless years—
> Drake's and Hawkins' buccaneers,
>   So do seamen say?

John Masefield in 'Sea Change' went farther than the seas and coasts of Britain:

> Them birds goin' fishin' is nothin' but souls of the drowned,
>   Souls o' the drowned and the kicked as are never no more;
> An' that there haughty old albatross cruisin' around,
>   Belike he's Admiral Nelson or Admiral Noah.

The eider drake is fortunate among males — he is to be seen swimming around usually accompanied by two ducks, their drab brown plumage in sharp distinction to his more dashing white and brown. Little guillemots, or 'tysies' as they are known in Shetland, scurry beneath the surface like rabbits going to ground on the approach of the 'Earl'. The traveller who knows and cares nothing about birds has a wide pleasant field of experience quite barren to him.

Yell is second to Mainland in size among the Shetlands. To give its length as 17 miles north to south is fair and true enough — as with Mainland which is 54 miles long — but so indented is Yell that a maximum width of seven miles gives no fair indication of its area. Mid Yell Voe into which we sailed cuts so deeply into the east coast that, coinciding with Whal Firth on the west, it leaves an isthmus only three quarters of a mile wide. Again we lay offshore. An ex-R.A.F. boat, 'John Tulloch,' came alongside manned by five islanders in dungarees. It brought us another white cow; the mail bags, an aluminium radiator, a large consignment of eggs, a sheet of hardboard, and several rolls of pig-netting. Two small boys jumped aboard us and looked round with great interest — neither had ever left Yell.

The customary provisions were loaded into the 'John Tulloch,' drums of petrol, bags of mail, boxes of biscuits, sacks of sugar and flour, and a roll or so of pig-netting which looked no different from that brought to us by the boat.

The afternoon was wearing on as we rounded the island of Hascosay and made for Brough Lodge, Fetlar. Home of the laird, Sir Arthur Nicolson, the Lodge presents the appearance of a low-built turreted castle, the only habitation visible from our anchorage. A thin road wound into nothingness through a landscape of gentle pastel tints on which cattle were grazing. Fetlar proudly claims the title 'Garden of Shetland,' and produces the best ponies and cattle in the islands. The boat which put out to us from the slipway below the Lodge was a sixareen, the typical old Shetland fishing-boat. Long and none too wide in the beam, it was pointed fore and aft, and rowed by six men in twos, with an oar each, crowded into the forepart. A seventh member of the crew steered with a long fixed oar. Whitecaps were advancing down Colgrave Sound, and when the sixareen pulled alongside it had quite an appreciable rise and fall. Nevertheless we unloaded into it most of our cattle.

Cows were manhandled from the 'Earl' onto the sixareen where their head tethers were quickly passed through rings in the boards and their heads pulled low and secured. Eleven cows were tethered side by side in this manner, having been shoved and hauled across without ceremony. A timid-looking girl squeezed into what slight room was left, and the rowers bent to no mean task in pulling such a load across the advancing seas. They reached the slipway safely and the cows filed out to graze placidly on the grass above the beach. Then the sixareen returned and there was more tugging at horns and pulling of tails while nine more cows were transferred. Then we turned into the seas and made for our northernmost point, Uyca-sound, visible six miles away.

This, then, was Unst, farthest north island of Britain if we except the tiny rock of Muckle Flugga which bears a lighthouse and lies just off Hermaness, Unst's northerly cape. Unst is 12 miles in length, and Uyeasound is at the south.

Ashore a little plantation of bushes rose near an amazingly sturdy house with a conservatory, and with daffodils growing in the garden as we could plainly see. On the beach a lorry was collecting shingle for making concrete. The usual traffic in goods was enacted, but this time one of the articles brought aboard was a spinning wheel. We also received our first consignment of girls for the Anderson Educa-

187

tional Institute at Lerwick. They had been spending a long Whit week-end on their remote island homes and were returning to the Bruce Hostel for Girls where they live during term, acclaimed the finest schoolgirls' hostel in Scotland.

Arthur Anderson, who endowed the Educational Institute in 1862, rose from humble beginnings to be Chairman of the Peninsular and Oriental Steamship Company. In a narrow Lerwick alley between the Esplanade and Commercial Street a rusting ring is secured to the wall, and to it Thomas Bolt, merchant of Cruister, Bressay, used to tie his boat. Mr Bolt employed the young Arthur Anderson as 'beach boy,' whose job it was to tend the stockfish drying in the sun. When little more than a boy Arthur decided to go forth into a wider world his employer gave him a motto: 'Do weel and persevere.' He did.

This ring is some 30 yards from the waterfront and is not the only evidence that the harbour at Lerwick has encroached on the Sound. Engraved on a wall, the width of the Esplanade from the water, one reads: 'The Old Lodberry, Grieg's Pier, built circa 1736.' Lodberry, derived from 'load' means a place from which goods were loaded directly on to boats.

At 5 p.m. the 'Earl of Zetland' sailed from Uyeasound. Skirting Fetlar we saw the cattle we had unloaded earlier cropping unconcernedly, and entered the little bay at Hubie, Fetlar, where we were confronted with a building more remarkable than Brough Lodge. It is a constant topic of debate whether the function of a house is to exclude the weather or to let it in. If there is any place more than another in Britain where I expected to see houses built for security it is in Shetland. Certainly I had seen some heavy rocks suspended over wooden or thatch roofs by ropes to help keep them on, yet Leagarth House, Hubie, once the home of Sir William Watson Cheyne, one of the foremost surgeons of Edwardian times, has a long glass verandah appearance on two sides. It stands in grounds enclosed by a wooden palisade, with signs of a plantation peeping above the boards.

Another sixareen approached us, this time carrying the implements of County Council roadmen — barrows, spades, and picks. Several iron bedsteads were also stowed aboard the 'Earl,' and another crowd of Anderson schoolgirls joined us. The shoregoing cargo included cement, an incubator, an old horsehair couch, and coal — there is little peat on Fetlar.

After an invigorating journey in the open sea down to Whalsay we made our last call there at 8.45 p.m., and picked up the people we had left there in the morning, several cycles, and a child's tricycle. As we headed for Bressay Sound and Lerwick misty yellow sunrays filtered into the valleys of Mainland, filling them with diffused light against which the ridges stood out in receding waves. We tied up at Lerwick at 10 p.m. — thirteen hours at sea for 14s.

* * * *

Mist over Muckle Flugga

THE OTHER WAY of reaching Unst from Lerwick is by the romantic-sounding 'Overland' — three buses and two ferry boats in a journey of four or five hours which leapfrogs the island of Yell between Shetland Mainland and Unst. This was how I proposed coming to journey's end, and shortly after mid-day I boarded the bus in Lerwick to do the first leg — nearly 30 miles to Tofts Voe. I did so with a heavy heart and little confidence, for Shetland had disappeared in so dense a sea mist that the bus headlights were switched on, and we travelled northward unable to see more than a few yards of heather on either side of the road. That I know much of the route and had done it not four years ago was scant consolation for the views I was missing. Although no spot in Shetland is more than three miles from the sea, Mainland has valleys which suggest the inland desolation of Rannoch Moor. Tetla Dale, one of them, can be traversed even in clear weather for six miles with no sight of human habitation, and with the sea always hidden by the hills. Elsewhere the sea intrudes at every turn, and even with a map one is hard put to know whether it is the Atlantic, the North Sea, or an inland loch facing him.

The deep fjord-like voes, biting far into the land, often have a string of low holms or skerries to seaward of them looking like the coils of a sea-serpent. Indeed it is from just such tiny islets that the legend of the 'kraken' is so rife in the Norwegian Lofotens, while several places in Shetland have their own 'sea-serpent.'

At Olna Firth a Salvation Army lass left us, carrying a concertina case, and the bus pushed on through the mist alongside Dales Voe, where the road climbs high round a brown hill and gives distant glimpses of Yell and Fetlar when visibility permits. Now the voe was just a presence, a sense of a long deep drop below our right hand, yet as we trundled down to the jetty in Tofts Voe there was sufficient lightening of the mist to reveal an awaiting boat. While certain drums and packages were put aboard I chatted with a man bound only for Yell. Learning I came from the Midlands he told me that within the past few years electricity had been installed on the island by a firm from Kidderminster. I can imagine the employees' astonishment on being assigned to an island with such a name as Yell. Of fuel Yell has an abundance, being one vast peat bank, and my companion carried a long brown-paper covered parcel which might have contained a tushker. The population of Yell has dwindled to barely 1,000, inhabiting 80 square miles.

I stood on deck swaying to the gentle motion of the ferry boat as we chugged through the mist and caught a hazy glimpse of the island of Bigga in mid-channel on the three miles to Ulsta at the southern extremity of Yell, where the mist had clamped down again on a post office, a school, a sprinkling of dwellings, a car or two, and another bus. This took me the most featureless 24 miles I have ever travelled — more the mist's fault than Yell's, and, returning next day I found the isthmus at Mid Yell, though still hazy, a pleasant place, with Whal Firth striking spear-like from the Atlantic to within barely half a mile of Mid Yell Voe, the inlet from the east.

The Yell ferry boat on the one mile crossing from Gutcher on Bluemull Sound to Belmont in Unst is called 'Shalder,' another name for that genius loci of these northern isles, the oyster-catcher. As it set me ashore on Unst I was treading the last and twenty-seventh island of my journey up the sunset coasts of the British Isles, counting Ireland correctly as one; Harris and Lewis less correctly as two; including Burray and South Ronaldsay despite the Churchill Barriers because I remember them as islands, but not counting Lamb Holm and Glims Holm, those tiny Barrier stepping-stones. Totting up my bag of islands as I sat in the third bus of my 'Overland' journey I reflected ruefully that the fine weather benediction of the Cross at Cashel had worn very thin in Orkney and Shetland, and that I had not seen a really colourful sunset since Jura went up in reflected flames from Colonsay.

To add to the anti-climax of these last mist-shrouded miles I dropped off to sleep and awakened only at Baltasound, the village capital of Unst. Within another three miles we were at Haroldswick, northern terminus of the 'Overland,' and there I was lucky enough to get a lift of two miles to Burrafirth, driven by a holiday-maker staying at Baltasound who, as I left him, warned me not to stray from a path through the heather which he remembered from his last climb up Hermaness a couple of years earlier.

'The path peters out on top of the hill,' he said. 'If you've got any sense you'll pack up there and not carry on to the cliffs in this fog.'

My map endorsed his advice. From the 657-feet summit of Hermaness Hill the ground seemed to slope increasingly steeply to the actual headland of Herma Ness. Assuring him that I would be sensible, I hunched my pack for the last time, crossed the bridge over a stream that runs from the Loch of Cliff into the great fjord of Burra Firth, and strode, with more confidence than I felt, into the murk. This was not how I had always pictured it — always in my mind's eye there had been a glowing sun low on a limitless sea horizon with impressive hills, cliffs, voes, and islets around. Fate, which had smiled so serenely on the beginning of my journey at Slea Head, a gannet's flight of 650 miles away, was dealing scurvily with me at journey's end.

I was 550 miles from my home in Birmingham, but only 180 from Norway. A story is told of the Unst farmer who posted an application to the Ministry of Agriculture for a free supply of some farming commodity. His form was sent back with a letter pointing out that he had omitted to enter the name of his nearest railway station. Would he please do so. He did — 'Bergen, Norway.'

I turned right beyond the bridge and first could sense, then later see, the firth beside me. But not for long. Soon a track moved up through the heather on my left. I could see only about 30 yards ahead so I had to take it on trust, hoping it was the one line of footpath marked on my map stretching two miles to the spot height of 657 feet. I certainly climbed at the expected angle, the path unrolling behind me, an escape route, like the thread which Theseus unwound as he trod the labyrinth of Crete, though mercifully my path was straight. Nevertheless I placed one stone on top of another here and there, and as the upward slope became less pronounced I took careful note that the breeze was hitting me on my right cheek, though the mist was so thick as to be scarcely affected by it. On the lower slopes I had experienced a sense of space beneath me on the right where Burra

Firth lay. My path veered a little to the left and I sloshed across the burn in Winnaswarta Dale, and so on to the flatter land of Sothers Brecks with a feeling of space now on my left also.

One thing about the mist — it was saving me from dive-bombing by the bonxies and terns, for Hermaness is a bird sanctuary, and Garry Hogg in 'The Far-Flung Isles' (Robert Hale, 1961) gives a lively account of the aerial attack to which he and his wife were subjected on the headland. Instead of the clamour that beset them I plodded along in a frightening silence broken only by the brush of my feet against the heather stalks, and the sepulchral note from time to time of the foghorn on Muckle Flugga. But for Out Stack, a rock half a mile north-eastward from it, Muckle Flugga is the northernmost point of the British Isles, and I began to feel very cross that I was going to be denied a sight of it.

I was now losing confidence in my path with numbers of sheep-tracks criss-crossing it, though the sheep were not in evidence, and when the undoubted thresh of the sea began to pervade the air I thought it time to call a halt. I was near enough the summit, I had done my best, and I had penetrated a giant's stronghold. But for the mist, as I came to the end of a journey begun four months earlier, I should have seen to eastward across the deep trench of Burra Firth the highest hill in Unst, Saxa Vord, rising to 935 feet. From this advantageous height a giant, one Saxi, is said to have indulged in those stone-throwing contests to which giants were partial with another giant, Herman, who gave his name to Hermaness. The litter of these bickerings lies on the surrounding hillsides in the form of rocks like Saxi's Baa on Hermaness.

As I dipped into my pack for some chocolate to celebrate the completion of my journey there was an audible beating of the air, and out of the mist swept a huge white owl. Three times it circled me, close enough for me to see its eyes a-goggle at the sight of a human on Hermaness in such conditions. I stopped searching my pack and began searching my mind, and the penny dropped. It was George Meredith in 'Love in the Valley' —

Lovely are the curves of the white owl sweeping
Wavy in the dusk lit by one large star.

A lush, exotic poem to remember in these grim surroundings. But poetry is my constant companion on the road; the greatest gift of my schooldays to my manhood. All day in the 'Overland' I had been conning over some more appropriate lines, lines from John Masefield's epic 'Dauber' about a sailing ship becalmed in fog off Cape Horn:

> *Denser it grew until the ship was lost;*
> *The elemental hid her . . .*

and

> *So the night passed, but then no morning broke,*
> *Only a something showed that night was dead.*

Now, in the last minutes of my journey, on an August evening in Unst, with the wind still blowing unerringly on my right cheek to tell me I was facing north across boundless seas to the Arctic ice, I stood like a wraith in the mist, seeing only

> *A wall of nothing at the worlds' last edge.*

Index